Change at Shebika

Change at Shebika

Report from a North African Village

by

Jean Duvignaud

Translated from the French by Frances Frenaye

Foreword by Cecil Hourani

Foreword to the Paperback Edition

by Robert A. Fernea

University of Texas Press/Austin

First published in the United States by Pantheon Books, a division of Random House, Inc., New York. Originally published in France as Chebika *by Éditions Gallimard, Paris. Copyright © 1968 by Éditions Gallimard. Published in Great Britain by Allen Lane The Penguin Press, London.*

International Standard Book Number 0-292-71041-0
Library of Congress Catalog Card Number 76-14079
Copyright © 1970 by Jean Duvignaud; copyright © 1977
    by University of Texas Press
All rights reserved
Printed in the United States of America

To Si Tijani Jejill,
who took me to Shebika,
and to the people of Shebika,
who wrote this book

CONTENTS

LIST OF PLATES

ACKNOWLEDGEMENTS

This work could not have been carried on without the valuable help of my students at the University of Tunis (1961–6) – Mlles Fenice, Belkhodja, Heinkele, Charrad, Mme Akrout, Messrs Boucraa, Hamazaoui, Hamouda, Akrout and Karoui.

Monsieur P. Roussopoulos, Christine, the young Frenchwoman whom the people of the village still call 'Christ', and my indispensable collaborator, Monsieur Khalil Zamitti, gave me their support at all times.

Monsieur Messadi, Secretary of State at the Ministry of Education, and Monsieur Abdeslem, Vice-Rector of the Faculty of Letters at the University of Tunis, made possible the concrete achievement of this study.

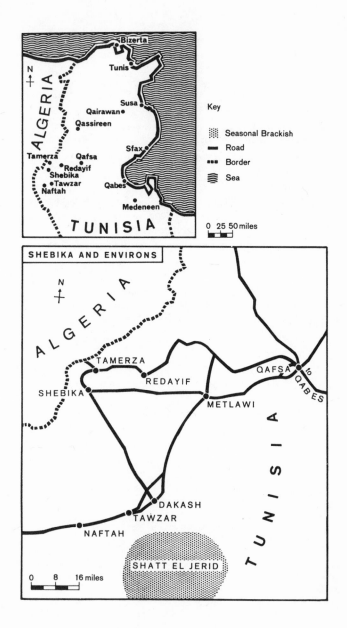

FOREWORD

JEAN DUVIGNAUD came to Tunisia to teach sociology at the University of Tunis, and *Change at Shebika* is the story of one of the two major tasks he set himself. The story of the second, which might be called *Tunis*, has yet to be told. When both are completed, they will constitute a major contribution to the understanding both of the social and psychological problems of development in a newly independent State, and of the relations between a western intellectual seeking a sense of community lost in the fragmented life of a capitalist industrial society, and a new ruling class seeking to form a new society in its own image.

Change at Shebika is a theatrical work in the truest sense of the word in which sociology – perhaps for the first time – reveals its full capacities not merely to study men, but also to change them. Under the probings of Duvignaud's group the villagers of Shebika slowly awoke to a new perception of their own values, and of their need for a reassertion of their collective life within the framework of the new Tunisia. At the same time the Tunisian researchers working with Duvignaud came to a gradual perception both of their own inadequacy to understand and to help a community which though formally Tunisian was in fact far removed from anything they knew or recognized as part of their national heritage, and of the inadequacy of the new governing class in Tunis to understand and to appreciate the real problems of a community which did not fit into their own scheme of things.

The dramatic denouement of the story came in what Duvignaud terms 'the incident of the quarry', in which the villagers opposed what appeared to them to be an arbitrary and unnecessary decision of the Governorate of the region to make them construct an administrative building when what they needed was the means to repair their own dwellings. The final outcome was negative: the villagers were forced by armed guards to cut the stones in the quarry, and at least one and maybe several died in the process; but the building has not yet been built. The story could be taken as a symbol of the final impotence of paternalism. Paternalism in government, installed in contemporary Tunisia, rests on the assumption that the authorities know better than the governed the interests of the community; but the concepts of the authorities are formed and shaped not by the real collective life and needs of the different communities which constitute the society, but by ideas which in part reflect the problems and experience of other societies, and in part reflect the interests of a new governing class anxious to maintain itself in power. The result is frustration. On the one hand the governed fail to appreciate the very real benefits which they receive and resent the price they have to pay for them: on the other hand the authorities become increasingly exasperated with what they take to be the ingratitude of the objects of their efforts, and come to despise and even to coerce in practice those whom they claim to love and respect in theory. From paternalism to tyranny the road is not long.

Change at Shebika is not a political book in the narrow sense of the word, but its underlying thesis is the necessity in the third world for 'social independence' to succeed and to complete political independence. This 'social independence' as conceived and imagined by Jean Duvignaud in the case-study of Shebika is his most important contribution to contemporary political and social thought. It is quite clear both from this book, and from his other writings, that Duvignaud's ultimate interest lies in the Western, industrial society of which he is a member. The 'social independence' which he imagined and to which he has given both form and substance in *Change at Shebika*, as a micro-society within Tunisian society, is what he also dreams of for western society. As a French intellectual of the left he can accept neither the myth of liberal capitalist society in which finally the individual loses all sense of community, and in which his search for private self-realization and personal happiness ends either in complete egoism or in despair;

nor the myth of orthodox Communism that a monolithic State or a party can create a free society.

Perhaps in despair of finding in western Europe the micro-cosmic elements for the 'social independence' of which he had dreamt Jean Duvignaud came to Tunisia and found Shebika. Its isolation, poverty and degradation were precisely what at-tracted him – not for the reasons that attract the slummer or do-gooder to poverty and misery, but because he rightly per-ceived that the villages and other collective societies of North Africa have preserved, through centuries of neglect and oblivion, ancient traditions and habits of communal life. They can be studied either as historical and social curiosities, and as objects of the 'folk-lore' which the Tunisian cultural authorities, like those of many other new countries, are trying to resusci-tate; or they can be studied as living organisms which have a right to a life of their own within a new framework, and which have a contribution to make to the new society of which they form part through the re-discovery of their own authentic per-sonality. Society as a conglomeration of Shebikas – the vision is valid for Tunisia, and why not for other societies too? This seems to be Duvignaud's message.

The impact of this study on the Tunisians, both villagers and researchers, and to some extent the authorities in Tunis, is care-fully and honestly analysed by Duvignaud. What we now await from him is the second part: what were the results of his years in Tunisia on himself, as western thinker and creative writer? We await his next book with impatience.

Geneva, July 1969   CECIL HOURANI

FOREWORD TO THE PAPERBACK EDITION

How are we to distinguish between the drama of theater and that of everyday life? Two years before publishing *Change at Shebika* in France, Jean Duvignaud wrote in *Sociologie du Theatre* (1965) ". . . the *dramatic situation* differs from the *social situation* insofar as one embodies social roles in order to assert its dynamism and modify its own structure, while the other represents action not in order to carry it out but in order to invest it with symbolism." Notice the qualification "insofar as." The writings of sociologist Erving Goffman have shown us how the interactions of daily life are richly invested with symbolic significance; indeed, his use of language of the theater to describe the daily presentations of self in society makes the practical consequences of complex social exchanges sometimes seem a secondary concern for both actor and observer.

Duvignaud's approach, like that of Goffman, is phenomenological. We are presented with scenes of daily life in Shebika, an oasis village in the desert of southern Tunisia, scenes in the house and courtyard, the grocery, the shrine of the marabout, the gardens, and the portico where time is measured by the drips of a water clock regulating the endless cycle of irrigation. Yet Duvignaud is deeply concerned with both the symbolic meaning of these scenes and the conditions of historic change which impinge on the existence of this postcolonial community.

Why does Shebika, a poor, relatively isolated desert village, so well match the interests of a sociologist or anthropologist concerned with the relationship between theater and society? Duvignaud went to the village in 1960 and for five years continued to visit and to undertake research there with the help of his Tunisian university students. The questions they asked, the formal methods of their research, were those of many other community studies undertaken by Western scholars. Yet the form in which their study is presented is not that to which the Anglo-American reader has become accustomed. The objects and subjects of study shift about. The first questions asked prove irrelevant as the relationship between what the Shebikans can say about themselves, the exchanges they make among themselves, and the ceremonies and rituals they perform all are seen to have less and less to do with the underlying conditions of their existence. The researchers, the government employees, the nearby tent dwellers, and the neighboring villages, as well as the Shebikans themselves, become part of what we witness and hear in a succession of scenes which at first seems to have little continuity and which resists attempts to reduce detail to abstract categories of social facts. We come to realize that neither the traditional culture of the village, which informs and structures the patterns of daily life, nor the conversations of the inhabitants have much to do with economic and political legacies of colonialism and the national state which have left this remote community in the backwash of urban-centered economic development.

Thus Shebika approaches the conditions that define the dramatic situation, and Duvignaud uses devices of the theater to reinforce this parallel. The Shebikans have no language with which to bridge the gap between their traditional beliefs about themselves and their world and the new ideologies that Tunisian nationalism proclaims (much less between them and the economic infrastructure that is replacing that of precolonial times). This is revealed in dialogues, narratives, commentaries, and theoretical excursions that Duvignaud weaves together in dramatic forms. The palaver of daily intercourse endlessly repeats and elaborates ideas and stories that seem uncontrolled by the tests of practical significance in coping with an increasingly degenerating condition of subsistence.

But of course the circumstances of Shebikan life are never the same from the day Duvignaud and his researchers arrive there. The latter are Tunisian; some of the young students themselves have come from rural areas and have moved into university life from circumstances not so different than those at Shebika. They are drawn into the existence of the Shebikans and are at the same time forced to recognize their own involvement in the patterns of change which have resulted in the theatrical detachment of Shebikan cultural life. With the students, the reader, too, perceives the self-defeating quality of traditional behavior in a national setting that is no longer traditional.

In a dramatic climax to the book, the roles of villager and researcher are transcended. The experience of having been the object of research is suddenly exchanged for the recognition of self in the eyes of others who are no longer objective researchers but instead have become participants with the villagers in the ongoing process of self-discovery. Has the theatrical distance of Shebikan cultural life from the impinging circumstances of modernization ended? The possibility is there.

The form of this study is a matter of great consequence for those of us who doubt that the objective categories of our academic social science preserve for us a privileged position vis-à-vis the people whose lives are our subjects. Increasingly, perhaps conclusively, we, the social scientists, follow the administrators and merchants of industrial capitalism into tribe and village where the changes for which our informants have no words are already well underway. We must cope with the gap between the ceremonies and rituals of their social life and the economic forces that threaten the efficacy of traditional belief and practice. Duvignaud, by combining the sociology of the theater of Georges Gurvitch and the search for *authenticité* of Jacques Berque, has confronted the dilemma of the anthropologist, who by training and theoretical orientation must see the organization of society reflected in the meanings of culture. If this relationship has been dissolved in the ongoing processes of world history that transcend the boundaries of the community studied, what is left of this traditional approach beyond a recording of dead artifacts, the piecing together of what once might have been, or the collection of myths forever severed from the circumstances that engendered them?

In his effort to discover the significance of change in Shebika, Duvignaud forces us to reflect on our own views of cultural meaning in a world where the boundaries of once-isolated communities have been shattered. By refusing to reify and categorize his information according to the conventional rubrics of traditional community studies, he forces us to think of people rather than abstractions. This is a rich text from which we can learn much about a North African community; the style, semiologically informed and theatrically aware, is well suited to the description of the alienated and the disinherited. *Change at Shebika* requires us to re-examine our own approaches to the art of ethnography.

Robert A. Fernea

PUBLISHER'S NOTE

Place names and proper names in North Africa are usually transliterated into French, a tradition which began during the intensive French colonization of the Maghrib. We have gone against this tradition, aiming to give, for English and American readers, a closer approximation to the sounds of the original Arabic, and to eliminate ambiguity. Thus 'Chebika' has become 'Shebika', 'Naoua' 'Nawa', 'Bechir' 'Bashir', and so forth. A few names already well known in French transliteration have not been changed.

Change at Shebika

THE 'TAIL OF THE FISH'

The Approach

The road leading east from Tawzar goes downhill across the desert-like steppe and through El Hamma, a paltry oasis spread out at the foot of a sandy cliff, eroded by wind and rain, whose crumbling mass threatens to fall upon it. Then it turns towards the *shatt* of El Bahri, which is smaller than that of El Jerid and covered not with a crust of phosphorescent salt, but with a coat of mud which, in the early morning hours, throws out bluish reflections. After this there is an expanse of sand, where the emplacement of the road shifts whenever a gust of wind covers up the gravel of its track and the sparse stalks of perpetually yellow esparto grass. The bed of the *wadi* has been dry for years, because dams, beyond the faraway mountains, the Jebel, to which the road is leading, have altered the course of the waters. Only in April, or during the autumn, does a mass of yellow, greasy liquid pass like a clot, through the unused passage, on whose clay banks, shaped by the winds, there accumulate tufts of the *euphorbia gruyoniana* in which camels occasionally seem to delight.

After the *wadi* the road enters a vast hollow which rolls up to the mountains to the north and west, and melts away to the south and east in a lost horizon haunted by a recurrent mirage of trees and strange shapes which resemble that of a ship cast up on the sand. Flocks of goats and camels, attracted by the esparto, wander slowly across it like moving hieroglyphs, the signs of an undecipherable tongue. The desert is not a solid mass, but a succession of unfolding plane surfaces, a nest of boxes, one inside the other, whose outlines continually dissolve, leaving the viewer with nothing but what he put into them.

The desert is not empty. On the contrary, it is filled with faint vibrations, with the ceaseless and frenzied movement of thousands of snakes, scorpions, lizards, and insects of every kind. The wide horizons fill the ears and lungs with a bulk that is weightless and yet oppressive. The oppressiveness lies in a sort of haunted suspense and a feeling of doubt even greater than that inspired by the sea. The desert, or rather the three unequally distributed deserts – of sand, gravel and salt – which fill the southern part of the Maghrib, often looks like a shore left high and dry by a low tide that never rises. Even in spring and autumn, or during the abrupt summer storms, the desert has always the same harsh, fleeting colour, which does not borrow the tint of the yellow esparto or of the occasional hills of sand or crumbling rock, but remains detached from any real object and even from the framework which should contain it. Only occasionally, after the rains or the fall of the cloud of sand raised by the south wind, are the few identifiable features of the landscape – plants or hillocks – animated by a momentary life of their own. Holes open up, cracks are filled and ripples flow in an uncertain direction. The movement of the sand, its crystallization into clay, its irresistible displacement and periodic disappearance into the gravel, are always unpredictable.

Then Shebika comes into sight, far away, like a splotch on the side of the mountain, which has become more and more transparent, with its ochre colour growing lighter and lighter. A saw-toothed mountain which, upon approach, gradually reveals its curious nature – a higgledy-piggledy pile of worn or crumbed rocks, an agglomeration of sand and gravel, taking on, at dawn and dusk, the colour of ripe fruit. Of Shebika itself, which at this distance is only a cluster of palm-trees, nothing can yet be said. We must wait until we have crossed a further stretch of the steppe, furrowed by crevasses, until we see that it lies between two spurs of the mountain, which open up over the desert. It is neither on flat ground, like the nomad encampments, nor on a hilltop, like the Kabyl villages of Algeria, but perched on a sort of platform which overlooks the *wadi*, the oasis, and a deep crevasse to the right, and slopes gently down to the desert. As we come out of the oasis the village is before us. It consists of two masses of ochre and grey houses, one grouped around a sort of postern at the left, the other to the right of a crude portico, whose entrance is raised up by two columns. They are not Roman columns, such as are to be found elsewhere in the area and might well exist at Shebika, which was a *speculum* of the *limes*, whence the size and movements of passing caravans were observed and reported by means of great mirrors which caught and flashed the reflections of the sun to other look-outs of the same kind. They are palm trunks which, curiously enough, have taken on, with time, the texture and patina of stone. Above these two unintentionally architectural masses the village is laid out in flat terraces whose criss-crossing levels are rounded off to fit the semi-circular pattern of the whole. At the left, starting from the postern, a succession of low walls lead down to the Mosque, which is on the edge of a ravine and therefore marks the boundary of the village on this side. On the other side the boundary is higher up, at the portico, whose walls, reinforced a few years ago with wire and iron staves, drop steeply on to the *wadi*.

On the big square at the entrance to the village there are only a square building (which had not yet been erected when we first went there in 1961) and the tomb of Sidi Sultan, a structure larger and more important than the Mosque, whose small, unevenly round dome weighs down heavily upon four low walls, sunk deep into the ground of an enclosure. This shrine, the only whitewashed building in the village, at the head of the steep path leading up from the oasis, shines out from afar amid the conglomeration of mud-brick houses which melt into the stone on the mountain.

In the cemetery, below, the dead are laid out by the families to which they belonged when they were living. Because it is at the same level as the school, children and the horses and donkeys of the Bedouins continually cross it, and the tombs have been trampled almost into the ground. Some of them barely stick up above the surface, and others have completely crumbled, so that after a period of prolonged drought the remains of what was once a living family are laid bare. Soon, however, the tomb is covered with sand and the bodies are gradually eaten away by insects and scorpions. Since we are in front of the school, the only modern building in the village, let us pause to look at the young teacher, wearing a regulation suit and tie and freshly shaved, like all government employees, as he opens the door to the classroom and imposes silence upon the sixty or more children who, under his guidance, are learning to read.

We approach the village proper either by the portico, where there hangs the water-clock which during six months of the year measures the allotments of water in the oasis, or by the postern. On the postern side is the grocery, the only shop in the place, a dark hole whose door is always open. Above this the main path rises steeply, splitting into three divergent alleys. The longest one, on the left, follows the outline of the village and winds up in a courtyard. The other two are subdivided further, each branch ending at a door. The doors furtively open and shut, and children, apparently very busy, run continuously from one house to another. There is, to be sure, always a birth, a marriage, a circumcision, or a commemoration of Sidi Sultan in process or preparation. The acts of everyday life assume great importance in this place where life itself seems to have none whatsoever. Olives and dates are piled into great mortars, amid shrill cries of women and children, and from time to time the beating of the traditional small, elongated drum calls the women together. Its echoes remain imprisoned in the courtyards, and the muffled sound is not a summons, but rather a call to some sheltered, intimate communion.

Thence, leaving the village above us, we penetrate a succession of gorges, with cascading waterfalls, in order to reach a last semi-circle of cliffs, at whose feet a spring runs out of bluish clay ground. Here shouting young girls bathe themselves, fill pitchers, and wash pieces of red or violet cloth.

It was in 1961, when we were at Tawzar, that Si Tijani Jejill first took us to Shebika, where he goes every year to organize wild-sheep and gazelle hunting. Si Tijani is a big, dark-skinned, amazingly young, sixty-five-year-old man. In his white suit he scours the desert for snakes and scorpions, whose venom is used for medical research in European laboratories. This veteran of the French army, this descendant of steppe and desert huntsmen, whose name is that of the noblest and most powerful of the mysterious sects of the south, the Tijaniya, is also a conscientious employee of the Tunisian Public Works Administration. Because he knows the region better than anyone else, the Administration holds on to him jealously, if only so that he can break in young engineers fresh from Tunis, teaching them to detect the movements of wind and sand, the shifting track of the roads, the course of the *wadis*, and to hire seasonal labourers, recruited on a percentage basis from the villages and encampments of the steppe.

Si Tijani has a high reputation throughout the Jerid, the area of *shatt* and oases which stretches from Qafsa and Metlawi to Al Wad and the frontier of Algeria on the south and to Douz and Tamerza and still another part of Algeria on the west. And yet this area is only a small part of that which he knows. He has penetrated the mountain gorges in search of eagles and wild sheep, spotted gazelles in the middle of the desert, tramped for hours with a stick in his hand, bending over to rout a scorpion out of its hole and imprison it in a cardboard tube, clambered over the rocks in order to catch a snake by its neck or tail and stuff it, all aquiver, into a sack, idled in the villages and encampments, talking of the latest births and marriages and deaths. There is no detail of the life of the Jerid that he does not know.

'I know the sort of people you care about,' he said, 'and I'll take you where you can find them. And they, in their own way, will respond. They may not know how to read and write, but they catch on quickly to what is wanted of them.' And then he told us that, in Arabic, Shebika means 'net' or 'network'; also 'narrows', the 'straight gate'.

Nawa

Nawa bin Ammar bin Shrayet is the first to wake up, long before the hour of prayer, when it is not yet light and the rocks of the cliff above the village have just begun to take on an ochre hue.

You could call it a bed, this stone slab some nine inches above the floor. Nawa calls it a *dukhana*. It is covered with a mat, and when she lies down she wraps herself in a blanket. Her daughters sleep on mats on the floor.

Nawa goes out into the courtyard to relieve herself, standing against the wall, with her skirt raised up over her old body. She shoos away the chickens, then pauses to stretch herself, like a child, crossing her arms behind her head. As she makes this movement she seems, at least from the rear, almost as young as when she first came from El Hamma to Shebika, nearly fifty years ago, perched on the back of a camel hired by her father. The French zouaves, who were still manning such small outposts, laughed as the two of them went by.

She goes over to the bucket of water and vigorously washes her face, without touching the cake of soap which her nephew has brought home, for his own use, from school. Still leaning over, she looks around her, frowning, to see if everything in the courtyard is in good order, and then dries her face with the inside of her dress.

Nawa's courtyard is comparatively large. At this hour most of the chickens are still asleep on the palm branches that have been tossed into one corner. This improvised roost is on the left side, if you turn your back to the low wall beside which Nawa was washing. Dropping gradually and unevenly down, this wall forms a right angle with that which, in the village of Shebika, is called a house, a cube of mud-bricks, held more or less together by crumbling cement and penetrated by the dust blown off the desert.

The roof, with its fifteen- to twenty-degree inclination (a reminder of the torrential winter and spring rains) is woven of palm leaves wrapped around trunks of the same tree. Everywhere in the Sahara people point out palm trunks several centuries old, and these must date back a hundred and fifty or two hundred years, to the glorious time when everyone was a landowner and given to profitable looting or *jaiysh*.

If the roof of the chicken-house has collapsed in the middle, as have most roofs in the village, that of the house where Nawa and her family live is still comparatively solid. No one moves a hand to stave it up; there is no telling when the beams will give way, and, fearing the worst, they simply wait for it to happen.

Moving from right to left in the courtyard we come to the gate, made of boards or trunks sawed lengthwise down the middle and held together by wooden bands. The gate swings on a wooden pin attached to the wall, and to open it one must pull and raise it at the same time. This is a gesture which Nawa learned to make as soon as she arrived, and once learned it is never forgotten. Still moving to the left we come to another shed, whose entrance is partly covered by a curtain woven of the same heavy cloth that is used for making tents in the plain. Here, against the wall, stands the loom, with a stone counter-weight to pull the cords. Occupying most of the space beside it on a baked-mud stand, there is an enormous mass of smooth stone, made of two parts that fit into each other. Inscriptions on the lower part reveal the fact that this is an ancient Roman press for olives or dates. Nawa uses this press in preference to the roller or *guersaba*, a small, round stone that has to be pushed by hand. She knows that the stone is an old one, from times of which she knows nothing, the *jahiliyya*, or age of ignorance, before the Prophet, when the earth was peopled by terrifying, not altogether human, beings.

The site of Shebika is, indeed, very old, going back to before it acquired the name of *Qasr al-Shams*, 'Castle of the Sun', because it is detached from both the mountain above and the desert below, fully exposed to the east. Here and there in the village there are remnants of ancient columns. All this is, to Nawa, very ancient, older than old. But what is she to do with ancient things? Travellers have proposed buying the press, but its weight discouraged them from taking it away. After that, to be sure, she saw it in a different light.

On the floor of this shed two young women, rolled in the same blanket, are sleeping. These are Nawa's daughters, who have married and live in El Hamma. The older one, Hafziyya, is pregnant and has come to bear her child in her mother's house. The younger one, Neila, who came with her, has no children yet. On the way to see her daughters Nawa passes close to the low wall running between the house and the shed. She glances down over the wall at the ravine below. There is a ravine on either side of the village, so that it is situated on what seems a sort of tongue stretching from the mountain into the Sahara.

This is the hour when the dog with the thick white hair and glaring yellow eyes comes back, always through the same hole in the fence, from her excursions into the steppe where, during the night, she has fought long and indecisive battles with jackals and small wolves. When the dog arrives it is day. Soon after this, from in front of the Mosque, the quavering voice of the *Imam* calls to prayer. 'Allah is great, Allah is great, and Muhammad is his prophet.' The two girls are already awake. Neila, the one who is not pregnant, puts on her red dress, pressing the wrinkles out of it with her hand, ties a plaited cord around her slender waist, and gathers her hair into the hanging part of her veil. Then she picks up two big earthenware pitchers.

At her mother's house she does the same thing as she does in her new home at El Hamma, 'when the stars are still in the sky' and her husband is still sleeping: she goes to draw water from the spring. Carefully she raises and pulls open the gate and closes it behind her. As soon as she reaches the unpaved square, still immersed in darkness, where a couple of men who have slept there all night emerge from the shadows, she leans forward and then pulls herself up straight again, making the traditional motion with which women raise their veil over their heads when their hands are not free to do so.

She walks diagonally across the square and down the graded path, where naked children are already throwing stones at frogs croaking in the puddles. The village lies above her, on a perpendicular escarpment, buttressed by terraces. Other women are already there, along the little canal which the villagers dug out a dozen years before, just after the declaration of Independence. Like them she puts her pitchers down on the edge and wades into the water up to her knees, raising her skirt as high as possible in order to wash. For the younger women this is the only chance to go out during the day; the older ones, followed by a motley throng of small children, circulate at all hours.

Meanwhile, up the hill, Nawa leans over the daughter who is still sleeping. She runs her bony fingers over her belly to estimate the growth of the unborn child since the preceding day. As she does so, she carries on a running conversation. She speaks of her distant cousin, the wife of Si Tijani, who lives in Tawzar. For two years she has been with child, waiting to be delivered. No use being impatient; she can only wait until the time comes for the baby to be born. Then she goes on to boast of the marabout of Shebika, Sidi Sultan, so much more efficacious than the one at El Hamma, which explains why Hafziyya has come here to be delivered of her child.

Usually, when Neila is not there, Nawa goes herself to fetch water from the *wadi*. She goes there, really, to hear the latest news and gossip. These, today, she will hear later on, going from house to house in her function of midwife. Two or three other women are currently in the same condition as Hafziyya. For Nawa and her husband a birth is an important bit of business. Her services are paid for by dates, or by extra water for the plot in the oasis during the summer. Besides, the baby, even before he is born, is indebted to the woman who brings him into the world.

Nawa piles up some pieces of wood between two big stones. The fire from the day before is still alive beneath the ashes, and bending over double Nawa blows upon it. For some time she remains bent over, her arms crossed beneath her breasts. Meanwhile, Hafziyya takes down an earthenware dish, called *tajin*, in which to heat some left-over couscous, which she stirs with a wooden spoon. Nawa stands up straight, takes over the dish and stirs it in her turn. She tells Hafziyya how hard she tried to please her husband when they were first married. On her ankle she wore a totally impractical silver bracelet, and she bought him cigarettes with the money given her by her father. Nawa laughs, and Hafziyya laughs with her. She is nonchalant and a trifle sad; this is her first child.

At this point Nawa's husband, Muhammad, comes on the scene. He makes straight for the couscous, and gives it an extra probe. Then he walks away, saying mechanically, as he does every morning:

'May Allah grant you a long life, and may he let us stay long together!'

Nawa and her daughter mumble the same phrases in reply, adding:

'May light shine upon your day!'

No one attaches any importance to these words, but they must be spoken. There would be a catch in the throat and an uncomfortable feeling in the whole body if they were not mumbled every morning. Actually Muhammad and Nawa have rarely said a word to each other, since the time when the children were very small and one or the other was ill. Now, except when they are harassed by an unpaid debt, they have nothing to talk about.

A few minutes later Muhammad comes back, squats in front of the fire and spoons up his couscous straight out of the dish in which it was heated. Then he wipes his mouth with the inside of his ghandurah. Neila returns from the *wadi*, pushing open the gate and crossing the courtyard with the pitchers of water. Muhammad takes one, and washes his face and hands.

It is at this moment that they hear the call to prayer. At once they turn towards Mecca, that is, in an easterly direction, towards the *shatt* and Tawzar. Even the pregnant Hafziyya wheels around with amazing agility. She is so large that the women of the village have mockingly predicted (*In sha Allah* . . .) that she will bear quadruplets – all girls. A cruel prediction, since the women, no less than the men, consider a girl of little worth. The midwife hardly dares tell a man that he is the father of a girl, whereas she runs joyfully to announce the birth of a boy. It is strange indeed, however, that the women should speak belittlingly of their own sex. 'A woman is just like a man, she's his equal,' says Nawa, 'only a man is better.' In the closed world of the women of the village (who do not communicate with their husbands except in the invocations we heard above) there is no deeper satisfaction than the idea that from their husband's embrace may be born a son.

As they are rising from their rapid prostration, the children of Nawa's sister (who died last year) emerge from the house and, paying no attention to the adults, take some hard olives from a calabash on the ground. They walk with their stomachs sticking out, clad in short, sack-like garments which leave their dusty legs uncovered. The caked dirt on their legs does not come off in the *wadi* no matter how often they bathe in it. It will stay on the boys until their father takes them to the hot spring baths at El Hamma, and on the girls, until, just before their marriage, the other women clean and scrape them with dried leaves and brushes until their skin is as smooth as a tanned goat-hide.

Now the mountainside takes on first a rosy and then a brick-red hue, and a covey of shrill, grey and yellow birds, a kind of desert dove, flies over. Beyond the wall hanging over the ravine the horizon takes shape, as it does every day at this hour. It widens in one direction towards the Sahara and in the other, which it outlines like the bed of a dried river, towards one end of the *shott,* which gradually whitens as the sun pumps the water out of its salt bed. In the distance, towards Algeria, the land is phosphorescent, as if the early light of the sun were refracted from the masses of darkness displaced to the west.

After the last words of the prayer Muhammad goes out through the gate, leaving it for Nawa or his daughter to close behind him. Men are all alike; they do what is expected of them. Nawa had two husbands before Muhammad, who died one after the other. Nawa finds little difference between what she used to be and what she is today, the mother of several married daughters and of a son who works at Tamerza, coming home at intervals, unannounced and without explanation. When she left El Hamma to marry Murad, a man from Shebika who gave her father a piece of the oasis with ten splendid palm-trees, she was a young Bedouin, proud of the tattooing on her left cheek. She had never seen Murad and was never to see him very often, although she bore him three children, who all died very young before their father was killed by the bite of a scorpion. After him there was Ali, who was killed in error during the passage of some French troops who brought Moroccan *goumiers* to burn the house of a villager suspected of having secretly helped a group of rebels hidden among the rocks.

But to Nawa there was no 'error' involved; she never asked herself the reason for all these deaths. She was brought up to believe that what must happen happens and that everything that happens coincides with what must happen.

When Nawa evokes the image of herself as a young Bedouin who arrived at Shebika thirty years ago she sees herself as she sees her daughter pushing open the gate, without substance or perspective. The two images are one and the same; between old Nawa and the young Bedouin there is no difference. She knows only that she can no longer have children, that she has arrived at the stage when she rules over the younger women, that she can go through the village with her face uncovered, and even joke with the men lying in the dust.

After Ali died she married Muhammad, and he is a good man, even if he gave her father no more than a dozen scrawny sheep and goats. She and Muhammad had the son who is now working at Tamerza. It was fortunate that Muhammad, the son of a tenant farmer, a *shreek*, of El Hamma, was indebted to Nawa's father and thought to repay him by taking in his widowed daughter. Such debts, transmitted from one generation to another, are real assets, when there is a marriageable daughter or one that has lost her husband when he was very young. Now Nawa, as a midwife, is rendering services that will indebt other families to her and to her children and grandchildren. She can recite these debts in chronological order, like the dried fruits that are strung on a palm stem for counting purposes.

Neila has called to her attention two women who think they are pregnant, although they are not quite sure, and she has a total of four or five midwifery jobs ahead of her. She picks up a pitcher and goes out through the gate, not so much in order to fetch water as to find out how things are going with the grocer's wife, who is due to bear a child. If Nawa is called in she will be able to liquidate the debts contracted over a number of months for sugar, tea, oil and tobacco at the only shop in Shebika. Three dinars, they must come to, and that is quite a lot of money. And there is no question of Muhammad's raising them by working the grocer's land. This would not be consonant with the dignity of his family. Hadn't his grandfather personally owned a large part of the oasis?

Of course Nawa doesn't go to the grocery. She has set foot

there only once in thirty years, at the time when she learned of the death of her second husband. All she knows about it is gleaned from her children, whom she sends there regularly on errands. Even some of the men never go to the grocery, probably because they owe money to Ridha, the only man in the village who can read, in a sort of chant, from the newspaper, and also the first possessor of a transistor radio.

Ridha often lets his fellow-villagers listen to speeches broadcast from Tunis, nodding assent to passages which they do not understand. In these parts the spoken word is limited to the few sentences learned at the *kuttab* * or commonly used in the home: 'May light shine upon your day!' or the even vaguer 'May Allah grant the fulfilment of your desires!', phrases to be uttered at a birth or a sick-bed or a final agony. The rest of the vocabulary is drawn from woman-talk, from jokes, from discussions of debts and tattooing, and the necessity of killing a goat.

Everyone knows, of course, that the radio conveys the voices of people far away. The French, the Germans, the Americans, and then the French again, all listened to it, and today the National Guards carry a transistor in their jeep. A boy who was employed for some months in the mines at Metlawi has a transistor, in a bright red case, which he carries around with him, even when he is working in the oasis. His family takes greater pride in this possession than in the ability to provide couscous for breakfast and stew for dinner.

Ridha and his wife are frequent subjects of conversation around the spring. First, because Ridha goes every month to fetch supplies from Tawzar, bringing news of El Hamma, which he passes on the way. He, too, as everyone knows, gives money to his suppliers. It is known that his two younger children go to the Shebika school and that his older girl is in a boarding-school at Qafsa. And it is known also that his wife has a mirror. This mirror is what sets Ridha particularly apart from his fellows, although his father and grandfather were *khammes* in the fertile land around the oasis and he played games with his contemporaries in the *wadi* and on the square. The fact is that

* The school for teaching the Quran.

no one in Shebika has ever seen his own reflection. Farther to the north, when the government moved the Bedouins of the steppe into a furnished housing project, where there were mirrors on the closet doors, the women, quite naturally, hung veils over them to ward off the evil eye. But Ridha and his wife have no such fears.

For some time the women down at the river have been saying that Ridha's wife is having a difficult pregnancy and will probably go to have her baby in the dispensary at Tawzar. Nawa needs to hear the latest gossip. She passes in front of the men already stretched out in the sun along the wall of the Mosque and scurries along the path, crossing the mules on which other men are riding down to work in the oasis. She won't find out anything definite of course – words aren't made for that – but there will be a little more reality to the service which – *in sha Allah* – she is hoping to sell.

Meanwhile, her two daughters have gone over to the loom, tightening the braces that hold it on its palm-trunk base, or *saddaya*. On the preceding days they have washed, by trampling them in the stream, the bits and pieces of wool gathered together – some of them by Muhammad during a trip to Tawzar – then hung them up on the wall, alongside strings of peppers, to dry, combed them with a *musht* and strung them on the *maghzel* or distaff. The idea is to add this wool to a piece already woven, which is to make a burnous that Muhammad has been waiting for for some time, perhaps since as far back as the marriage of his first daughter. Everyone knows that, for lack of wool, weaving is a long-drawn-out affair. The town price of the amount necessary for a burnous is far too high. There is no other resource but gifts, swaps, scraps picked up in the street and the left-overs from the annual sheep-shearing. There is a slender hope, too, that visitors from the town, impressed by the weaving ability of the village women, may bring with them some good wool and buy back the finished cloth as they do from the Bedouin nomads. But the Bedouins are always on the move, and travellers always make more money than stay-at-homes. Doesn't the Quran say: *'Seeru fil ardh'* – 'Walk out over the earth'?

As they fit the ends of the recently acquired wool into the loose ends of that which is already woven, before pressing them together with an iron comb, Hafziyya, giggling, teases Neila for not being a mother. If she goes on this way her husband will repudiate her and she will come back and grow old in her mother's house, as many of her relatives have done before her. And Neila, giggling in her turn, repeats the prediction that, with such an enormous belly, Hafziyya is surely going to give birth to four baby girls. They laugh together and then fall silent. Outside, the children shout as they run after the chickens. Little Ali rolls in the mule's straw and runs, his protruding stomach covered with dirt, to see his aunts. No one dreams of scolding him. Ali is a boy. Hafziyya leans over the loom and asks Neila if she has noticed how developed Ali is for his four years. Soon he'll have to be sent off with the men; his mother would be proud if she could see him. Neila catches hold of Ali and pats him as if he were a little animal, while he laughs and struggles to get away. Neila takes a particular delight in caressing the little boy.

When Ali has run away, Neila pulls out of the bundle which has served her during the night as a pillow a long piece of black cloth with yellow embroidery, a *tarf* on which she has been working since her marriage, without ever having enough thread to complete it. Once upon a time gold thread was used, and certain Bedouin women sell in the city elaborate *tarfs* from their great-grandmothers' dowry. From the loom Hafziyya tells Neila that she won't finish until she's an old woman, like Nawa. And Neila retorts that Hafziyya will never have even the cloth to embroider, because her husband is too poor to buy it.

Here is Nawa, back again, with the pitcher of water on her shoulder. She hangs it beside the others and leans over to pick up a big earthenware pot with a cover made of braided esparto. Over the fire, which is still smouldering beneath the ashes, she re-heats the couscous, adding to it some olives and cooked peppers. As she turns the spoon in the pot she tells her daughters that they are lazy and their husbands will scold them. But this is just talk. A man never speaks to his wife, even when they lie down together on the mat at night during the first ten or fifteen years of their marriage. He cares little for what she likes or what she may be thinking, any more than she cares for what he likes, beyond the likes of a normal man : a hot couscous when he comes home and healthy children. Theirs are two separate worlds, which pass without touching.

Now, when Muhammad comes back, he pushes open the door and sits down, waiting to be fed. The women greet him with a '*Sabah el kheir*' and go back to their work, except for Nawa, who squats down in the dust beside him. The mule pushes his way in and sniffs at the loom; the children follow, and lie down, with their eyes on Muhammad. The sun is oppressive, although it has disappeared from sight, lost in the throbbing sky, which seems to spread light and heat from one end of the horizon to the other. Below, the Sahara, behind the low wall, has melted away into a grey haze.

Muhammad conveys the spoon to his mouth, using his free hand to supplement it. He says, flatly, that – *in sha Allah* – he will go the next week to Tawzar with the grocer, in the National Guards' jeep. He wipes his mouth with his left hand, dries it on his ghandurah, goes to look at the mule's stall and kicks the dog, which responds with a happy bark to this unusual demonstration of interest. The tent-dwellers of the steppe, on the contrary, care more for their animals; they delouse their dogs and feed them well. Nawa has boiled some water and poured it over the tea, bought loose in small quantities, from the grocer. To this she adds powdered sugar, which she keeps in a secret place for fear the children, or even her grown daughters, may steal it from her.

The heat pours down relentlessly. The chickens cackle, the mule whinnies, and Muhammad emits a couple of loud burps, to which Nawa responds with a blessing. The great silence of noon falls upon Shebika. Nothing is comparable to it. 'At this hour one penetrates the mysteries of Allah,' that is, the feelings and imagination and all that which carries man beyond the dust amidst which he drags out his existence, rises to the 'steady motor' that is God. The village surrounded by mountains, the strait, triangular gate among the red rocks overhanging the desert, is the work of God, and the villagers know that they have this to show to strangers and that no one else has anything like it. One day Muhammad pointed out to a soldier who did not speak Arabic the portion of the sky cut out behind the irregular ridge of the mountain, and for a long moment neither of them spoke.

Muhammad squats to drink tea. Nawa and her daughters sip at theirs as well. The tea has a bitter taste which the sugar does not disguise. In the old days, it seems, the tea was better; it was accompanied, then, by *takruri*, the Indian hemp or hashish which everyone smoked or chewed before Independence. At this hour, in those days, the whole South entered into a state of weighty contemplation. Along the hedges, at the foot of walls or palm-trees, the smokers and chewers no longer noticed the women passing by with water from the spring, or their companions returning on muleback from their work below. They saw only what they called God, this shimmering balance of the cosmos in the heat of the noon.

After this Muhammad goes away. A few moments later, without consulting one another, the three women get up and go to the main house, where they put on a *bawta*, a long black dress which covers them so completely that only their feet are showing. In this garb they venture outside the gate.

On the square, in front of the Mosque, men, rolled up in their *ghandurah* or burnous are sleeping, with their heads in the meagre shade. Only the indefatigable children are running, hither and thither, after a little girl who has caught a lizard and put a string on its tail. There is no real shade except for the narrow strip at the foot of the walls, and the grey houses seem to have melted away into the rocky texture of the mountain.

The three women turn to the right and go around the square and down the path leading to the *wadi*. They turn upward, alongside the portico, where men are talking together, veer to the left on a path of beaten earth, then to the right again, and enter a courtyard, similar to their own, where four or five other women are sitting around a pot of tea. This tea is even more bitter than that which is served by Nawa, but the women claim to savour its genuine taste. By dint of economizing on sugar they have come actually to like this strong, bitter brew. Stretching out in the dust they wait for it to act upon them.

There is no definite programme. But at a certain moment little Fatimah appears with her *durbakka*, a small drum with a goatskin stretched across it, which gives a hard, clear sound. She beats it, first with a folded finger and then with her whole hand. Each beat calls forth another, and all together they inspire a slow movement of the body, they phrase a sort of invitation which women alone know. Time goes by. How long a time? The yielding heat generated by the tea and the stifled beat of the drum allows for no punctuation.

But the beat of the drum creates an atmosphere of suspense, of something that must be expressed, that only women understand. They drink more tea. The sun still bears down heavily upon the closed courtyard, where the chickens sprawl in the dust, raising their heads from time to time to peck at a flea, a gesture which is occasionally made by the women also. Finally old Nawa rises, not completely, but half-way. Throwing back her head and rolling her hips, at first hesitantly, she twists herself in a way that seems to detach her motionless and slightly separated legs from the rest of her body. Because it is her privilege, as a woman who can no longer bear children, Nawa transforms herself into a warrior. Out of an old stick she makes a sword, with which she feints, while her body is revolving. Old Qaddura comes to her side and joins the dance, warding off the thrusts of the imaginary sword. And the others accompany the drum-beat, clapping their hands and calling out, as if they were men: 'Watch out!' 'Look sharp!' 'I'll split you from stem to stern!' 'Curses on you if you give in!'

Dust flies in the little courtyard, and the chickens take refuge in the shed. The children, who had stretched out, naked, to sleep, come to look on and clap their hands. One of the Qaddura girls, who has joined the dance, raises her skirts, laughingly displaying the tattooed palm-tree on her shaved intimate parts. The other women laugh, too, at this obvious hint to her husband that he should get her with child. Nawa twists more and more slowly. She knows that she is not a man and never can be, but her movements are purposefully calling up a man's presence, the presence of a warrior.

Soon the women fall back, laughing, on to the mats and speak of other things. They relax and doze off, in spite of the drumbeat. This is the only time when Nawa dreams. In her dream she calls up the image of the man that she is not, the man whom her mother held up to her as an ideal, the man capable of begetting many children, of going to war, if need be, of carrying her off on horseback, like the hero of a Bedouin song. This man into whom she has made herself is playing his part for her benefit; he is behaving with her as did her first husband in the early days of their marriage, rolling joyfully over to her mat during the night. She feels something more than the satisfaction of receiving the seed that will bring forth a son, something whose fulfilment lies perhaps in the mere fact of being a man. ... It is only a passing dream, and at her age quite futile. But this, she knows, is what draws her to old Qaddura's house, to hear little Fatimah beat the *durbakka*.

When the women get up the sky is almost blue, because the sun is no longer so strong. It is sinking towards the horizon, outlining the Sahara – the double wasteland of the salt lake, where nothing grows, and the steppe which turns into sand. Fatimah has long since stopped beating the drum; she pours out more tea, but the tea is cold. Everyone is silent, for it is time to go. Nawa manages to inquire about the grocer's wife, but no one has had news of her for several days.

Nawa and her daughters go back to the square. The men are coming up from the oasis to have a cup of tea at the grocery. Back in her own courtyard Nawa finds the children still asleep. Her daughters resume their weaving. Hafziyya teases Neila again about her sterility, and Neila repeats the quip about the girl quadruplets. Nawa ties up the mule and feeds him a mixture of wheat and straw. Then she too takes her place at the loom. Here, too, time passes quickly.

When the sun grazes the Sahara, the plain opens up, as if to receive its first red and then violet light, the same colours as those which Nawa extracts from the grain grown in the oasis for the purpose of dyeing dresses. The Bedouin tents below the village stand out so clearly that one can make out the women shooing the chickens and the men driving the camels. The tents take on colour, although they were grey during the heat of the day, with bands like those woven by the women of El Hamma when Nawa lived there as a little girl. That was the time when, in both summer and winter, long camel caravans set out, by way of Tawzar and Naftah, to far-away Libya or to the even remoter area of oases bordering upon the Black Men's land.

Nawa stands leaning against the wall, her head resting on her right arm, looking at nothing in particular. Ever since she passed the age of child-bearing she has stood here at this hour. She is thinking of the torrential autumn rains, which arrive just in time to flood the oasis, and of the spring showers which cause wheat to sprout almost at the edge of the desert. The coolness which arrives with the decline of the sun is agreeable in the same way as the expectation of something new and life-enriching. Nawa thinks (and says so quite frankly) of the *takruri* that people used to smoke and chew before Habib* said that it was a poison brought in by the colonialists and inappropriate to 'a new and healthy country'. He was right, of course, for the men have changed since the abolition of the hemp habit. They work harder, even during Ramadan.

She has heard talk, over the radio, of the city. The city, of course, is Tunis, where a family from Shebika went to work and has not been seen since. The city is a collection of houses, like Tawzar, but much larger, since it seems that one can walk in it for hours without ever seeing the country. At least this is the account of it given by Si Tijani, who goes there from time to time on business.

The sun is touching the edge of the Sahara, which is now the colour of crushed olives. Hafziyya and Neila are preparing a stew made out of the meat of a kid which was killed a few days before and put to soak in a big pot. When Muhammad comes Nawa may learn from him whether the grocer's wife intends to bear her child at Shebika or whether she will go all the way to Tawzar.

* Habib Bourguiba, President of the Republic.

Turning back from the wall Nawa reflects that she has seen a great many things in her time. The French spahis, with their red trousers and burnouses, their heavy trucks and horses, the Germans with their enormous helmets and darting yellow cars, then the Americans, who left a trail of gasoline cans, tins, clothes and shoes behind them, and now the uniformed Tunisian 'brothers' of the National Guard. A 'new age' is beginning, she has been told, and she believes it. But exactly what is new?

In the South night does not fall, it comes up out of the earth, creeping like a fog over the desert. A last remnant of day still lingers at the hour of prayer, a prayer which she has not said for a long time and which the others barely murmur. Nothing has much meaning at Shebika, now that they have been told that everything must change, even if as yet the change is invisible. People have no respect, any more, for tradition, that is true. Marriages are haphazard affairs, holidays are celebrated with indecent haste, hardly any money is given for the marabout of Sidi Sultan, and the young people talk of nothing but the city. Yet nothing new has happened. Everything goes on, but not the way it did before.

There is very little doing these days at Shebika. Once upon a time there were the religious holidays, and the marriage rites, and even a traditional way of working. Now the women stay in the courtyards, occasionally dancing, and the men sleep on the square. They are waiting for they know not what. The radio says they must wait, that everything is going to change. Surely the voice from afar is not mistaken.

Now the sun disappears over the edge of the desert, which is the colour of oil. Night settles in, like a thick and palpable object. In a few minutes Muhammad will push open the gate, leaving it open behind him. And she will close it, with the gesture that she learned to make when she first came from El Hamma, a young Bedouin girl, with tattooing and bright eyes. Muhammad will sit in front of the fire and eat his stew, without saying a word, and she will look at him, just the way she always has, to see if he is satisfied. No one speaks while he eats his meal, running his fingers over the bottom of the empty dish and sucking the oil from them. .... The others will eat only when he has finished.

Then Muhammad will go to his room and stretch out on the mat. Nawa will stay for a while with her daughters, speculating about the wife of the grocer. Everywhere night will outline the shapes of the houses. Now everything is swallowed up in silence. There is nothing but this time and place, on the road traced by God, where there is nothing to do but wait for better days to come. But how? Once upon a time she knew what she was waiting for. But for years now Muhammad no longer comes to her mat to bestow a rapid and silent embrace upon her.

Muhammad

Muhammad wakes up to the light clatter of the water pitchers, to find that it is very nearly day. The first thing he does is to roll up the blanket in which he was sleeping. Once or twice a month, although awakened by daylight, sounds from the court-yard, or sheer habit, Muhammad pulls the blanket around him and prolongs his sleep. This is usually because he has had to go down to the oasis during the night, to attend to the distribution of water in the plots of which he takes care. But this second early morning sleep is never very satisfactory, and he prefers, particularly during the summer, to nap during the afternoon. Most often he gets up when Nawa comes back from the foun-tain. Beside his bed he finds a terracotta bowl, a *maajana*, in which he washes his face and mouth and hands, inhaling water into his nostrils and blowing it out again with a loud noise.

Then he goes out into the courtyard and draws a deep breath to see from which direction the wind is blowing. If the sirocco is blowing up from the Sahara he can calculate that for the next few days (his calculations, even about money, never cover any large span) he will get little work done. The mule that he shares with old Ali will be stubborn and rebellious and swarm-ing flies will buzz about his head.

Turning round he sees Nawa and his daughters, who imme-

diately hide their faces. He looks, then, in the direction of
Mecca, focusing on a cliff, which is now ashen in colour, but
will become red when the sun falls upon it. This cliff was
pointed out to him at the age when he began to say his prayers,
just as it is pointed out to the children of today, *'Bism Illah il
Rahman il Rahim:* In the name of God, the gracious and merci-
ful. . . .' This first line of the Quran which Muhammad repeats
morning and evening, is of itself unimportant, but there is more
to it than the mere words, as commonplace as the gesture of
breaking a stick every time he passes in front of a hedge said to
be inhabited by a spirit or *jinn.* But the phrase reveals (not too
clearly) two simple certainties: first the profession of faith,
the *shahaadah,* and second, al-Islam (submission to God), the
Law. These are associated with the prostration of all the faithful,
from Shebika to the far-away Occident, the Maghrib, on the
one side, and, on the other, beyond the desert and the marabouts scattered through the clusters of fig trees of Barbary, to
the Orient, the Mashriq, the site of Mecca, 'from which we all
come'.

Thus nothing is confused or uncertain. From dawn the world
falls into this pattern, which makes of everything he knows
and everything he does not know a solidly and definitely built
structure. These certainties obliterate for a moment the cares
of the day – the question as to why old Ali dug his trench in
the oasis a little behind its usual emplacement, although if
questioned he will never say; the problem of obtaining enough
tobacco for at least three cigarettes, in exchange for hoeing
around one of Rasheed's olive-trees (that is, if Rasheed has not
already given all his tobacco to his son) – and re-establish that
unity which Muhammad is incapable of putting into words but
which he feels so stably and concretely around him.

Now, at last, as he puts on a belt given him by his brother
who served with the French army, he returns Nawa's greeting:
'Tesbah ala kheir!' (Good morning) meaning the most material
of gifts, daily bread, just as *Kheir Rabbi,* the Lord's gift, is the
rain that revives the plants. Muhammad talks in a mumble. All
the men speak between their teeth; this is part of the role which
they attribute to themselves. The women are easier to under-

stand. Actually, what a man says is, with rare exceptions, entirely predictable.

When he has finished his couscous Muhammad gets up, murmurs something, as usual, incomprehensible, cleans his teeth and, as he goes out, takes down a sort of hoe, or *masqa*, considerably shorter than the kind used in the olive groves to the north. He pushes open the gate and leaves it swinging behind him, then, holding his hoe by the middle of the handle, in an upright position, looks around the village square. Here he is more truly himself than he is at home; he is a man of Shebika. In the courtyard he may refer to himself as 'I', but on the square he is bolstered up by the consciousness of belonging to 'us', of being one of the group of the men of the village, even if the others are not actually there.

The square is hexagonal in shape, adjacent on one side to the Mosque, a low-set, crumbling edifice. It is outlined by a wall which rises on the left side along a rough path leading to a postern, behind which is Ridha's grocery. At the far end there is a sort of portico, resting on palm-trunk columns, which must have been discovered half-sunk in the ground. Here is installed the *qaddus*, the water-clock which measures each man's allotment of water in the oasis. Across the way the hillside drops steeply away over the *wadi*, some ninety feet directly below. The stones that hold it up have been reinforced by heavy wires and staves, whose installation was 'the first thing we worked at all together after Independence, and a good thing it was, too'. Hence, the square curves round and breaks off at the brink of a cliff, which overhangs some of the oasis gardens before sloping in terraces, down to the rest, and, farther to the right, to the desert.

On the square, at this hour, there are only the two children of old Ali, who have caught a sand-lizard and tied a string around the base of its tail. If a National Guard passes by they will try to sell it to him, that is, if the lizard survives. Just then a white shadow appears beyond the postern leading to the grocery. Muhammad is always embarrassed by the sight of Ridha. They played together, years ago, on the square, but since then Ridha has become a travelled man. He has taken numerous trips on the Jerid and even, so people say, as far as Tunis.

Ridha must have foreseen the course of what the radio called the 'events' leading up to Independence, the demonstrations in the big cities and the battles with the *fellahin* in the mountains. Because the village had openly shown its sympathy for the rebellion and furnished volunteers for the guerrilla warfare, which recalled the *jaiysh* of ancient times, celebrated in song for its mixture of heroism and looting, a French-led column of Moroccan *goumiers* was sent to 'restore order'. The Moroccans have little use for the Tunisians, and when they arrived the women escaped to the mountain caves, where their great-grandmothers had taken refuge when the men of Tamerza or Redayif came on plundering expeditions, or the troops of the Bey of Tunis arrived to recruit soldiers or collect taxes.

The *goumiers*, finding the village empty, set fire to the only building which seemed to them of any importance, the grocery shop of Rasheed (who wasn't yet 'old Rasheed') alongside the marabout of Sidi Sultan. Later on Rasheed touched a certain sum of money called 'war reparations', which must have disappeared like water under the August sun, because he never spoke of it.

It was after this that Ridha appeared on the scene with his pack and installed himself, as if he were in hiding, in the dark corner behind the postern. Here he set up a counter and wooden shelves, where he displayed the goods he had brought with him: powdered sugar, tea, salt and oil. Soon people fell into the habit of going 'to Ridha's' to buy small quantities of these staples. He wrote down their names in a big notebook, and by now there is nobody unlisted. Ridha has become the most important man in Shebika, not only because he fills day-to-day orders, but also because he is willing to lend five or six dinars for some more sizeable purchase. Such loans have to be repaid with interest, because Ridha is always complaining that he is penniless. But there is no alternative. A man has to live, and Ridha has become as indispensable as the water which makes for work in the oasis.

Ridha's latest enterprise has caused a great deal of talk. In a jeep belonging to the National Guard he brought back a fifty-year-old sewing-machine and set it up in the doorway of his shop. Since then young Abdelqadir, who learned how in the army, has installed himself every day at the machine and mends clothes brought in by the customers of Ridha. He doesn't work the whole time; he talks and drinks tea, but he puts in about a dozen hems a day.

Muhammad takes a few steps on the square, and young Bashir comes out of the portico where the water-clock is hanging. Bashir is twenty-five or thirty years old, and a Frasheesh, like Muhammad. But Muhammad puts little stock in family relationships. 'For some time now people have been moving around too much for a man to know where his relatives may be.' Much less stock, anyhow, than Nawa who, like the other women, 'speaks of nothing else, when she is with her friends, and, when she opens her mouth, even at home'.

Bashir walks down towards Muhammad on the dirt path. His bare feet slide on the gravel, because they are hardened by his lack of shoes. 'May God's gift be with you!' he murmurs, and Muhammad echoes his words. Bashir has in his hand a hoe just like Muhammad's. He too is a *khammes*.

The word *khammes* or *shreek* is heard in all the oases of the Jerid. It gives Muhammad his identity, and he uses it as if it were his name in speaking to himself or to others. *Khammes* comes from the word *khamsa*, five, and signifies that he does not own the piece of land which he works, but is entitled to a fifth part of the harvest. This does not hold true in larger oases, like Naftah or Tawzar, where the owners do not give a fifth part of the harvest to their *khammes*, but a share which still bears this traditional name. When was this division established? It is hard to say. Much longer ago than what is called the 'old days' it probably had to do with the division of the five essential elements learned at the *kuttab*: earth, seed, harness, tools and work. It goes back to the *jahiliyya*, the age of ignorance, when everything was part of an unbroken whole with God. But there was also a more recent period when landowners lived with their tenants, the *shreek*, or their day-labourers, the *khammes*, when they worked and ate together and divided the fruit of the land.

Now Muhammad, like all the men of Shebika, is a *khammes*, a day-labourer on a piece of land whose three owners hold interminable discussions about the exact proportion of their gains, in January from dates, and at the end of the summer from other produce, particularly peppers, which sell at Tunis for twenty times the local price. The three owners are a man from El Hamma (the purchaser of the land with which Muhammad obtained his various wives from the hands of those who disposed of them and who, in their turn, became *khammes*), a miner from Redayif and a nomad from the tents. The same state of affairs exists at El Hamma, Naftah and Tawzar, except that the parcels of land are larger, and the *khammes* more numerous and obliged to keep longer working hours. The owners live in Qabes, Qafsa, or Tunis; they rarely visit their land, and leave the care of them to an overseer.

Something would be lacking in Muhammad's life if he didn't occasionally see one of the owners, or at least think of him, if only in the hope of a word of approval, especially after nights when he has had to go down to the oasis and channel the water. The owners are men like himself, wearing the same sort of blue overalls or a burnous just as ragged and greasy at his; in short, they, too, are poor.

Of course, in the time of his grandfather, Muhammad's family had land of its own, as did all the families of Shebika. This was a long time ago, before the advent of the French. And in the back of Muhammad's mind there is a core of stubborn certainty of having once owned the land on which he now works for somebody else. His condition of *khammes* seems to him somehow temporary, because there is an order and balance of things, set forth in the Law of the Quran, by virtue of which the land must surely be his again some day. He says this to himself over and over when he is at work. At the time of the 'events' he said vaguely to himself that now he would recover the land of his grandfather. But nothing changed, and the owners are the same as before.

Still Muhammad thinks of the land as his; between him and

it there is a sort of intercourse of which no one but himself is aware. In his passage to and from the oasis, his back-breaking work, his efforts to squeeze out the last drop of water. . . . The associations that weave themselves in a man's mind while he is walking or riding are curious indeed. Muhammad believes, for instance, that his to-and-fro journey is reminiscent of what the Quran teaches about 'the night of power which brings on fate', the night of the 27th of Ramadan, the *Leilat al-qadr*, during which the Quran comes down to earth and the Prophet, in his turn, goes to join God in the course of a long 'night-time journey', the *Leilat al-miiraj*. Surely this coming and going is the same for all things created.

Muhammad and Bashir go down to the oasis. First they skirt the external wall of the marabout of Sidi Sultan, Shebika's most precious possession, but one which has no more purpose, because everything deteriorates and even old customs are forgotten, and this is just as well. Instead of following the track which crosses the oasis from one end to the other, they take the steep path which leads to the most important branch of the *wadi*, the one which was made into a canal at the time of the 'collective work', so vividly remembered. Along the way there is an abandoned wild palm-tree; frogs perch on the roots and leap in every direction. Here the two men retrace their steps, every day, and every day frogs leap into the transparent stream, letting themselves be driven by the current for a few inches, then striking out with their hind legs in order to return to where they were before. And every day Muhammad gives a great burp and spits into the water.

On the other side of the *wadi* they enter the gardens of the oasis. There is no definite path, because every segment of land is surrounded by a sort of ledge which holds back the water during irrigation. Various plants grow on these ledges, some of them as stiff as willow branches and others easily pushed aside by the hand. When they cross a segment of cultivated land Bashir and Muhammad walk along the ledge, in order not to trample the peppers or break the branches of the cherry and almond trees. In January, when the dates are harvested, the fruit trees are in flower, and as the *khammes* shake down the dates these fall among the red and violet haze of their blossoms.

After the two men have crossed the three parcels of land along the *wadi*, Bashir halts and, without saying a word, begins to hoe. Before the two of them part company he ventures the idea that 'if the drought continues the tent people will come up out of the desert in the direction of Shebika, and there will be plenty of them'. And Muhammad speaks of the transistor radio which Ali's son has brought back from the army and hangs on a tree while he works. Even now music drifts through to where they are standing. This is all they have to say. They are together, and they are happier than if they were apart. In any case, words have little significance.

Muhammad has to cross another piece of land before arriving at his own. At Tawzar and Qabes there is a man to every two and a half acres, but here the sub-divisions are smaller and Muhammad has less than he could actually handle. Nevertheless, he comes down to the oasis every day. The date-palms give him considerable work for about a hundred days out of the year. In winter, after the dates have been gathered, the trees have to be pruned; in spring he has to climb up two or three times to loosen the pollinated flowers and tear off the now useless male organs; in summer he climbs up again to spread fertilizer. And then there are the summer and spring nights when he has to assure the passage of water through the canals, for it is at this time of the year that irrigation is measured and controlled.

Muhammad works with goodwill and indeed with pleasure. He likes the idea that every growing thing must ripen, for this is God's will, and he, Muhammad, is called upon to effect it. The vegetables and everything else that needs watering bring him every day to the oasis, not only because the profits from them go to him rather than to the owners, but also because they feed his long-standing dream of possession. He must hoe the earth and keep the canals in such a condition that the water can flow freely through them, regularly in autumn and winter and irregularly in spring and summer. Otherwise the peppers, peas and beans would dry up as quickly as they do in the desert.

In the oasis there is perfect silence; an occasional muted cry

is barely heard among the branches. In this late spring season
the flowers of the fruit trees form a dense wavering cloud at a
man's height in the air and the violet shade of the palms protects Muhammad from the sun, at the same time isolating him
from his fellow-workers. He is sheltered, even if not completely
hidden, by the thick, uncut foliage. Even the exhalation, reminiscent of that of sewerage, which arises from the clay bed
of the *wadi*, is overpowered by the odour of the flowers and
the almost sickly-sweet smell of mint.

He knows, too, the source of the slightly bitter odour that is
wafted towards him at intervals while he is hoeing, from a
hemp plant which he tends along with the others, although to
grow it is strictly forbidden. There was a time when he used to
come upon his father, during the summer, stretched out with
his head in the shade and a hemp cigarette between his lips in a
state of complete relaxation. In those days the smoking of
takruri was tolerated, or at least very slackly watched over
throughout the South, and the summer days went by in a
dreamy torpor, to the accompaniment of the buzz of flies and
the shrill sound of a shepherd's flute in the distance. Life was
altogether different, and although Muhammad does not exactly
regret it (since Independence the radio has proclaimed that this
period was one of shame and that the French settlers encouraged
hemp-smoking in order to keep the natives quiet), yet he looks
back almost nostalgically, as if to a lost paradise.

In the oasis he feels protected; this calm, humid, closed
place shelters him from the world. He has been told that the
hammam, or baths, in the cities are places where a man likes
to linger for the same reasons. It seems natural that the people
of the boundless steppe should like enclosed, sheltering places.
Sometimes the Mosque is one of these.

At intervals Muhammad observes the flow of the water in a
saqia, or trench, and with his hoe, frees it of encumbering
clumps of dirt or grass. In this season when there is abundant
water, it is sufficient to open the sluice-gates blocking the connexion between the trench and the smaller lateral canals and
direct the flow into the cultivated beds. Muhammad cuts out
squares of grey-blue water, one after another, and they sink

slowly into the sandy soil in which trees and plants are growing. The sluice-gates have to be watched and built up again by hand when the current tears them down. Muhammad does not mind kneeling down in the mud. The mud is good, and life-giving; it makes the dates and peppers grow; in short, it makes food.

Water is precious, above all in spring and summer. It belongs, legally, to the owner of the land and it is a grave fault to let it be lost or wasted. There is nobody to watch over Muhammad's work, certainly not the old man from El Hamma, who never shows his face, or the other two owners, from Redayif and Tamerza. And yet Muhammad works as hard as if someone were watching.

He knows that one day (according to the story they tell in Tawzar) a young boy reported to a land-owner that his *khammes* was wasting water. But the owner was angry with the tale-bearer and punished him. Didn't the wasted water remain in the soil? Yes, it did. Then it was still one of God's blessings, and there was no waste!

Sometimes the water goes into a hole. The hole has to be filled in and the land around it consolidated. This is a different kind of work, but Muhammad does not dislike it, because it breaks the monotony of the gestures which he is accustomed to making.

Muhammad is so used to bending over almost double that his back no longer hurts. When he was a young man, working with his father, he used to have pains that he thought he could not endure. Many young *khammes* leave the oases and go to seek their fortunes in the cities. But if this radical step does not enter their minds or they find no occasion to take it, they get over their pains. Today, as the old men say, Muhammad is 'bearing down on his kidneys'. With one foot on dry land and the other in the mud, he moves slowly along. Between his legs, the live, blue-grey water runs into the bed and percolates through the soil.

Working in the oasis of Shebika is nowhere near as hard as in those of Naftah and Tawzar where, during the dry season, the *khammes* is threatened with curses and even a beating-up if the land-owner arrives at a moment when the water is spilling over, as it often does, into the property of his neighbour. Here everything is easy-going, but the production is slimmer. Here, too, as in the larger oases, in the summer there is always the fear of a spill-over, and the *khammes* is in a state of constant anxiety, even if no one is watching over him, especially if it occurs when he is not on the spot.

Working conditions are continually tense. The fruit and vegetables mature simultaneously but at different rhythms and each one requires a particular kind of care. And in summer, the season difficult above all other, the distribution of water often takes place during the night. The *khammes* waits in the portico, near the water-clock, a jar suspended over a basin cavity dug into the rock, from which water falls, drop by drop, and is renewed, as many times and for as long a period as the piece of land is entitled to irrigation. When it is his turn Muhammad runs down the path, hoe in hand, to the oasis, opens the sluice-gate and waters his plot until it is the turn of his neighbour.

Today, as he drains off the water into his plot, Muhammad reflects that the date-palms and the vegetables have got off to a good start; he can save water which will be credited to him three months later, when it is most precious, and exchange it for tobacco with the grocer, whose land is farther from the .wadi and less happily situated in regard to irrigation.

Future favours and exchanges are added to those of the past. There is the sugar which Ridha promised but has not yet given in return for Nawa's services at his wife's childbirth the year before (this should surely be recuperated on the arrival of the new baby). The tea he owes to old Ali (which prevented him from asking Ali to his face why he had changed the course of the water, an action which may have concealed some hidden intent), the favour he did Bashir during the winter, when he brought him back some medicine for his eyes from Tawzar and Bashir promised a vague 'something' in return.

These things are the very fabric of life. Everyone has such exchanges on his mind. Sometimes Muhammad thinks it would be simpler to pay cash, but in these parts money is a scarce commodity. And what would people talk about if exchanges were not the chief topics of conversation? Their minds are constantly on the give and take of commodities and favours. What do they talk about in Tunis or other such places, where these transactions are unknown? This is life, or at least it is the chief spur to taking an interest in everything that goes on.

When he has finished with the irrigation Muhammad plants his hoe in the ground and sits down under a palm-tree. The passage of the water has had a cooling and freshening effect, and the smell of flowers is mingled with that of damp earth and decomposing mud. Mosquitoes move to the attack, but Muhammad does not stir a finger to chase them away. They buzz without biting, and if they do bite he hardly feels them. Within reach is the basket, prepared by Nawa, which he picked up from beside the fire earlier in the morning. The contents are always the same: a piece of dry cake, baked in a mould, the *tajin*, which gives the cake its name, and a slice of paste made by crushing dates in a goatskin and drying them out until they are so hard that, several months later, they have to be cut with a hatchet. Muhammad eats slowly, slipping his tongue between his teeth in order to extract the bits of food stuck there. His teeth are bad, like those of all the men of the Jerid. A dentist on the medical truck, which passes occasionally by Shebika, told him that four or five of them should be pulled out and replaced. But what can he do about them? The dispensary at Tawzar is too far away.

After he has eaten, Muhammad drinks some goat's milk. Then, leaning against the palm-tree, he rests. But his fingers mechanically busy themselves with braiding stalks of esparto into a sort of rope with which to tie up his mule or camel, or to bind together the dried palm branches which he takes home for the fire. The mosquitoes continue to buzz, an unknown bird (strange enough for him to notice it) chirps in the tree-top. The smell of the flowering trees is almost inebriating, with its sugary sweetness, which attracts the flies and the bees. Muhammad is drowned in a transparent haze, now green, now reddish in colour, according to the angle at which the sun strikes the palm branches. In the distance the camel utters a cry.

At this season the only remaining job is to hoe the bean rows and pull up the weeds. At a certain period of the spring the palm-trees call for attention. Muhammad plants the sharp blade of his hoe in the trunk and pulls himself up with the handle, his free arm around the tree and his feet gripping the bark, which sticks out beyond the base of the lowest branches. This is the time for *tathqir*, or insemination, which is achieved by attaching the male stems, with their long, yellow, claw-like protuberances, to the female stems. The operation is time-consuming.

When Muhammad has finished with one tree and before he begins on another, he digs a hole with his hoe, builds a fire around three stones in the centre, and sets on it an old tea-kettle, which he left behind a clump of grass the day before. In the pocket of his overalls he carries an old matchbox, containing the half-dozen match-sticks which he has managed to collect for this express purpose. It takes considerable scratching to get a flame and when he has one he leans over it, hunching his shoulders, and sets fire to the dry grass and sticks.

If this is the season of insemination he tackles another tree. If not, as today, he proceeds to weeding. He squats down, seizes a weed with his left hand, and sticks the point of his *manjil*, or sickle, under the root, using the handle as a lever. He pulls up one weed after another, with as much care as if he were caring for them rather than destroying them. He is constantly scratching the earth, and as a result his hands are covered with a permanent layer of dust, almost like a second skin, and the tips of his fingers are hard callouses. Manipulating the earth as he does, every day, he is aware of how it depends on his attentions. By its obedient response to his touch it gives him a feeling of power and something like possession.

At harvest-time birds sweep down upon the oasis. Muhammad stands up, looks around him, and emits a yelping sound – the verb is *ihahi* – awakening a response from the men in the other sectors around him and, if it is night, the barking of dogs awakened from their slumber.

In the summer Muhammad goes back up to the village early, as soon as the sun is at its zenith. Some of the *khammes* sleep all afternoon under the trees, in spite of the flies and the humidity which makes the undergrowth into a steam-bath. But this is usually because they live far away, or because a caved-in roof or the presence of chattering women makes it difficult to sleep at home. Often the men gather together on the square, between the two posterns, between the Mosque and the marabout. They roll up in their ghandurahs in the narrow band of shade at the foot of the walls or assemble in the portico of the water-clock, where a current of fresh air is blowing.

Muhammad stretches out on the smooth stones. The heat obliterates the grey elevations of the desert, beyond the cemetery, and the silence is broken only by the dripping of the water-clock. Occasionally one of the men rolls over and starts to talk – of the Bedouins who come, with ready cash, to make purchases at the grocery, of the fact that the date-harvest will not be as good as it was the year before, so everybody knows and is saying. Sometimes the elders instruct a young fellow who has just come back from military service in the duties that await him when, like his father and grandfather before him, he enters the estate of *khammes*. Irrigation (because 'water is life'), insemination (an expression of God's will), weeding, hoeing the bean patches, driving away grasshoppers and sparrows, assuring the flow of the water in the trenches and the functioning of the sluice-gates. 'God is the real owner of the land, and the work of a *khammes* is more important than that of a road-worker or bus-driver, because it helps everything that should come to birth to be born, and this is God's pleasure.'

When the elder who is enumerating these duties leaves one out another man rises up and puts in, almost angrily : 'And the animals to be tended and put out to pasture, and the cords to be woven for the *mashia*, what of those?' And the elder protests that he knows all these things, that he is 'swallowing his words', in order to continue, to speak of the cutting of wood, the preparation of *surgho*, the cleaning of tools and the feeding of the animals. And the young apprentice nods his head in assent as he listens to these words which he has heard a thousand times over.

At other times there is no talk; the men doze or sleep. Above all in the month of Ramadan. During this sacred month the village vegetates. The necessary work is done at night or early in the morning, fatigue permitting. After that there is a tendency to rest, although it is said and written that no man must take refuge in sleep from the temptations of the day. But who respects the conventions, in these times? How can a man be as scrupulous as his forbears, when Habib and the radio proclaim that a new life is just around the corner? And how can a man hold out when, just before dawn, he has eaten only a fistful of couscous or a few morsels of kid stew? The whole body calls out for sleep.

Everyone knows that work slackens during Ramadan. There was an occasion, a long time ago, when a cloud of grasshoppers descended upon the oasis in the month of Ramadan, which was during the summer that year, and no more than two or three *khammes* were willing to go down, in the heat, and beat the ground to drive them away. The harvest was destroyed, and everyone lost out, including the land-owners, but they understood and did not complain. Such things happen.

When Ramadan falls in the rainy season or during the winter, it is a different matter. Everyone does his usual work, taking care only not to make the mechanical gesture of chewing a blade of grass or drinking a handful of water from one of the canals. The difficulty of working under these circumstances is increased by hunger and thirst and the craving for a cigarette. Men's nerves are on edge, and they break out into sudden, swiftly appeased quarrels, *hasheeshet Ramadan*.

In ordinary times, even in summer, when the sun has sunk lower in the sky, and the Bedouin tents stand out among the rocks where they are nestled, Muhammad and his fellows pick up their hoes or sickles and go back down to the oasis, jokingly taking leave of the old men who stay dreaming or talking without end at the base of the wall. In summer, after the extreme heat of the mid-afternoon, the atmosphere of the orchards is damp and foul-smelling; in winter it is sometimes cold.

Muhammad rakes together the grass and weeds that he has uprooted during the morning and ties them into bundles with the rope that he braided during his noon rest. One of the land-owners has a donkey which he bought from the Bedouins, and Muhammad uses it rather than the old mule he inherited from his father, which for some reason he keeps in reserve. The donkey is pastured in the 'waste land' of the oasis, the patches along the river, above the date-palms, which belong to no one in particular.

Now he loads the bundles of weeds and some pieces of wood on to the donkey's back and goes back up to the village. Part of the wood goes on to a pile stacked up in one corner of the courtyard for the benefit of the owner who works in the mines at Redayif. For three years he has not been able to find an animal to carry it to where he lives, and probably he never will. Meanwhile the wood continues to accumulate, providing a home for a large number of lizards. The owner comes to look at it every year during the date-harvest and palavers for hours on end with the men of the village, although he knows perfectly well that none of them will carry it on his back for fifteen miles over the mountains. Occasionally he thinks of selling it, but there are no buyers. Every now and then Muhammad helps himself to a piece to be used for heating his tea.

By the time Muhammad gets back to Shebika the sun is setting over the Sahara. The light lingers on the plain, outlining the village houses against the reddish mountainside. The colour of the sky passes from green to ochre to a silvery grey, all very rapidly, because twilight is short, and soon Shebika is ashen and dead.

All the *khammes* have come home. (Muhammad notes that Rasheed has preceded him.) Their mules do not need to be led; they make the climb on their own all the way to the gate of their own courtyard. This is the hour when the men gather together for discussion and the settlement of any disputes there may be among them. They debate such questions as whether the son of a Frasheesh and the daughter of a Qadduri should marry or how to comply with the request of the representative of the governor of Qafsa at Tawzar that five men be commandeered for road-building and chosen on the basis of their family situation. Often they talk about taxes. Because money is scarce it is up to Ridha to advance it, on the assurance that he will be repaid in working-time or in extra water for his parcel of land in the oasis.

Sometimes Muhammad lets the donkey go home without him and pauses at the Mosque, which is next door. It consists of a large room with a partly collapsed ceiling. A few corroded columns surround a sketchily decorated *mihraab*. The mats are ragged, but the *Imam* conscientiously spreads them out in the sun every day with the result that in the evening they are still warm. On the floor there are a few loose stones. Everyone knows that religion does not authorize trafficking in the simple magic of throwing a stone into the air and from the place where it falls predicting such events as the payment of a debt or the birth of a child. But one or two old men are always casting stones, although no one has much of an idea of what conclusion they come to.

Muhammad prostrates himself and says his prayer. Of the five obligatory prayers – *al-subh* (morning), *al-dhuhr* (noon), *al-asr* (afternoon), *al-maghrib* (sunset) and *al-aasha* (evening) – he says only the fourth. It fits the best into his schedule and he considers it quite sufficient. A dozen men are prostrated on the ragged mats as darkness creeps into the Mosque, swelling the size of the columns and the height of the ceiling, which has not been whitewashed for years, for lack of money. As the men finish their prayers they get up and leave, one by one. In the last resort each one of them prays for himself alone.

Muhammad goes out on to the darkened square. Ridha, the grocer, in his whitish ghandurah, walks by, and tells Muhammad that he has just received, from a passing traveller, a certain quantity of tea and tobacco. No traveller has passed by for weeks – his presence would surely be noticed – but Muhammad knows what the grocer means. He has changed his mind about taking his wife to give birth in the city, and probably this very afternoon someone from his household has told Nawa that her services will be wanted. Muhammad pretends not to understand, even when Ridha roughly tells him that he can come to the grocery. He makes no answer, but lets the donkey in through the gate, leans his hoe against a post, and puts his basket down beside the fire, where he will find it filled again in the morning. Then he makes his way to the grocer's.

The first thing he sees there is two Bedouins, wearing ghandurahs and a sort of turban that comes down over their eyes. Their eyes are keener, more restless and also harder than those of any man of the village. The two Bedouins are very tall and, except for their darting eyes, quite still. They are talking, very deliberately, on their feet, to Ridha, who is rolling up a bottle of oil in an old newspaper. The first of them is saying that he has noticed that the pasturage below Shebika is better this year than usual. His *arsh*, that is, his family, has been pasturing the animals not far from the *shott* this season.

Ridha, in his turn, observes that the sheikh, or village chief, of Shebika, Ali the Sheikh, is presently away, looking after his affairs at Redayif. The second Bedouin observes that the weather is not unfavourable for moving the sheep down from the highlands and that the *shatt* where he will pasture them is no more than a night and a half's walk from the foot of the mountains.

Ridha has folded the newspaper and is standing with his hands on the counter, like a watchful animal, when Muhammad enters the dark and smoky room. Animals can graze where they choose in the desert, Ridha says, and the details can be discussed later. The taller of the two Bedouins, the one that spoke first, pulls half a cigarette out of his ghandurah and lights it with an old lighter which he has to tap several times against the counter before it produces a flame. His companion extracts a hand from his enveloping garment and puts down some change, which Ridha absorbs, as it were, by covering it with his sleeves, while the Bedouin tucks the bottle of oil away.

The light of the candle is so yellow and smoky that Ridha can barely make out Muhammad's face. The faces of the two Bedouins shine in the darkness. They draw back, with a snake-like movement, towards the door. A moment later their horses are heard whinnying from the little square above the portico, where the grain is threshed in season, and there are always left-over bits for the chickens to peck at. Finally the horses' steps ring out clearly all the way to the cemetery below the village.

Ridha picks up the tea-pot which is boiling behind the counter, with its steam arising between himself and Muhammad. He remarks that a man may owe money, but that it can always be repaid by some other means. Muhammad nods assent and quotes what he has been told that the Quran says against usury. Ridha agrees, complaining of the usurers to whom he is indebted at Tawzar, who ignore the needs of the people of Shebika and refuse to give him anything on credit, in spite of the fact that he pays up regularly as best he can.

Muhammad says that it is difficult for a man to pay if he has nothing, and Ridha agrees with this as well. They drink their tea in tiny sips, blowing to cool it off. The tea is very black, having boiled for some time in the water, and it leaves a bitter taste in the mouth. But how could they do without it? Muhammad stares into his glass and says it's right for a man to want to wipe out a debt with a single stroke, but isn't it wiser to take what he can get and leave part of his debt outstanding? Ridha assents to this too. He pulls out a scrap of paper from which he reads aloud that Muhammad has acquired, since the winter, almost two dinars' worth of coffee, sugar, salt and oil. He hands the paper to Muhammad, who examines it attentively. Muhammad does not know how to read. Ridha knows how to reckon a bill and write it down, and he knows, of course, that Muhammad cannot read it. When Muhammad hands back the dirty scrap of paper he tears it into pieces. Then he takes out another paper and jots down the prices of two pounds of sugar, a packet of tea, and a bottle of oil. This adds up to quite a lot, half a dinar, but the rest has disappeared.

The grocer refills the glasses with tea, gets up with difficulty, leaning against the wall, and disappears behind the counter, where he can be heard rustling papers and shifting boxes. There is almost nothing on the shelves except for some loose cigarettes and sheets of newspaper. Everything else is in boxes, underneath the counter. Muhammad musters up his courage and says he needs a few cigarettes. Without hesitation Ridha hands them to him, as a *sadaqa*, or gift, in Allah's name.

Muhammad tucks them carefully away in his overall pocket and takes the parcel from Ridha's hand. Ridha sits down again and they silently sip more tea. Finally Muhammad sets down his glass. 'May God give you a son!' he says, and Ridha replies: *'In sha Allah!'* As Muhammad goes away both men raise their hands to their lips in a brief gesture of farewell.

It is dark outside, and Muhammad gropes his way along the wall parallel to the path. He pushes open the courtyard gate. Nawa and her two daughters are waiting, their faces outlined by a candlelight as yellow as that of the grocer's shop. Muhammad hands the parcel to Nawa, who calls down Allah's blessings upon him. Here, indeed, is a good provider! When Muhammad has sat down he learns that this evening, after the moon has risen, Nawa is to go to serve as midwife to the wife of Ridha. But the birth bids fair to be difficult. He notices that she has filled a basket with herbs and ointments and readied the mat on which she kneels to invoke the spirits. Meanwhile he eats his evening stew, sopping up the gravy with a piece of bread made from the grey, local flour.

When Muhammad wipes the bottom of the dish with the forefinger of his right hand it means that he has finished his supper and the women can begin theirs. They are sitting apart, beside the loom, with their elbows hugging their sides, their hands on their knees and blank eyes. Nawa remarks that no one can tell what sort of a child heaven may send or whether it will send one at all, and Muhammad recommends leaving the matter to God. Nawa says that Ridha's wife told her that Qarawi, the land-owner from Redayif, must be coming to Shebika because she saw him taking a rest in the grocery at Tamerza. Muhammad shoots a glance at the wood outside. It is unlikely that Qarawi has found anyone to take the wood away, but he may intend to sell it in the village or give it to him, Muhammad. Why not? It seems unlikely that he should travel so far simply in order to give the wood away. But you never can tell; stranger things have been seen and nothing is impossible if God wills it. Probably he is coming simply in order to put in a short period of work on the land, as he often does when he has had enough of the phosphate mine. At such times he lives in Muhammad's house and buys supplies from the grocer. He has a way of saying that he intends to move permanently to Shebika and work on the land. Muhammad knows that Qarawi's family has lived for a long time at Redayif and that he makes as much money in a single month as he, Muhammad, in two whole years. The story of moving is a fabrication. But he always nods approval and repeats with conviction: 'Of course. . . . You are quite right.'

After supper Muhammad lies down on his mat and rolls the blanket around him. He remembers the cigarettes that were given to him by Ridha, takes one out of his pocket and lights it. The effect of a cigarette is stronger than that of tea. For a while he can hear Nawa chattering and laughing with her daughters; then the great silence of the steppe prevails. Muhammad stretches out his arm and crushes the cigarette stub on the dirt floor. Then he turns over and starts to go to sleep. There are vague sounds from the Mosque, which is on the other side of the wall. Perhaps the *Imam* is restless, or else he is throwing stones into the sand in an attempt to read the future.

The Meeting

Ali, Muhammad and Qaddur, the old man who has almost lost his sight, have settled down in the narrow band of shade at the foot of the wall of a shed built on the incline between the village and the marabout of Sidi Sultan. The bright light causes all of them to blink, and Muhammad is falling asleep, because he worked all night at irrigating in the oasis. Old Qaddur is no longer active. He lives with his brother's children and pays in prayers and blessings for his portions of couscous and stew and the mat on which he sleeps in the corner. He says the blessings in a loud voice, so that all can hear, and says them well. In this way he often earns half a cigarette or a glass of steaming tea. Qaddur is imperturbable. For him Shebika has become an agglomeration of yellowish stones with human forms moving across it – clothed in black when they are women and in white robes or blue overalls when they are men. Most of the time he is content to keep out of the sun, blowing his nose at intervals with the thumb and forefinger of his left hand.

The pressure of Ali's bony leg against his knee does not bother him. Like the sleepy voice of Muhammad it is a link connecting the parts of the whole in which he lives and has his being. He has always felt better in such close company than dragging himself about the village streets or even in the company of his own kin. Everyone in Shebika has links of this kind; the fact is so well known that it isn't worth discussing. Similarly, old Qaddur knows and performs all the gestures that are expected of him – from the morning, when he receives the greetings of his great-niece, to the hour when he enters the Mosque and embraces the *Imam* and then comes to stretch out in the shade until it is time for supper. Everyone at Shebika lives the same way, but no one talks about it. How could it possibly be expressed?

In sleepy, unfinished sentences Muhammad is talking about the water he lent to Bashir, which Bashir repays in small packets of salt or else by letting him pasture his donkey on part of the land which he works, and of the fact that the National Guards no longer come to Shebika as they used to do in order to list the latest births and deaths. Ali contradicts this assertion. Just the day before he saw the Guards stop at the school-house and speak to the teacher, parking their jeep near the cemetery, which is not clearly visible from the square. The teacher is now the one to gather birth and death data.

'When do they usually come by?' asks Muhammad, but neither of his companions makes an answer. Muhammad was not really curious to know the exact dates (it is very rarely that he rides in the jeep to Tawzar); he asked the question just for the sake of asking. All three men are silent. They have come up against the intangible partition around the here and now, the elastic barrier composed of the accumulation of days and nights each one exactly like the one before, with nothing to mark them off or divide them. What is fundamentally lacking are the words with which to identify the partition, to pierce the fog. No one makes any effort to find the words or to wonder what might be behind the barrier if it were to disappear. Everything is taken for granted. For a long time women were imported from El Hamma, but now they are found at Shebika; every now and then a marriage is celebrated or a man who has worked uninterruptedly for thirty or forty years of his life is laid in the ground. But around these events there has always been a dense fog, of whose presence no one was aware. The voice that comes over the radio from Tunis has made it barely perceptible, but no more.

Already the question about the dates of the Guards' visits has been left behind. Ali speaks of a wild goat, which some children saw up in the mountains, beyond the spring. They told him that the animal was wounded and had fallen into a hole. It might be worth going after. But none of the three men makes a move. There is a time for everything. In the evening some young man will offer to go and look, in return for a large portion of the meat. Why worry?

At the time when they were building the stone wall which prevents the village from falling a hundred and fifty feet down into the *wadi* during the rainy season they ate wild goat every day. Part of the project involved disengaging and channelling the river and digging around the spring, and in the process a wild goats' refuge was discovered in the ravine. Si Tijani of Tawzar (who is vaguely related to several families of the village and considered a big brother because he has obtained construction jobs for so many of the young men) had a huntsman's practical advice to offer. He said: seal off the lower end of the ravine and wait for the goats to come down from the mountain. After that there would be meat for the taking.

This job was a communal one. It was surprising for the men of the village to find themselves all together, each one with shovel in hand and the assurance of a weekly pay-cheque. The exact date of this vividly remembered episode is shrouded in the fog of which we have spoken. Winters have come and gone, who knows how many? Only the taste of wild-goat stew remains in the mouth, and the warm feeling that goes with a full stomach.

When Ali, Muhammad and old Qaddur speak of this period they say 'we', but the pronoun is limited to themselves alone.

Ridha, the grocer, who is crossing the square on his way to the Mosque, and Ali's wife, running along with her face covered and half a dozen children at her heels, are not included. They do, of course, belong to Shebika, to 'those of us that live here in Shebika', as they are described to an outsider. But the real 'we' refers to the ordinary men of the village, when they are gathered on the square. Even the school-teacher, who is just now coming up from the school, is not of their number.

The sun narrows the band of shade in which the three men are reclining. The smell of frying meat is wafted in gusts from one of the houses, followed by the smell of burning rags. Perhaps the meat smell was an illusion. Ali sniffs the air, stretches himself, and sticks one foot out into the sun, alongside that of old Qaddur. Then he pulls himself up and brushes off the flies that have clustered on his face. These are not yet the aggressive flies of mid-summer.

Meanwhile the school-teacher has covered the distance between school and the square. He wears a jacket and a shirt, open at the neck, but he is shod like everyone else, with his toes sticking out of his shoes. He comes from Sfax, on the coast, and his family owns a piece of land in the oasis of Tamerza. Ever since he arrived, fresh from his examinations but not too scared because he was already familiar with the region, he has been lodged in the school itself. He uses an upturned wooden crate for a desk on which to correct his pupils' papers, sitting cross-legged on the floor in front of it, in true peasant style. He owns a transistor radio, given him by his older brother when he was appointed to this job. Regularly every month he sends half his pay to his mother and the mother of his fiancée at Sfax.

As he goes by, swinging a plastic bucket, he gives a rapid greeting to the men on the square before going on to the *wadi*. At Shebika they treat him like one of their own, set aside by his teaching function and the fact that he reads both Arab and French books. Every morning the sing-song recitation of the school-children rises up into the air. The rhythm is not the same as that of *kuttab* of earlier days, but still it is a sing-song recitation.

Ali remarks that the other day, at the grocery, he heard

Habib talking on the radio about the schools and saying that within ten years everyone in the country would know how to read and write. This would mean a different sort of life. Muhammad looks in the direction of the school and old Qaddur coughs several times over. The radio spoke too, of the seeds that would be distributed to the peasants. At this old Qaddur's body is racked with alternated laughter and coughing. The seeds will never arrive unless the governor, for the sake of his own popularity, makes a solemn distribution. That's the only hope, for who cares about Shebika?

Muhammad reminds him that the governor has made one visit since the previous summer, bringing medicines with him. But old Qaddur remains sceptical. Nobody is likely to come to Shebika, and even if somebody did come, what could he do? The roofs of the houses are caving in, and no one has money to buy seeds, because it is all spent on dowries. Nobody is coming to Shebika, and for a good reason. Shebika is good for nothing; everything is dead or crumbling. Perhaps it is God's will that it should fall apart.

The school-teacher comes back with his bucket full of water and pauses in the sun, before the three men. His young face is shiny, probably because he washed it in the *wadi*. Only children go into the water, and occasionally the girls, on the sly, when they are washing their clothes. The school-teacher shifts his weight from one foot to the other. He reports that the Bedouins have changed the site of their encampment on the steppe, probably because they want to protect the newly sown wheat from the birds. The transfer took two whole days, although the distance covered was no greater than that between the Mosque and the school-house. But the Bedouins have a great many possessions. So many that they have little to gain from dealing with the people of Shebika.

The school-teacher kicks at a stone, puts down his bucket and sits down in a fragment of shade. He is a man of the village, but he was born in the city. When he was a child his father, who worked for a French company, took him for the holidays to visit his family in a village almost as poor as Shebika on the road that goes over the mountains to Douz. It was only through his acquaintance with a European teacher that he was able to finish elementary school and go on to the *lycée*. He sits and talks like the others, but he is different from them. He is like the men with yellow eyes or a hump on their back who go from village to village, singing and performing tricks. The fact that he knows how to read and write cuts him off from the people of Shebika. Only Ridha, the grocer, really talks to him, not only because the school-teacher pays for all his purchases in cash, but also because Ridha is an important man, in touch with the Destour Party * and hence in a position of power. His word carries much more weight than that of the elected Sheikh, a poor devil who is never on the spot, but constantly travels between Tamerza and Redayif, from Tawzar to Shebika, without knowing what he is really after.

The others, like Ali and Muhammad and old Qaddur, hold out against the school-teacher as they held out, once upon a time, against the seeds, in pretty packets with pictures and written instructions, given out by some foreign organization. How can a man recognize a living plant from a motionless, printed picture? The seeds rotted away in the back room of the grocery, because nobody knew how to read (the young men were away doing their military service and the school-teacher was on holiday). And the few seeds that were actually sown produced nothing but flowers.

The school-teacher remarks, in a neutral tone of voice, that an old woman is said to have died in the Bedouin encampment, but that nobody seemed to know her name. Ali, Muhammad and old Qaddur, all talking at the same time, enumerate the names of various families, but none of them satisfies the school-teacher. All he knows, anyhow, is that the old woman is to be buried in the cemetery and that a boy has been sent to fetch from the Mosque the shroud in which her body will be wrapped for carrying it there.

After a moment of silence Ali raises his voice to observe that it threatens to be a hot afternoon. The school-teacher stands up

* The Neo-Destourian Party was the party of Independence, founded by Habib Bourguiba in 1942. Today it is called the 'Destour Socialist Party'.

and there appears a car like that of the National Guards, except that in this case the occupants are wearing civilian dress. Muhammad is the first to say: '*Shnuwwa?* What is it?' The car sways from side to side on the rough track, turns, slows up and, finding no spot of shade, comes to a stop in the sun, near to where the three men are sitting. The National Guards' jeep has a steel body, a rusted hood and a distinctive red mark on the doors. The fact that this mark is lacking and there are no soldiers inside is puzzling. Instead of getting up to investigate the three men raise their hands to their eyes in a self-protective gesture, such as they would make to ward off the dazzling sun, and simply stare. They remember vaguely other visitors to Shebika – doctors and nurses in a big white truck, agricultural experts, and even an occasional carload of tourists, which no sooner arrived than it turned around and went away. Suddenly Muhammad exclaims:

'Si Tijani!'

All of them recognize the man whom they call 'Ammi', or 'Uncle Tijani', a tall, dark-skinned fellow, invariably clothed in an oversize white corduroy suit with a ghandurah rolled around his shoulders. As he gets out of the jeep he waves the big stick with which he routs snakes and scorpions out of their holes. Tijani is with the Department of Public Works, and he often hires men from Shebika for a two- or three-month stint of road-building. When he comes he usually brings medicines for the women and children and hands out general advice. The men help him to find the serpents and scorpions which he sends, in sealed boxes, to laboratories in Europe. Once, when Ali was stung by a scorpion, he took him in a Public Works truck to the dispensary at Tawzar. Generally a man survives such a sting only when there is no poison in it. Otherwise he dies in the attempt to walk the thirty miles to the town.

Now, in Tijani's honour, the three men rise and pronounce the great blessing, touching their lips with their hands. Behind him they see two Tunisian girls in European dress, a blonde woman (such as Muhammad has seen only in a passing tourist-car at Tawzar), a European man of medium height, and two thin Tunisian men, also dressed in city style. Everyone stands stiffly, waiting for a conventional spoken word to fill the silence, to put everything in place and wipe out the feeling of uneasiness caused by a sight or event entirely unprecedented. After pronouncing the ritual greeting Tijani shakes the ghandurah off his shoulders. From the passageway leading to the grocery, and the portico which houses the water-clock, half a dozen villagers gather round, eyeing the familiar figure of Tijani. The engine of the jeep is still turned on and simmering, as if at any moment it would go away.

At this moment the procession escorting the body of the old Bedouin woman winds its way up from the plain. The corpse is wrapped in what appears in the sunlight to be a lavender bag (the shroud fetched from the Mosque) and carried on the back of a camel. After it a few men are running. Already the school-teacher and another man from the village are digging the grave. Only a few eroded white stones distinguish the unfenced field as a cemetery. Usually a few men and a bevy of children go down to a funeral. But this time the car from the city is a greater attraction.

Muhammad, Ali, Qaddur and the grocer are waiting for further words to dispel the awkwardness of the surprise visit. From time to time they look distractedly in the direction of the cemetery. The Bedouins unload the body, as if it were a big, round parcel, from the camel's back, and carry it unceremoniously to the shallow grave. The dead are buried near the surface of the dry, pebbly ground, where scorpions and insects feed upon them. Now the body disappears from view as the mourners form a circle around it. Finally they go away, leaving only a stone, some six inches high, designating the grave as that of a woman.

*

Si Tijani is the first to step forward. Leaning on his big stick he looks around at the people of Shebika. The children start to gather about him, while he advances to the middle of the square before coming to a halt. He begins by saying that he has brought with him the eye medicine that they asked for when he was last here. The men nod, and laugh. Then he says that we have come from Tunis. 'You must have heard,' he tells them, 'that in the capital there are schools where young men are acquiring the kind of learning that will allow them to become the leaders of the country.' The men nod again; two or three of them come up and shake hands, pointing in the direction of their own school. 'In a few years everyone will know how to read and write, and everyone will have a chance to acquire learning.' This is not the moment for visiting the village school, and so the subject is dismissed with a handshake.

Si Tijani goes on to say that our group or team is going to stay here for a period of time and to come back at intervals in order to get to know the village and to tell the outside world about it. We shall talk to them and ask them questions, and all they need do is answer. This will be to their advantage, for they will no longer be so isolated as before. We shall report to Tunis and find ways of helping them.

There follows a moment of confusion. The men talk all at once, and two or three of them start running down to the cemetery. The funeral is over. The Bedouins have broken their circle, and one of them is trampling the earth over the grave, while the camel goes back, riderless, to the encampment.

Meanwhile, the others agree that it is a good thing to tell Tunis about Shebika. In spite of all the promises that were made, the village has been forgotten. The governor of Qafsa has occasionally sent his delegate from Tawzar, but he came and went in a hurry, after inspecting the frontier posts, which were placed in a state of alert because of the war in Algeria.* As for the

---

* During the early years of our visits to Shebika, we felt the excitement and anxiety caused by the war in adjacent Algeria. 'No-man's-land' was near by. Once, when we were driving on the mountainside, on our way back from Tamerza, where we had gone to get some registers of vital statistics, a low-flying French plane followed us. The consequences, if any, were felt only after our return to Shebika. During our third or fourth stay there a stranger in overalls appeared in the village and looked us over. We were told that he was an inspector of the 'Front' in Algeria. He questioned the local people and somewhat roughly interrogated Salah and Khalil, our researchers. Then, when he realized what we were doing, he greeted us from a distance and went away. For the rest, we soon won tacit acknowledgement of our scholarly status.

Sheikh of the village, he is rarely there at all. He was chosen only because of the fact that he had provided supplies to the *maquis* during the struggle for Independence.

Once or twice the governor's delegate proposed hiring some men from Shebika for a far-away construction job. But why should they go to work far away, they asked themselves, when there was so much to be done at home? And they didn't accept his proposal. This was something we were given to understand at our very first meeting. We were told insistently : 'There's no place to live and work but Shebika. No other place is half so beautiful.'

Si Tijani explains again that we shall be asking questions. On this point there is some discussion, but meanwhile the two groups have got together. We are perched on the hood of the jeep, and the men of Shebika are pressing around us as only desert people do. They inquire as to what sort of questions we shall ask; whether, for instance, we shall ask about money, in which case we shall have no answer. We laugh. Of course we shall ask nothing of the sort. We aren't tax collectors. We have come to find out how they live, and those who care to tell us will do so of their own accord.

In any case, for all of five years, the apparently most abstract questions aroused the greatest interest. The Arabs, even if they have benefited from nothing more than the sketchy teachings of the Quran, attribute to words the same importance that we give to ideas. Contrary to general opinion, where there is a paucity of substantial or 'consumer' goods there is a greater wealth of intellectual speculation. In the cities of Tunis and Sfax and their squalid suburbs (which, since Independence, have been rebuilt or ruthlessly but all too slowly razed to the ground) the Bedouin at grips with urbanization finds certain words, heretofore indefinite, charged with various meanings in the form of a choice of actions or of desirable objects. The suddenly awakened need of *things*, the sight of the busy streets and of comparatively modern working conditions roots words in experience and in a multiple variety of implications.

With this goes the prevalence of an urban religion, influenced by Turkish rites and Turkish social forms, chief among them the women's veil, which takes on the meaning of accession (even if by miserable gradations) to a higher social status, that of the middle class, still dominated by the signs and symbols of Ottoman colonial penetration. In these new surroundings the man of the steppe passes from an ingenuous idealism to a shameful nominalism. Even if he can now connect things with words, he cannot make these words replace the things that this miserable condition allows him to crave but not to obtain.

The men of Shebika continue to stare at us. They are curious now, not so much about what we have come to do, but about who we are. Needless to say, they are intrigued less by the Europeans of our group than by their fellow-Tunisians. Si Tijani extracts a packet of tobacco from his trouser pocket, rolls a cigarette, and mutters something almost incomprehensible. Tunisians have changed, in recent years, he says; now they take an interest in their country. The bystanders nod their heads in approval, and Si Tijani introduces the first of our group, Khalil, a tall fellow with the face of a Sicilian.

Khalil is from Tunis, but his father is an agronomist and his uncle owns land at Zaghwaan. One or two of the men approve, because they have heard talk of Zaghwaan, a small town south of Tunis, at the foot of a mountain which in Roman times supplied water to the city of Carthage. Khalil is experienced in the work he is to do at Shebika, because he has already taken part in a research project at Ain Sareen in the region of Beja.*

Khalil touches his lips and his heart in greeting to the peasants while Si Tijani lights his cigarette and proceeds to introduce Salah. Salah's is a different story. He is the son of a Bedouin of the Qassireen region; as a boy he tended sheep and would have continued to do so if a school-teacher had not become aware of his unusual intelligence. His father and the rest of the family came to seek their fortune in Tunis and settled in the suburb of Melasseen, on the edge of a *sebkha*, or lagoon, which fills up every winter with salt water from the sea. There the parents and seven children live all crowded together. Because Salah is

* With Jean Cuisenier, *L'Ansarine: Contribution à la Sociologie du Développement* (Paris : Presses Universitaires de France).

of the same kind as the men of Shebika he is the prototype of what their children may some day become.

Salah puffs, motionless but tense, at his cigarette. He has come back, somewhat bitterly, with us, to the world which he had left behind him. 'At first,' one of his colleagues told us, 'he asked the most superfluous and aggressive questions of all, taking umbrage at the fact that the peasants slit the throat of a sheep and sacrificed it, treating the old men roughly and intimidating the young. It took him two or three years to get into the atmosphere, but eventually he worked with an enthusiasm which led to an unexpected broadening of our research.'

The third person introduced by Si Tijani is a young girl, Naïma, the daughter of a civil servant at Tunis, an enlightened man since he has encouraged his daughter to live as a free woman and to take part in an enterprise such as ours. Only a few years ago it would have been inconceivable that a better-class Tunisian girl should go off with some young male students on an expedition to the south. Now, with her friend, Munira, a doctor's daughter, she has come to study conditions at Shebika and to see what can be done to better them.

One of the peasants is saying that these young people will make their mark in the world one day, which is not true of the young people of Shebika or of the tent-dwellers in the plain below. No one from here has ever been known to fame. At this everyone laughs, except Si Tijani, who is handing out and lighting cigarettes, as he waits for the laughter to die down, so that he can introduce the two Europeans who are working in Tunisia.

By now the two groups are completely mingled, shaking hands and lighting cigarettes. Then silence returns, and with it a certain torpor. Now that the unexpected has actually happened the villagers don't know exactly how to take it. Tijani repeats that we are going to stay around for a while to see the way of life at first-hand, that we shall live with them and share their life, that we shall bring medicines and cigarettes and make ourselves useful in whatever way we can.

Old Qaddur, who was blinking at the sun out of his almost blind eyes, laughs and taps the ground with his stick. He doesn't understand what it's all about, he says, although he's willing to talk. The fact is that nobody, not even in Tunisia, is interested in Shebika. Shebika is a pebble in the desert, an agglomeration of poor people and stones. Waving his stick and laughing aloud, he concludes:

'Nobody cares about Shebika. We're the tail of the fish . . .'

2

THE LABYRINTH

The 'Castle of the Sun'

'We've always lived here, as far back as you can go, to our parents and grandparents and great-grandparents. It's an old place, nobody knows how old. There are canals that an engineer told us were built by the Romans, and some Roman millstones. The engineer told us that the Romans came before the Arabs. We're Arabs, of course. There are some tombs at the foot of the mountain that contained rusted iron weapons, which we used to make a plough. And the Roman stones you see in some of the houses, they're ours to make use of now. Finders keepers, as they say on the steppe. An Arab makes use of anything that falls into his hand. They aren't evil, those stones.'

'What do you mean, they aren't evil?'

'There's no evil spirit in them, as sometimes happens. Those people lived here before we did. It must have been a very long time ago.'

It seems that the former name of Shebika, Qasr al-Shams, or Castle of the Sun, refers to its exposure; the sun shines on it from dawn to dusk. Already at sunrise the light changes the colour of the mountain and seems to lift Shebika up out of its pedestal of tawny stone. They say that here was an outpost of the Roman *limes*, the boundary line and bulwark of Africa to the south, and this supposition is borne out by the discovery of eroded military remains. The outpost is said to have been called *Ad speculum*, because of a metal mirror with which signals were flashed, in time of danger or just as a matter of routine, to other outposts of the same kind. In any case, the Tunisians are not interested in Roman archaeology, as were the French or are the Western tourists who still go to visit the ruins of Carthage and Sbeitla. Westerners may consider themselves the heirs of ancient Rome, but the Tunisians hark back to Islam and its traces are those that – when they think of them – they quite naturally cherish.

'Castle of the sun', of course; it's a matter of geography and orientation. Would that the name had a cultural context as well! But it has none; Qasr al-Shams is not known, like Tawzar, as a meeting-place of mystics and poets. It calls up – if anything – the legendary figure of Abu Saïd, 'the man with the donkey', who left the Jerid to attack the cities on the coast, pillaging everything along the way, raping the women in the Mosque of Qairawan, massacring the men and endangering the fragile dynasty of the Fatimids, until he finally fell into a ravine and was skinned alive by his conqueror, El Mansur. 'The man with the donkey' is the prototype of the man of the South, the symbol of the enmity between the steppe and the city. He precedes by a century the arrival of the Hilali, who came from far-away Syria, driven westward by the Sultan of Cairo, who wished to get rid of them. Of the Hilali, Ibn Khaldun * speaks in the same terms as of the Arabs:

> For instance, the Arabs need stones ... as supports for their cooking pots. So they take them from buildings which they tear down, to get the stones. ... Wood, too, is needed ... for props for their tents and ... as tent poles. So they tear down roofs to get the wood ... the very nature of their existence is the negation of building ... [they] plunder whatever other people possess. ... They recognize no limit.†

Does this covetousness and nihilism of the South stem from the Zenata, the Islamized Berbers who settled for a time in unstable empires and then faded away, to the peculiarities of the plains, the fields ... of the steppe and the mountain valleys?

* Ibn Khaldun (1332–1406) is the greatest Islamic historian, or perhaps we should say sociologist. His *Histoire des Berbères et des dynasties musulmanes*, translated from Arabic by Baron de Slane (P. Guethner, Paris, 1925–34), and *The Muqaddimah*, although they are dominated by the concepts and language of Aristotle, are the only analyses of the Muslims by one of their own.

† *The Muqaddimah, an Introduction to History*, translated by Franz Rosenthal (New York: Pantheon, 1958), pp. 302–10.

Little does it matter. Memories of the past, when they survive, take on a man's face, they turn into a character whose dramatic actions become a source of beliefs and crystallized dreams. When we study the formal structure of 'myths' we too often forget that the logical language hidden behind their imaged pictorial and often confused expression provides a framework that is valid only for a Western observer. Certainly there is an internal logic in these combinations of words, a logic comparable to that which a psychiatrist perceives in the apparently incoherent speech of a schizophrenic. But this logic is valid only for the therapist, whose purpose is to cure, that is to adapt to a certain background whose norms and lines of force are defined, without his knowing it, by the mental make-up and even the ideologies of his own social world. The internal logic of the structure of a myth guides us to a common participation whose shapes and aspects it defines; it is like an apparently confused Rorschach test, which guides the psychiatrist's projections and interpretations. The participation created by a myth remains contained within the limits of a society determined by its original type and configuration. It gathers together the individuals rooted in it and is not easily communicable to strangers to its social system, who are involved in different forms and modes of participation.

More meaningful is the structure of a myth or an 'historical' story when it nails down a certain content or – with a varying degree of success – brings to life a definite experience. The terms of a myth are sometimes contradictory, but they relate to the awareness of an event which is linked to the collective and individual life of the group, to something it *might* experience. These implicit contents, whose development is always contingent, serve as so many means for an unhistoried group or society to order the relationship between the cosmos and its own internal organization, through the systems of partial classifications. In an *historical* society the myth becomes demiurgic in character; it responds to the implicit awareness of this society's capacity to modify (either directly or through an individual) its situation in a certain environment. But in societies without a history the myth remains the restless manipulation of forms of classifications which allow man to broaden the narrow sector of his actual experience by a mixture of perception and imaginary reality whose content and finality are never within his powers of verbal expression.

Thus the myth-memory of the man-with-the-donkey, as it survives, however confusedly, in the minds of the three old men who bring it up in their conversations (the younger men must have heard of it, but they never say so) is broken up into several schemata, equivalent to so many unusable suggestions of potential experiences. It is perhaps the intense frustration of being cut off from the realization of these possibilities that causes the myth to survive.

The first of these schemata is that of the old man riding off on a donkey to the city. It was old Qaddur that put us on its track by talking of 'men that gallop off on their donkeys and go everywhere, even to Tunis and Tripoli'. Shouldn't we see here the image of an innate force of the men of the South, who without either car or camel, can launch out upon a measureless course, the representation of their effort to overcome and abolish distance? 'They are men on the run,' says Si Tijani, 'and for them the miles do not exist. Unaware of the time of day, of light or darkness, they spur on their donkeys.' The man with the donkey seems to be the basic image of the man of the South, symbolizing his power to conquer space.

The second aspect of the myth is that of the permanent grudge which the steppe bears to the city, the continuous resentment which the man of the desert feels towards the man of accumulated property. The Bedouin's tenacious memory of Abu Saïd may bear witness to the ambitious dream of the conquest of established and dormant wealth by the galloping aggression of a little Southerner. Behind this dream of power there lurks the passionate love of pillage and *jaiysh*, the capture of booty. There is an element, also, of pure hostility towards the city and those of its representatives who seek to impose their authority. Frequently, in the North African past, the steppe has besieged and plundered the city. Of these long-ago victories there remains only the floating symbol of future action, real or imaginary.

The third aspect is that of permanent defeat, symbolized by the death of Abu Saïd. 'That's it,' Qaddur and Ali tell us, 'that's the way it ends. The man with the donkey knocked his head against the walls of the city, and his head was broken.' This defeat impels and hastens a retreat into impotence. 'We amount to nothing, and we can't even talk, because the government doesn't like it. We don't know what it is that we fear. That's something no one ever knows.'

The fact that the myth of 'the man with the donkey' maintains its power reflects a consistent attitude of the people of the South, and of Shebika, as they seek to justify their weakness. This weakness hides the true content of the myth (not its logical structure, which is not typically Southern), that is, the resentment which the steppe feels towards the accumulated and inactive riches of the city, the dream of pillaging them and, at the bottom of it all, a permanent and irrepressible hunger. The 'we' employed in the narration of Abu Saïd's story revives its drama and reflects a fundamental attitude of the desert and the desert people. In it are inextricably mingled the dream of waste on an heroic scale, of a great feast (for the pillage of ancient times was a feast, an orgy of consumption) and the certainty of an eventual defeat, bound to follow upon this momentary victory.

But the man of Shebika does not live by myth alone. He knows that he is implanted in this mountainside village, facing in the two fundamental directions, south and east, the Sahara and Mecca, the latter being every Muslim's spiritual home. He knows that the village belongs to him, that once he enjoyed the rights of ownership, but that now he is a miserable *khammes* on a land no longer his. 'We, the people of Shebika' implies a feeling of dispossession and decay.

'We owned the palm-grove; we had well-built houses with solid roofs. The marabout of Sidi Sultan was filled with gifts; caravans from Algeria camped at the foot of the mountain before going on to Tawzar.' Old Ali is speaking. He assures us that Shebika means 'net' or 'narrows', and this because the passage of the river valley is difficult; the village is well protected and, please God, it always will be. That his forbears lived here since time immemorial, and so, with two or three exceptions, did those of all the village families.

The Polarizations of Shebika

To all appearances Shebika is a simple enough proposition – a sort of triangle with the mountain as its apex and the desert and the oasis as the two points of its base. Children swarm over the square and in the orchards; women pass quickly by with a pitcher or jar on their heads or against their hips; men go down to the oasis and ride back on their mules.

The population is two hundred. But this is an approximation. When we read in the official statistics that in 1961 the population of the 9,000 square miles of the region of Qafsa was 279,100 we are amazed at such precision. We were literally unable to calculate the exact population of Shebika. We were told it was made up of thirty families; Ridha, the grocer, calls it 'around two hundred people,' and the National Guards spoke of two hundred and fifty. At Tamerza, the administrative centre, we were shown the census sheets of 1956 and 1961, which give no definite figure but only an approximation of two hundred and twenty. In the office they told us that no exact count could be made, 'because only burials, not deaths, are recorded; there is no record of still-born children, and the girls of a family are never declared to the census-taker'.

Like any figures relative to the South, ours are somewhat a matter of guesswork. The only definite figures are those of thirty-one families and fifteen single persons over forty years old. The thirty-one families have about ten members each, but there is a shifting population of girl cousins, daughters-in-law and children old enough to work, who come and go, staying as long as six months at a time. It seems that the most accurate count varies (and did vary from 1961 to 1967) from two hundred and fifty to three hundred, that is if our calculations reflect all the changes that occurred.

One thing is certain : few people die at Shebika. 'Old people, that's all,' the government employee at Tamerza told us, 'be-

cause the air is so pure.' And at Shebika itself they say the same
thing: 'The air is very healthy; there's no sickness. It's God's
own air, with no evil spirits, any more than there are in the
water. The spring is pure.' The truth is somewhat more complex. Only the deaths of old men and women are reported, either
to Tamerza or to the school-teacher. We examined his statistics
and found them strictly approximate, since there were no
undeclared deaths among them. The young man didn't want to
get mixed up in village affairs, and he simply put down what he
was told. He had been there only six months when we first
questioned him in 1962 (before then we had never seen anyone
of his profession), and in 1963 he had gone away. We tried to
add his successor to our group, by training him as a researcher,
but the administration objected. It was considered undesirable
that he should acquire a skill which might tempt him to leave
his job. This second teacher, in his turn, was transferred elsewhere. The third was willing to tell us all he knew, but he
could never find the statistics kept by his predecessors, and
apparently these had not been transmitted to Tamerza either.

There is an intangible element in the inaccuracy of death
records, and that is the fact that the phenomenon of death
itself does not have the same importance as in a Christian
country. As for the difficulties of census-taking, we may give
the following example.

'There are seven people in my house,' Nureddin told us; 'my
father, my two brothers, my mother, my married sister and my
two sons.'

Nureddin is a particularly amenable subject. He answers
questions readily and precisely. On this occasion we reminded
him of his three daughters (of whom Naïma had told us). 'Oh
yes,' he conceded, undismayed by his apparent forgetfulness.
He had not counted them and, for that matter, he would not
have reported a death among them either. This does not imply
a systematic disregard of women. The fact is that a son, as we
have already said, is a cause for rejoicing and, to his father, a
source of triumph; he will perpetuate the family, work at his
father's side and swell the number of believers at the Mosque.
A daughter belongs to another world.

A break-down of the population statistics is not easy to make either. Of the three-hundred-odd people of the village between 120 and 150 are women and girls; there are over a hundred children and young people under twenty years of age and some thirty old men, most of whom are no longer the heads of families but bachelors and widowers, who live with a son or cousin. Death, caused by either illness or accident (a snake-bite or a fall from a tree) seems to strike the men most often between the ages of forty or fifty. If they survive this decade, there are prospects of their living for many years to come.

These three hundred people live in an area of the sub-pre-desert steppe, where geographers note the accumulation of modifications and erosion caused by the wind, the paucity and irregularity of rain and the intrinsic disorganization of the flow of water.* We have here a dialectic of aeolian erosion and entropic erosion, the result of a conflict between wind and water. 'The destruction of ligneous or thorny drought-resistant plants, even if it does not bring about the destruction of the thin soil which provides a meagre pasturage (for goats and camels), may have serious results because of the shifting of the sand.' †

Under these difficult and often pitiless conditions only 'group solidarity' permits man to survive or merely to exist. Geographers know well that geo-morphology alone cannot give a satisfactory picture of life in these regions. We must take into account the nature and quality of the challenge with which the natural surroundings confront the collectivity in its simplest units, those of the village, the encampment, the oasis. By 'surroundings' we mean the sum of the hostile forces which, apparently, left to themselves, present the collectivity with an obstacle which has to be hurdled every day. What was called in the last century 'adaptation to surroundings' implies a complex of elements based on continuous readjustment. These readjustments do not stem from the accumulation of previous re-

* J. Poncet, *Les rapports entre les modes d'exploitations agricoles et l'érosion des sols en Tunisie* (Publications of the Department of Agriculture, No. 2).

† ibid., p. 78.

adjustments; they do not make for a synthesis achieved with the passage of time and continuously self-enriching. On the contrary, it is characteristic of so-called 'backward' societies to be ignorant of acquired experience and its transmission. The very nature of backwardness and the 'archaic' is defined by the limitations which external surroundings impose upon a group which never succeeds in overcoming its unfavourable and negative situation. Each generation has to repeat the same struggle, without any increase of the ability to deal with it. If there is any accumulation of experience it develops on the level of mental classifications which (along with the lingering memory of successive adaptations) establish a straight line, represented in the manner of a non-existent past. Social classifications, as they are variously manipulated, seem to correspond to a magic and somewhat pathetic intention of reconstructing human history under circumstances where there is only the mechanical repetition of sporadic efforts to overcome a steadily deteriorating situation.

It is, then, in the unity of the living group that we find the reasons for the survival and indeed the very existence of Shebika. But this group, this *we*, this Shebika, is not so simple. Not only because the morphological aspect of the village, its division into various sectors: the grocery, the portico with the water-clock, the three or four houses where the women meet in the afternoon, calls for a morphological analysis, but above all, because we learned from five years of research and observation that the reality of the village is dissimulated behind the morphological pattern, that there are levels of analysis tied in with an area of collective experience which is constantly shifting ground. If, as the philosopher G. Buchelard says, there is no science except of that which is hidden, then everything here that escapes the eyes fans out in the path of vectors which orient the life of the collectivity in different directions. The 'hidden' aspect consists of all elements of the collective existence, each one diversely accentuated at different times and in different individuals. It implies not only an apparent logic (which a crude and insufficient language does not always render) but also the fact that an important part of the collective life is *played out*, on the occasion of holidays or events imposed from the outside. Thus our stay in the village deeply modified its life. Upon our arrival, the deteriorated and depressed village group felt impelled to act the essential roles inherent in its social organization. This dramatization, as we shall see, had serious consequences.

If these masked elements do not emerge on the surface, then we must analytically reconstruct and develop the various levels of reality in an attempt to explain the group life by breaking it up into its basic components. For the masked elements correspond to different levels of the collective existence.

The facts recorded during five years of investigation may be grouped around these various levels of experience, according to a diagram proposed by Jacques Berque for the analysis of the villages of the Maghrib. This is a series of concentric circles or, rather, lest these circles seem to be closed compartments, a sort of spiral which gives the idea of circulation between one division and another. Every one of the windings of this circle corresponds to a set of significant facts whose concrete meaning is at this plane of emergence alone. We may still refer to them as circles: *the circle of marriages*, which relates Shebika, across the desert and the fluid stretches of the steppe, to other groups, by means of a conventional code which is still more or less in force even today; *the circle of work in the oasis*, which brings into play not only agricultural techniques and the division of labour but also the whole system of land-ownership and the resulting poverty of the *khammes*; *the women's and family circle*, which extends into the various houses and certain points of the village and takes in the question of incomes and budgets. In the middle of these concentric circles Berque places the living heart of the village, located, paradoxically enough, in such fundamentally inactive places as the grocery, the portico of the water-clock and the Mosque, where the men gather idly together. These concrete points (which vary from one village to another) are important not for themselves alone, but for the intimacy which brings *khammes* and small land-owners (there are no large ones) together at all hours in the apparently passive state where the real life of the community develops, a state of waiting or expectation. This diagram fits the demands of rationalization and reconstruction of the collective experience, insofar as each one of its categories groups together the multiple pieces of information which (for the men of Shebika and for the observer striving not to project his European classifications) are implicit only at the levels distinguished therein.

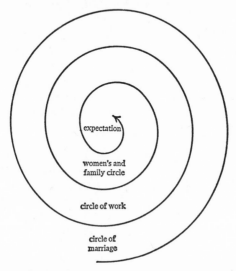

We must also examine – and eliminate – the polarizations to which the villagers spontaneously admit and of which they speak quite easily, because they belong to a primary morphological experience. The near-by places – the desert, the mountain passes, the north-western plateaux, Tamerza, Redayif, El Hamma, the *shatt* – define a lie of the land so familiar that everyone has a *language* in which to describe it.

For Muhammad, Qaddur, old Ali and Nureddin (the head of an important family in whose house the women most frequently meet in the afternoon), the village belongs to an area that is both fluid (in its borders) and set (in its nomenclature). 'The desert is all around us and the mountains behind, with a pass leading to Tamerza, but we look out mostly in the direction of El Hamma and Tawzar.' Or, more definitely: 'Mecca is that way [pointing vaguely towards the *shatt* and the East], and then there are Tawzar and El Hamma. El Hamma, because that is where we have the greatest number of relatives, and Tawzar because we go there for supplies.'

It is natural to go down to the desert and El Hamma, and understandable that they should lend their names to this direction. When there is mention of Redayif and Tamerza, they are indicated not only as being in another direction, but also in a hazy and embarrassed fashion. 'They are far away and difficult to reach,' says Muhammad. But Qaddur and other younger men say merely: 'They're just like Shebika, and it's not worthwhile to go there just to see the same things all over.' Young Bashir was the one that finally gave us the clue. 'Once upon a time the people of Redayif and those of Shebika were always at war, and if they went up in the mountains it was only to take one another by surprise and stage a fight.'

It is impossible to pin down the date at which this hostility between Redayif and Shebika started. It seems to have been a long time ago, and nobody knows the reason.

'They were always stealing our flocks, and during the wars of *jaiysh* they went after the things we were after.'

When we went to Redayif we asked the same question. The people of this little town, now a centre of phosphate-mining, said:

'The men of Shebika are chicken-thieves, and because their chickens are not so fine as ours they used to come into our territory and steal from us.'

One of the sheikhs of Redayif had a more pondered and likelier explanation. At the time of organized pillage, the route of the Algerian camel-trains passed through the gorges of Redayif and Tamerza on the way to Qafsa. The interception of a caravan going to Al Wad or Naftah required covering a considerable distance across the desert. And so the men of Shebika, quite naturally, sought their fortune in the mountain gorges which Redayif considered as belonging to its own private preserve. Hence the fighting.

Later on, we came to realize, there arose another rivalry. Many peasants of Redayif work in the mines or in some way profit from their presence. The standard of living is incomparably higher, and the six or seven hundred miners make as much as ten silver dinars a week, a sum which no one except Ridha, the grocer, has ever even seen at Shebika. The miners put money aside, and a dozen of them, although the sons of poor peasants, have bought up parcels of fertile and well-cared-for land in the oasis of Shebika. It is understandable, then, that the men of Shebika do not care to look in the direction of the road to Redayif. Over it travel land-owners whom they regard as enjoying rights which they themselves lost in consequence of an inexplicable catastrophe.

One of them told us of yet another manifestation of the enduring hostility, which under the rule of both the Beys and the French was reduced to a war of words rather than of weapons. At one point, at a certain season the people of Redayif started going up to a plateau in the mountains, half-way between the two villages, taking with them abundant provisions. They set out some bread, and then hid behind the rocks. Soon after, the people of Shebika, also bringing provisions, arrived upon the scene and pretended to snatch the bread. The owners rose up from behind the rocks and threw themselves upon them in a mock battle, after which they all sat down, exchanged titbits and ate together.

This custom was still observed 'quite recently, until just after the return of Habib [that is, the achievement of Independence]; since then we haven't had time and it no longer seems such fun'. In it we see the superposition of various elements, which we may break down as follows: cessation of the traditional enmity and its replacement by a mock battle; metamorphosis of violence into a game, exchange of objects formerly stolen, and fraternization, at a half-way point, between the populations of the two villages. These are outward signs in which we perceive a change, for a change is never seen as such but always through some fundamental element of a former reality, transposed or, we might say, sublimated. The discontinuance of a period of traditional action is not seen as the rupture that it actually is with the past. Thus the end of the fighting had to become a mock fight before it could make way for a new and different human relationship.

The two opposite directions, El Hamma, 'where we have cousins', and Redayif, 'where the owners come from', are complicated by other equally contrasting polarizations, such as that of the encampment on the desert recently set up by a dozen formerly nomad families, whose members frequently come to the village but are not liked there. 'They're people like ourselves,' admits Qaddur, 'but we prefer strangers like you.' 'Arabs are like lice,' said Muhammad; 'they swarm all over the place and eat up everything.' We object that all of them are Arabs, but he, like the city-dwellers and all those 'sedentary' people who live in one place, reserves this designation for the people of the steppe, who have no fixed abode. 'They come up here when they please,' says a younger man, 'and we don't try to stop them. That's all that matters. We shouldn't mind exchanging talk, but they come only on account of the grocery.'

The above polarizations are recognized by the people of Shebika themselves as being parts of their daily life.

'All the researchers were struck at the start,' Khalil tells us, 'by the bad feeling towards Redayif and Tamerza, and the resentment towards the Bedouins. But these are commonplace differences and distinctions. You would find them elsewhere in the Maghrib and in other countries as well.'

In any case, the collective experience of the people of Shebika is at another level.

The Circle of Marriages and Ancestry

'We and our fathers and our fathers' fathers and grandfathers are from Shebika or El Hamma. Among ourselves we call such-and-such a one a Bu Yahia, a Qadduri, an Imamiya, a Zam-mamera, or a Nasiqa, but it's all the same thing.'

Old Ali is speaking, but the others do not all agree. The three or four old men talking in the shade of the portico and Ridha, the grocer, who occasionally intervenes to simplify and sum-marize their discussion, hold it necessary to justify, beyond the relationship which in our imperfect biblical terminology, we call that of the 'tribe', a genealogy more complex and imprecise, *because it is a complete invention*, which attaches all these families to that of the Prophet and to the Arabs of Medina or Mecca. We cannot fail to appreciate this effort. Doesn't the Prophet himself say: 'Learn your genealogies', in speaking of the interminable 'historical' links that make for a bond between the country of origin and the province of the 'far West', the Maghrib? This bond is a complete myth, if we stop to think of the North African past: Berbers and Kabyls converted successively to Judaism, Christianity, and finally to Islam, which came to them from the East, Hilali from Syria, passing over into Egypt and then driven westward and absorbed in the confused disparate mass of the continent. . . . This Babelic confusion obviously precludes any idea of ethnic continuity. But this bond, this long succession of generations, whose protagonists are known only by their first names, incarnates, in bodily form and sexuality, the mystical connexion with the sacred original site and obliterates the distance between the place of exile and the kingdom, which only a pilgrimage can attain. Genealogy, because it links the man of today to the essence of the Arab East (something quite impossible, of course, when it comes to Bedouins who were born in North Africa or have for centuries broken away from Mecca and Medina), defies and wipes out this physical removal and integrates the individual with a religion and a civilization.

These conversations occupy hours at a time. The men love to manipulate genealogical classifications, even if – indeed because – they are invented. Actually they are elements of rational thinking, since they are aimed at imposing a logic upon the confusion of the generations. When the talkers are brought back to consideration of their concrete connexions, those of cousinship, which are at the base of every partnership and every marriage contract, without a moment's hesitation they shift from one plane to another, from the mystical to the real, without showing the slightest unease, without any apparent awareness that they are leaving the realm of fiction for the realm of reality.

But even on this subject the discussion rambles on, never

ending. It comes round to the question of the origins of the Bu Yahia.

'We've been told,' says Khalil, 'that the Bu Yahia tribes are a branch of the Hamami.'

'Yes, the Bu Yahia belong to the Hamami that live near Qafsa at Aamra,' Ali replied, 'and then there are the Bu Yahia who live at Tawzar as well.'

'Didn't the Bu Yahia who live near Qafsa come to Shebika?'

'No, they are Berbers,' says Muhammad. 'We think of the Hamami and the Zlass as Berbers.'

'Oh no,' says Ali, 'I wouldn't say that they are Berbers.'

'To us they're Berbers, because they've kept up the old Berber habits. They still live in caves! Houses and an easy life don't suit them at all. They feel they're in prison the moment a roof is over their heads.'

'Do you mean to say they're nomads?' asks Khalil.

'Yes, the only life they'll live is in the desert, and the only thing they'll do is graze their flocks.'

'In your opinion, then, the Bu Yahia are descendants of the Hamami?'

'Yes, the Bu Yahia are a branch of the Hamami.'

'Do you know anything about the Zamour?' asks Khalil.

'The Zamour? I know they're over in the east.'

'Are they Berbers or Arabs?'

'As far as we're concerned they're Berbers. To us, they are real Berbers, they're mountain people, the true descendants of the Berbers, they're the "chieu". I'm certain the Bu Yahia are part of the Hamami, it's not just hearsay. They're not just a small group; the descendants of the Bu Yahia are a huge family.'

'Can you tell us the names of any of the families?'

'There are some tribes that have been going for a long time, the Majar and the Frasheesh. One of them rebelled against France.'

'Who was that? Ali ben Othman?'

'No, Suhaili. We say that the name of Frasheesh is always associated with the name of Majar. There are two "saddles", the saddle of Majar and the saddle of Frasheesh. The saddle is the symbol of the chief.'

'Of the chief or of the tribe?'

'Of the chief that governs the tribe. It used to be that the saddle of the Frasheesh was occupied by a chief called Ali al-Saghir. He was very well known when the French were here. As for the Majar tribe, it was governed by a chief called Ali Abul-ghudayl.'

'The one that rebelled against France?' asks Khalil.

'You've forgotten the rest of the tribes,' says Muhammad to Ali. 'You spoke only of the Frasheesh.'

'No, I haven't forgotten; they're all Frasheesh and Majar. The ancestor of the Frasheesh had three children: Naji, Ali and Wazzaq. Naji's children are Almula, Khamssiah, al-Haj Mahmoud, Hamza and Barki. Ali's children are Ismaïl, Marwana, Kamata, Hawafiz.'

'You've forgotten Altamanusha,' says Muhammad, without laughing at the long enumeration. 'The Altamanusha are neighbours; some of them used to live in Tunisian territory, inside the frontiers.'

'You mean that before the frontiers were staked out they all used to live together?' asks Khalil.

'Yes, but they were enemies. The Frasheesh and the Majar had a chief who used to attack the other villages. When there was a quarrel between the Frasheesh and the Namamsha they used to submit it to Morokoa.'

'Was he the chief of the Namamsha?'

'No, Morokoa was a chief of the Frasheesh, a descendant of Wazzaq. He lived a mile away from the Namamsha. The petty chieftains of the Frasheesh couldn't attack the Namamsha without Morokoa. They'd go to him and say "The Namamsha have trespassed on our land. They've stolen cows and sheep and dogs ..." '

'So Morokoa was the chief of the tribe, was he?'

'Yes, he was the chief of the tribe, the invincible iron horseman. He was wild about horses, thoroughbred horses. He had a stallion, and everyone that had a mare took her to be mated with him. It was a great honour to have a foal from Morokoa's thoroughbred. ... The quarrel between the Frasheesh and the Namamsha was a very old one; for a long time they had

been attacking each other. There was a Namamsha called Bin
Maryam, who had a mare that produced very fine foals. One day
his mare was stolen and fell into the hands of Morokoa. Bin
Maryam had to go to his enemy and ask to have his mare mated
with the Morokoa's stallion. This was done, and she had a foal.
After that the two clans stopped raiding each other. They
considered there was a relationship between them.'

'A relationship through the horses?'

'Yes, they said it was a mixture of blood. After the birth of
the foal the raids stopped.'

'Why don't they intermarry?'

'They're enemies, and they don't mingle. After the foal was
born Bin Maryam invited Morokoa to come to see him. The
Bin Maryam live in hair tents, and so do the Morokoas. The
important men of the Bin Maryams live in larger tents, with
pillars that hold them up in the middle. The women of the Bin
Maryam wear veils and never go out; they're kept well hidden.
Bin Maryam's tent was divided into four or five rooms, and he
gave Morokoa one of them. Then Bin Maryam went out to find
a ram or a sheep to be slaughtered in his guest's honour. Bin
Maryam's wife had a strong character. She was virtuous and
painstaking; she was manlike. When she caught a glimpse of
Morokoa she was surprised to find him so short and had an
urge to measure him, beginning at the feet. When she got to
his heart Morokoa woke up and said: "Stop there, it isn't a
man's height that counts, it's the size of his heart." She ran
away. After her husband had come back, and their guest had
finished eating and retired to his room to sleep, she told Bin
Maryam what had happened. "That's real virility for you!" he
exclaimed.'

These discussions are infinite in number; they are held in the
spoken language of the interminable conversations that take
place in the portico or in the shadow of the Mosque. They are
like a game of chess, in which the villagers manipulate names
as if they were chessmen, with complete imprecision. The
name of an unlikely and unproven ancestor (prestigious because
he can be joined up with the sacred genealogies) is that which
designates a family group. If we grant that consanguineous

marriage between families linked by cousinship is the basis of relationship in the Maghrib and if, on the other hand, we can measure the expression of the family by the unwillingness of two human groups to consider themselves as brothers (*khuwiya*) or as sons (*awlad*) of a common ancestor, then we can establish the names of the present-day families of Shebika. But the double play of designations compels us to draw up our diagram in two ways: one reproducing the expressed relationships and the other starting from the actual families, such as to define the *background* of connexions concretely shown in the relationships of marriage, work and property. Thus we have the family picture of Shebika not just as the villagers *wish* it to be when they play with their designations of relationship, but as it is forced upon them by facts, *independently of words*, which last are for the most part in disagreement with the diagram and bear witness to the difficulty of pinning down the variables of the village's oral tradition.

It will be noticed that we do not use the confusing term of 'tribe'. Jacques Berque calls attention to the difficulty of applying this term to the societies of the Maghrib, when he says: 'The legislator's decision to substitute a territorial unit for the patriarchal grouping of "the Sons of so-and-so" all over the country presupposes not only an analysis but a judgement as well.'* A judgement which breaks with the mentality of the colonizer, who saw the life of the Maghrib through his memory of the Old Testament, or even the New, and explained it in terms of 'tribes'. It may be interesting to recall, at this point, that the word 'tribe' might belong to the same category as 'totemism', both of which Claude Lévi-Strauss criticizes as follows: ' "Totemism" is primarily the projection outside our universe, in a sort of exorcism, of mental attitudes incompatible with the demands of the discontinuity between man and nature so essential to Christian philosophy.' † We may say that the term 'tribe' reflects the wish to order non-Western

* Qu'est-ce qu'une tribu africaine? in *Mélanges*, Lucien Febvre, (ed.), (Paris: A. Colin, 1952), vol. 1, pp. 261–71.

† *Le Totémisme, aujourd'hui* (Paris: Presses Universitaires de France, 1962).

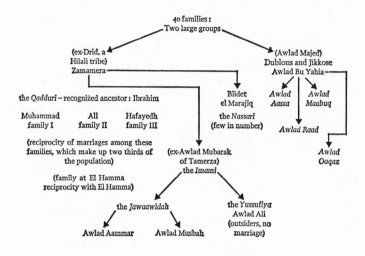

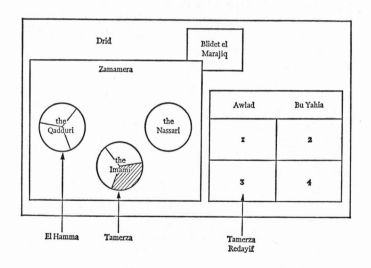

human phenomena according to the model of the so-called patriarchal, biblical family. Their picturesque and unfamiliar quality calls up certain mistranslated Bible stories.

We must call attention, too, to the inextricable confusion of 'tribal' names all over North Africa. As E. F. Gautier says, 'Every name is found everywhere.' * This confusion should make the analyst aware that the term 'tribe' is an actual block to the understanding of the social realities of the North Africa of today. 'The same group names occur all over the Maghrib. Their geographical interlacing, at the family level, so much more intricate than it appears on the map, causes them to pop up in the most unexpected places.' †

In the case of Shebika we must distinguish three different and often contradictory levels of denomination.

The first is that of the designation of family ties or, in more precise sociological terms, of 'fundamental allegiances'. For instance, the six contemporary Qadduri families (which are regrouped in three different units – awlad Muhammad, awlad Ali, and awlad Hafayedh) have a fundamental allegiance such that they are continually helping one another, freely rather than on the basis of an exchange of services, and marry only within their own circle. The three families called Imami, although they claim a common ancestor, do not have the same close ties. The two Jawaawidah families – awlad Aammar and awlad Musbah – constitute an organic unit, but the Yussufiya are considered strangers to the village and do not intermarry with the Jawaawidah.

'Who are these Yussufiya?' we ask awlad Ali (Qaddur), a thirty-five-year-old *khammes*.

'To us they're nothing, they're people from outside.'

'Where do they come from?'

'Who knows? People arrive, with their belongings. We let them settle here. They're free to do so as long as they stay on their own.'

'Would you marry off your son to one of their daughters?'

'No. Why should I?'

* *Le passé de l'Afrique du Nord* (Paris: Payot, 1962).
† Jacques Berque, op. cit.

We ask the same question of our old friend, Si Qaddur, who has taken back his family name and enjoys the prestige of belonging to the strongest group of Shebika.

'They're strangers,' he tells us, 'but nobody cares. They live beside us. They pray in the Mosque and work in the oasis and come to our celebrations. We don't marry them and they don't marry us.'

'Are there any differences between them and you?'

'Differences? No. They're two families living in the same house, up there; they live the same way we do.'

'Then why don't you intermarry?'

'It's never been done. The Yussufiya marry awlad Bu Yahia if they want to. The awlad Bu Yahia are strangers, too, but not the same kind.'

'What do you mean?'

'They've always been around. My grandfather married one of them.'

We met a young awlad Ali, a Yussufiya, and he told us that he would eventually marry a girl from the tent encampments on the far side of the main road, towards Dakash. His brother, on the other hand, wanted to marry a local girl. He had saved up his money from the time of his military service, and wanted to buy a few date-palms in the oasis of Shebika.

'Why a girl of Shebika?'

'She'll know what to cook and what to do.'

'Won't your wife know these things?'

'No, my mother will have to teach her.'

'No one in your house has ever married a girl of Shebika?'

'No, never.'

Here, then, the family is defined by its frontiers; its name or denomination is determined by marriages and cousinship, in the sense which Germaine Tillon gives to this word.* We must look for the family in the internal workings of a narrow allegiance, based on the cohesion of the group unit, an allegiance which we have seen holds up the Qadduri, the most numerous of such groups in Shebika, and enroots them in the village.

The second determinant is geographic. The villagers say, for

* *Le Harem et les cousins* (Paris: Seuil, 1966).

instance, that the Qadduri are Zamamera, but also that 'there are Zamamera elsewhere', particularly at El Hamma, where they form an important fraction of the population, concentrated towards the east, in a section adjacent to the road between Tawzar and Shebika and stretching as far as the hot spring 'bathing establishment'. (At least this was the case as recently as 1962.)

'Those are cousins,' says Qaddur, 'cousins with whom we intermarry. All the Qadduri women come from El Hamma. They are always coming here, and we are always going there. We are at home with them, and they with us.'

'But do your women ever go to marry and settle at El Hamma?'

'They do, very often.'

'As many as those you bring as wives to Shebika?'

This Qaddur doesn't know. We tell him that out of the six Qadduri families of Shebika (actually fifteen, if we count the young couples that live with their parents), we have counted, since 1961, twenty married women of all ages who are from El Hamma but only two Shebika women (of the awlad Ali family) who have gone to marry and settle in El Hamma. He, as a Qadduri, ought to know the reason for this discrepancy. But Qaddur doesn't see it, or at least he does not reply.

'Could it be because the Qadduri of Shebika are better off and can barter for their wives with land in the oasis, whereas the Qadduri of El Hamma have nothing to offer?'

'It's true that every time we marry a woman of El Hamma we cede some of our land or our water rights in the oasis.'

'And do you marry often?'

'Before the passage of the law* we married two or three times, always a woman from El Hamma. Now we marry more than once only when our first wife dies or, having no children, goes back to her father.'

'Or if she stays in your house to do the cooking?'

'Sometimes.'

'And if you had a son would you approve of his taking a wife from El Hamma?'

* The law prohibiting polygamy, passed after Independence.

'If I can't find him one in Shebika.'

'So Shebika is your first choice, is it?'

'Yes; first Shebika and then El Hamma.'

The Qadduri marriage connexions with El Hamma are paralleled by those of the Imamis with Tamerza, where they claim to have awlad Mubarak cousins. In their case, too, there is a consistent record of marriages (five in the span of four years), but there is greater reciprocity, perhaps because the Imamis of Tamerza are better off than the Qadduri of El Hamma.

In the geographical context of the region it is plain that the function of these matrimonial exchanges is to strengthen the life of the village by integrating it with other villages. When an Imami says: 'We're from Tamerza', and a Qadduri: 'We're from El Hamma', it means that over fifteen miles of desert or ten miles of mountains the two groups are affirming their cohesion and unity. Family relationships counteract these distances and overcome them, thus asserting the power of society over an inert but aggressive nature. It is fitting, somehow, to abolish space and broaden the social structure by the bond of intermarriage. May we not say that family relationships reveal, by this means, their fundamental opposition to nature?

The third determinant comes out of the background of the two others. To speak of the Qadduri and Imami families is to call up a very real, domestic allegiance. Geographical extension symbolizes the effort to achieve integration and cohesion in the face of the dispersion and fluidity of the steppe. When a Qadduri states that he is a Zamamera and that the Zamamera are Drid, that is Hilali; when the awlad Bu Yahia say that they are awlad Majed and that their group lives at Ziqu, their words have a deeper meaning. The meaning of this denomination lies in the will to attach themselves to a major group of the Maghrib, the one which most often determines the signs of facial tattooing. Whether this is a remnant of Berber connexions (perhaps preceding Islam) or an equally mythical connexion with one of the more or less known groups existent during what E. F. Gautier calls the 'dark ages' of North Africa, this oneness has no foundation in reality. The broad sweep is one of verbal suggestion, a human sweep which binds together large family groups and religious beliefs over a vast area. It would be an error, obviously, to consider these statements true when they are simply utopian escape from the hardships of daily life.

'We are Hilali,' says Qaddur. 'The Hilali came from Mecca, bringing religion with them. Everyone around here is Hilali. That's our real family.'

Remnants may endure of the plundering, nomad peoples who were converted to Islam in Syria, emigrated to Egypt, where they made nothing but trouble until finally the Caliph let them loose among his unruly vassals of the Maghrib, where they systematically destroyed the technical substructure left by the Romans and maintained by the early Arabs. But it is highly doubtful. They were led by their Sultan, who imposed unification (for the only time in history) on the Maghrib, into Morocco, taking with them their disregard for culture and their fanatical religion. Their survivors in ancient 'Ifriqiya'* must have been lost among the Berber masses. But little does this matter. To identify with them makes for a link with Mecca and an image of ethnic unity in a universe where dispersion is the rule. We have here an effort to unify and classify, in some logical pattern, even if it flies in the face of reality, the diverse elements of a picture of confusion.

The area of experience formed by family relationships, both concrete and mythical, gives the village a reason for being rooted in a definite geographical location. It ensures a permanent and continuous contact throughout the successive generations and the ruptures between them and broadens the web of allegiances and connexions. But, contrary to what we might believe, it does not have the function of deepening family intimacy. What it does is to order, according to the laws of a classification both simple and complex, mythical and concrete, a series of contacts and exchanges which combat geographical distances, the hardships of daily life and the helplessness of man before the cosmos.

Marriage relationships extend Shebika beyond the narrow circumference of the village and the oasis, they open it to and

* Name given to the area of the Roman provinces of North Africa.

integrate it with the South. *Through them Shebika is more than just Shebika.* No other social experience has the same enlarging and integrating power. When we speak of family connexions we may do so in statistical terms and content ourselves with giving them graphic representation. We forget that this collective experience has a double significance. It morphologically extends the group to the geographical horizon, and at the same time negates space and welds different and dispersed men into a coherent whole, the embryo and dream of an as yet unachieved greater society. By its marriage relationships Shebika tries to escape from the isolation and loneliness of Shebika. It is far from successful. But there is an effort to overcome the boundless distances of the steppe and to give the people of the village the feeling of belonging to something greater than themselves, which enlarges their image of man.

The Circle of Work

The oasis follows the course of the *wadi*, and wild palms grow at random along the running water. It is beyond and below the village that this forest turns into cultivated gardens, spreading out as far as the incline of the school-house and stopping short at the edge of the desert as if an invisible sea had outlined its coast. The parcels of land are infinitely smaller than those of Tawzar, Naftah and Dakash, where for generations large landowners have taken over the distribution of the water for their own profit. Thus, at Naftah, with its 18,000 inhabitants, sixty owners have gradually acquired complete control, and the single parcels are only fragments of a great complex. The small owner is reduced to working as a *khammes* on land which was once his, or to selling it.

Here at Shebika the average parcel is no more than thirty paces square, surrounded by water-willows, improvised fences and barbed wire, intended to keep off animals and marauders. There are no paths; three trails fan out from the marabout of Sidi Sultan at the left exit from the village and two others lead from the school-house, at the right, to the road at the farthest extremity. From these the *khammes* climb over or around the fencing and make their way cautiously across other parcels to their own.

The names given to the parcels are the same as those at Naftah and Tawzar, although they more often individualize the land and connect it with the man that works it. There is *hussah*, the parcel, usually followed by a qualifying word – *hussah hrasa* the 'parcel of the donkey's saddle' – or by a name – *hussah bin Sassi*, or *hussah Harbi*, the latter designating a family of Algerian origin, which before integrating with the group of Shebika had for a long time been considered as foreign. There is *hussah minqa*, named for the watering hole, near the *wadi*, where horses and mules come to drink, and also, as in every oasis, an orchard, known as *Iinan Ibrahim*, the 'paradise of Ibrahim'.

There are 176 parcels in all, belonging to forty-seven owners. The establishment of this fact was one of the thorniest parts of our investigation. For nearly a year *the men of Shebika would not admit* that they were no longer owners of the land, that almost all of them, including the oldest and formerly richest, had sunk to the status of *khammes*. It is easy to understand their bitter distress. They hold that their impoverishment stems from the fact that certain men, 'men from around here, flattered the French in order to obtain jobs from them, and with their pay bought up the land'. Considering themselves victims of colonialization they waited for Independence to restore their holdings. But in this they were disappointed. Expropriations were infrequent and those that were affected did not give back the land to the former small owners. This was for several reasons: the idea of socialist planning, aimed at setting up large-scale development projects, the more or less successful attempt to create agricultural cooperatives, the understandable difficulty of choosing between poor, landless peasants, and peasants of greater means, with greater capacities for production. On the other hand, it is possible that the expropriations were purely imaginary. However it may be, the people of Shebika date their ruin to colonial times. Only five of the heads of families – Yunis bin Hajayid, Salah bin Aamr, Muhammad bin Aamr, Mustafa bin Muhammad and Ahmad bin Aamr – are land-owners today. It is strange that Ridha, the grocer, who definitely has land of his own, is never named among them. Can it be that the people of Shebika are unwilling to speak of a man whom they see and talk with every day as one of the real owners of the village? Do they, perhaps, wish to hide, by some obscure magic, the fact that they owe him money? Are they unwilling to admit his importance? In any case, this sixth land-owner is shrouded in silence. The reason may be that Ridha is the son of a *khammes*. There were never land-owners in his family, whereas all the others inherited their land.

The peasants' concept of the land is far from simple. None of the *khammes* or the owners (who are equally or even more poor, since they have to pay taxes) looks at his piece of land as we do in the West: as a possession which yields a certain profit. For fifty or sixty of the eighty workers whom we questioned, land is a part of the divine creation which, through man's work, participates in the transcendent, mystical process that leads every living thing to behave according to its essence, that is, to sprout and grow. The notion of gainful work exists only in a few of the young men who have performed their military service and learned the relationship between human labour, the investment in technical tools and the possibilities of material profit. The others take part in a vast mystical action, in which property should have a place. The fact that it has none is a permanent insult, a sign of deterioration.

'Everyone has taken advantage of us, and we've had no benefit,' says Aamr, who for fifty years has worked the land of an outsider. 'Once upon a time we had everything, and now, even if we give Allah his due, we are obliged to work for someone else.'

Or, according to Aazzuz, who is only thirty years old but was judged unfit for military service:

'People have exploited our poverty by buying the fruit of our work at starvation prices.'

'No one has ever tried to give us our due,' says another, 'the due of Shebika.'

The villagers that own land are regarded with respect. They

live as miserably as the others and work just as hard, and their ownership brings with it financial burdens which the productivity of the land does not allow them to bear without borrowing. But they are the only ones who, in spite of all difficulties, have maintained a moral claim to the land.* For the claim is moral or spiritual in nature; it is a mystical factor of cosmic existence rather than a legal and economic right.

The other land-owners, the 'outsiders', are of four kinds. First those of El Hamma, who acquired their land through marriages with their cousins, fifteen miles away. Second, those of Tamerza, who have other and larger palm-groves besides. Third, nomads installed on the near-by desert. And fourth, half a dozen miners of Redayif. Each one of these categories corresponds to one wave of the take-over of Shebika from the outside and is an instrument of its degradation, the degradation which threatens all the small oases of Southern Tunisia and bids fair to affect the larger ones as well.

Of the present-day heads of families of Shebika, about twenty have married women from El Hamma. In the preceding generation there were as many as sixty. This is because, as we have seen, an important branch of the Qadduri family lives at El Hamma, and its women are bartered for a parcel of land. The marriage relationship, besides making for social integration and human exchanges between two groups settled at a distance from one another, has also made for economic damage and hastened the process of decay. The conventional system, instead of strengthening the group's possibility of survival, has in this case imperilled it. The take-over on the part of El Hamma is the oldest and perhaps the most important of all. It is not the first case in which we may note that *the observance of tradition is actually a factor in the dissolution of structures.*

The second wave of invaders is composed of 'the people of Tamerza', the large village at the far end of the gorge that leads towards Algeria, which was an important station of the caravan route, before the advent of roads and railways. As a

* K. Zamitti calls to my attention that at Shebika, as everywhere in the South, a government employee enjoys little esteem and is often called, belittlingly, *Khadim ed dawlah*, 'Servant of the State'.

frontier post during and after the period of French colonization, this village of two thousand inhabitants, with a relatively
rich oasis on the banks of a *wadi* that runs through scenic
gorges, has an importance infinitely greater than that of the
proud and lonely Shebika, which is oriented, geographically if
not administratively, towards far-away Tawzar.

Here in the South, account is taken of the distinction made
by Muslim law between the land cultivated by the human hand
and the 'dead land' which belongs to no one. But the two
notions are applied with some confusion and there are not the
distinctions made in the North among different types of
property: the *milk*, land owned by an individual, the *milk* of
the *baylaq*, or representative of the Bey and the *habus*, or con-
secrated land, private, public, or dependent on a *zawiya* (sort
of cloister).* Here ownership is more fluid and less rigorously
defined, modified by debts and services. Even in the North, in
spite of the legal restrictions imposed by the Turks, the Beys,
the French colonial regime and the new independent government, complex and shifting human relationships interfere with
the administrative structure which French jurists, versed in
Roman law, economic experts, and the new administrators
have sought and are seeking to consolidate. Modification of the
structures begins at the level of the multiple exchanges among
individuals which, whether or not they are actually carried out,
constantly upset the elusive 'tradition'.

The land-owners from Tamerza, even when they are cousins
by marriage of the people of Shebika, have treated the oasis
just as the large land-owners of Naftah and Tawzar have treated
the smaller owners of their own towns. They have bought up
land, put the parcels together into larger units, and set groups
of *khammes* to work on them. This recent transformation of
social relationships in the oasis explains the protest movements
of 1955.† The possession of lands more extensive than the
original parcel creates a new situation among the 'partners',

* Cf. G. Salmagnon, *La loi tunisienne du 1er juillet 1855 sur la
propriété immobilière et le régime des biens fonciers.*

† Benno Steinberg-Sarrel, 'Les oasis du Djérid', in *Cahiers inter-
nationaux de sociologie*, No. 15, XXX, 1961.

or, rather, gives a new form to the relationship between the owner on the one side and the 'partners' on the other. Nowhere more plainly than here do we see the hypocrisy of the 'partnership' concept, viable, perhaps, in the Middle Ages. It is fundamentally a question of 'salary', but the owners make profits from glossing this fact over.

At Shebika, then, the absent owners from Tamerza have snatched up most of the land not owned by the villagers themselves: one third, to be exact; some of their blocks include six, seven, or even ten conventional parcels. There are also, of course, properties held in common with owners from El Hamma. Such co-ownership is frequent, and two or three men may share a single parcel's profits. This is most often a matter of water rights, which are rented, bought, and exchanged. When the right to a certain quantity of water, or watering-time, is greater for one parcel than for its neighbour, then the latter comes to depend on the former.

The largest of these properties is that of Aamr bin Ali, who was the local sheikh under French rule. It consists of twelve parcels, worked by the greatest number of *khammes* dependent on any single owner. About Aamr bin Ali himself opinions differ. 'He took everything, because he had the French on his side. Because he was in charge, everything passed through his hands and he knew when there was a chance of buying up a water right or a piece of land.' Another opinion is more violent, but there is no proof to substantiate it: 'When he wanted to grab my uncle's parcel, he buried a grenade in the ground, and it exploded when the French gendarmes were making their rounds. My uncle was sent to prison and the sheikh confiscated the land and then bought it for a song.'

In any case, Aamr bin Ali seems to have built up his holdings by exploiting his real or pretended prestige with the colonial administrative or military authorities. Even if he is no longer the sheikh, he has held on to his lands in both Tamerza and Shebika. His *khammes* do not feel the same hostility towards him as the smaller land-owners. Quite the contrary. One of them says that he 'consults him about family affairs and borrows money from him'; another that 'Si Aamr knows the country better than anyone else and you can ask him for anything you want'.

We made the acquaintance of Aamr bin Ali in the one small café of Tamerza, next to the headquarters of the local administrator, a single, very clean, whitewashed room, where sacks of flour with 'U.S.A.' stamped on them are piled up, ready for distribution to the workers. He is a man some sixty years old, and thin, with a hatchet face and gleaming eyes, clad as simply as the poorest *khammes*, in a flowing, dirty ghandurah. On this particular day we found him talking with a group of other men, and laughing aloud, something which is in these parts very unusual. He sat with us for some time, telling us about his hunting of wolves, foxes and, above all, wild sheep, and proposing to take us to hunt mountain eagles, which he said he was quick enough to catch by the claws. We realized at once that he was a typical village braggart, and the winks of the bystanders confirmed the fact that he was putting on a performance for our benefit.

When we questioned him again, a year later, we discovered another man playing the buffoon, a role that he had played to advantage during the colonial period and kept up in the form of a parody, inventing exploits of the most impossible kind. The most surprising of our discoveries was that this relatively important land-owner did not behave according to the pattern current at Dakash and Tawzar. He turned out to be quite incapable of anything like economic planning, for he contents himself with picking up bits and pieces of palm-bearing land, which he never so much as visits, and turning them over to the care of the *khammes*, from whom he collects the money due to him on the occasion of a chance meeting. This indifferent attitude probably explains both his *khammes*' appreciation and the hostility of the small land-owners of Shebika.

We have here a problem of which Aamr bin Ali represents but one example. For many men of the South, and of the Maghrib in particular, the urge to acquire land is not accompanied by any capacity for planning, much less for the development of modern techniques. They are not up to making good use of their acquisitions, but stop short at the invisible frontier which divides the old social structure from the new. It is not a question of hesitancy or incompetence; it is simply that a tentative gain of social status is not accompanied by a shouldering of the economic role that goes with it. Nobody at Tamerza takes Aamr bin Ali seriously, because of his more or less wilful incapacity to become the real and active owner of the land that he has, by hook or by crook, put together. This attitude is more frequent than is generally believed. It is enough to make us wonder whether the economic norms which Europeans and European-educated North Africans try to apply outside their natural industrial context really have a transferable and universal validity.

After the owners from El Hamma and Tamerza, there are the Raqaariqah, the nomads of the Sahara who have pitched their tents at the foot of the mountain and now own one sixth of the oasis of Shebika. Whether they are awlad Sidi Abid or the members of some other family, they are the most exacting and suspicious of proprietors. At harvest-time they come to the oasis and watch over each and every tree, as their *khammes* pluck dates and pile them together. They exercise this supervision not like the other owners, who are themselves but a step away from the condition of *khammes*, but like men of the desert who are fearful lest the 'settled' men cheat them.

These nomads are not popular in the village. They go to the grocery – particularly the younger men who in some cases work the land – and gather in front of the Mosque, but their hardness and exactitude set them apart. They are owners in the modern sense of the word, employers, not unlike the rich men of Dakash or Tawzar, harnessing to a new economic attitude that which is all too facilely termed their 'greed', which is, in reality, a keen attention to *things*, a mixture of suspicion and the brusqueness that goes with it.

Sometimes they come in person or send their sons, in the dry season, to check on the distribution of water, as it is measured by the *qaddus* or water-clock. When this happens, the men of Shebika, ordinarily talkative, stiffen and are silent. As the Bedouin takes up his stand they notice that he has good shoes, sometimes riding boots, and often a watch as well. He is by nature nervous and abrupt, a meat-eater, rider, and huntsman, whose relation to the land is different from theirs.

Where the Bedouins are concerned the discussions between owners and *khammes* are the sharpest. It is a fact that the nomads have acquired their parcels of land at Shebika in payment of outstanding debts – for sheep, goats, chickens, or tea – or else because some small village land-owner cannot raise the fifty or a hundred dinars in cash which he needs on account of an illness in the family or the marriage of one of his sons. The Bedouin does not go in for long palavering; he is more concrete than the man of the village and insists that the discussions result in deeds rather than words.

The fourth and last category of absent land-owners is that made up of the half-dozen miners from Redayif. They are not as easy to distinguish as the others because the people of Shebika scarcely recognize their status as land-owners and only refer to them as such in the course of the most searching discussions. It took us two years and a long visit during the season of the date-harvest to find out who they were.

At the time we were in the oasis, sitting with Muhammad on his plot of land. Two men arrived at the same moment, the one a tent-dwelling Bedouin whom we knew by sight, the other dressed like all the *khammes*, but to all appearances somewhat poorer. Someone started talking to him :

'Yes, I'm from Redayif, I work in the mines. My brother worked for a while at Shebika and he still has friends here, especially the grocer Ridha, whom he knew from Qafsa or Tamerza. When I was working in the mines, I began thinking, after a while, about Shebika, because it is pleasing to God to work the land.'

'Because working in the mine is not pleasing to God?'

'It depends what job you're doing in the mine.'

'The job that you do.'

'I don't dig out the phosphate, I have to push forward the wagons that carry up to the station what the others have dug out. It's ten hours a day. I don't know that that is very pleasing to God.'

'What does please God?'

'To recite the prayers, observe the fast-days ...'

'No, as an occupation.'

'As an occupation? Certainly to make the earth bring forth something fruitful.'

'That's why you bought some land?'

'I share what is included in this plot with another man from Tamerza, a man from the awlad Sidi Abid and an old man from El Hamma who never shows up.'

'And what do you make from it?'

'I don't know ... Two or three qfeez.* Just a few dinars. Ten or twenty ...'

'And you prefer this to the mines?'

'If I could, I'd live here, like the others, and increase the fruits of the earth. But I can't. My house is at Redayif.'

'House' (dar) means 'wife and children'. In any case, the miner had walked for a whole Saturday from Redayif. He would walk back the next day and turn up for work at the mine on Monday. Of the half-dozen miners he is the only one, except for one of his cousins, who pays regular visits to Shebika. The money due to the others from the sale of dates at Tamerza is taken to them. Other phosphate-miners buy and sell land in other oases. It isn't that their work in the mines doesn't yield them sufficient income. They are too much a part of the land to resist plunging into it in order to draw from it a strength which their religion tells them is linked to the invisible power of God as he works to raise nature to his level.

These worker-owners, as we have said, are actually very close to the small owners of Shebika. They are khammes of a very slightly superior kind, and probably even more weighed down by their obligations. And even if their land is an integral part of their beings they draw no more strength from it than do the ordinary khammes, as things are today. For they all of them hark back to the past, to the golden age when everyone owned land. They are, after a fashion, sociologists, for they believe that with the ownership of the land restricted to a minority, the over-all social structure of Shebika cannot change and that

* A qfeez is 200 pounds, which sell for between 3 and 6 dinars from one year to another.

only if the village had the oasis to itself could a new way of life ensue.

The four layers of ownership which we have described above are linked to four different and often diverging economic attitudes, four kinds of integration and activity, whose relation to innovation is critical in the present-day South and in all of Tunisia. The 'social electron' of Shebika is a focus of interests which may bear upon the 'socialist' reforms which the government is introducing.

The owners from El Hamma keep up very little with the land which they have obtained in exchange for their women, contenting themselves with the receipt of the profits, at highly irregular intervals. Those from Tamerza are more demanding, but they do not exercise continual supervision like the Bedouins who, because their discovery of the modern economic system is so new and innocent, insist on making it work with unwelcome precision. As for the miners of Redayif, their salaried status is so recent and they are still so close to the small local owners, and even to the *khammes*, that they do not make the full claims of ownership.

These four different attitudes correspond to four possibilities which are open to the people of the South under the changing circumstances of the present day. It is striking that the only one in tune with modern development is that of the nomads who, coming from the abstract world of the steppe, where words are deeds, bring to the mechanism of modern economy a spirit far more practical and concrete than that of the 'settled' peoples.

This should prevent us from projecting our own attitudes and categories, from speaking of a 'primitive economy' or 'economy at subsistence level', when the form and philosophy of life implied by these terms has no real bearing. Every type of society has its own system and the function of its activities varies so widely that we cannot lump them all under the same designation without giving proof of a most unscientific ingenuousness and an inappropriately dogmatic spirit. When we speak of the development of new societies we must place ourselves at the borderline between the present of yesterday (which seeks to prolong itself) and the present of today. We must not think along the lines of a 'subsistence economy' as opposed to a 'modern economy', because these terms belong to European categories, crystallized in a purely subjective image. If, in the wake of certain remarks of Marx, we try to define the necessary stages of economic hardening that hold true for all human societies, interposing gradations in the succession of events which the author of *Das Kapital*, after Hegel, holds logical and inevitable, we are flying in the face of reality, translating everything into an alien language (our own) and insisting that life conform to its pattern. Analyses of the Asiatic manner of production * are interesting, but they are arbitrary. The succession of types of society does not obey, over all the planet, the peculiar logic that Hegel imposed upon Western intelligence and which this intelligence has made into a postulate. This succession depends upon the history of each type of society, and every such type secretes the impulse of de-structurization and re-structurization according to its own internal composition. Every history relates to the internal combination which defines the overall form of a society, and it can be measured only if we place ourselves at the boundary-line between the old system ('tradition') and a system which is as yet undefined, even if government administrators claim the right to lay down, quite arbitrarily (and always imperfectly), its laws.

The people of Shebika, then, are tugged at by at least three conflicting forces: that of the system of large-scale exploitation of the land, prevalent in the oases of the Jerid, that of modern economy, and that of stagnation in the precarious equilibrium of poverty. No one can yet say which of these forces will prove to be the strongest and will spell out the form or rhythm of eventual change.

At least the circle of ownership, bound up as it is with the family and the means of production, brings with it its own existential organization. It defines its own duration, measured by seasonal labour, a cosmic accord with plant and animal

* K. Wittovogel, *Le mode de production asiatique* (Paris: Editions de Minuit).

life, and the multiple accidents and chances of nature. When we say that Islam is ignorant of the role of chance in economy, and that this is why it has not known capitalism, we forget that we are speaking of a rural world and that the peasant is more subject to the rule of nature than any other man. It seems inevitable, when we think of the reality of human groups, that Islam should have excluded from its theory of money the notion of chance in which it is cosmically enveloped. Only to a superficial observer, a European 'expert', or a European-educated Tunisian government official (who is more remote from his origins than an objective local investigator), is this un-thinkable.

Obviously these three opposing forces do not make for a climate of calm and sincerity. Especially as, at the same moment, the radio and visiting public officials declare that a radical change of habits and customs is under way. It is often said in government circles: 'We choose to change men in order to change institutions rather than to create institutions for men who cannot yet adapt to them.' This change, or rather awareness of this change, makes for a trauma whose importance must be taken into account. The present regulation of property at Shebika, like that of the family, is a factor of social dissociation and decay. There are societies which destroy themselves by obeying their own interior impulse, that which is often called their 'structure'.

The Women's and Family Circle

Work, property, and marriage connexions culminate in the family circle. Here is surely the most elusive part of the village life. When we count up the time which the men spend at work and either under the portico or at the grocery we may wonder how much there is left for home. If we draw up a rough schedule of a *khammes'* or a small land-owner's day, we shall see that it is very little.

Summer: 6 AM to noon: work in the oasis

Noon to 6 PM: under the portico or at the grocery; siesta, discussion

6 PM to 8 PM: work in the oasis

8 PM to 9 PM: supper with the family

9 PM to 10 or 11 PM: on the square, before going to bed.

Winter: 7 AM to noon: work in the oasis

Noon to 2 PM: on the square

2 PM to 5 PM: work in the oasis

5 PM to 9 PM: on the square or at supper before going to bed.

Of course, we have not counted the hours spent watching over irrigation. Our schedules are strictly tentative, since the villagers do not work by the clock. But we can see that, apart from the time spent in sleep, family life fills no more than an hour or an hour and a half of the day. And, as we have said before, husband and wife barely speak to each other.

And yet, as five or six heads of families bear witness, this area of collective experience holds a very important place in a man's life and he would be thrown off his balance if it were missing. Indeed, the personality of the man of Shebika seems to rest on this shaky and belittled foundation.

'The family's a gift of God. Without his family and his sons, what would a man do? He'd run from town to town, living in any old place and scrambling for food like a beggar.'

Ali is speaking, and Muhammad says about the same thing:

'I've had two wives, one after the other. A man needs a woman to make the couscous and dry the peppers and wash clothes. Those things have to be done.'

'I was away from Shebika for a long time,' says the *Imam*. 'One year, or five, I don't remember, but my family was here, and I came back. That's the way it is. We have a home, and it pleases God to keep it for us. I lost my wife, and now I have another, a cousin. She's the one that takes in and distributes the gifts to the Mosque. How else could I manage?'

'My family is up the mountain,' says Nureddin. 'When our ancestors were attacked they put their families in the caves. That was the first step to take. Family and children are the most important things. When a man goes away he takes them with him. That's all we have.'

'Do you often take your family somewhere with you?'

'To Tawzar, yes.'

'Which do you care more about, your land or your family?'

'My family.'

All thirty of the solidly based families of Shebika live in the same way; in a ramshackle house with a tumble-down roof, which no one bothers to repair, since they have been told that the whole village is to be rebuilt soon. Everything is gradually crumbling. The average house of this kind provides more or less space for from five to eight people, not including passing friends and relations and cousins who have been taken in permanently. There are seventeen other units, which cannot properly be called families, where the wife has died without being replaced and the man shares his house with a son or brother. Then there is the woman pedlar, who sells thread, needles, shoelaces and sweets; she comes every two months to stay for several days or, in winter, several weeks, in a house occupied the rest of the time by two elderly female relatives. A small group of bachelors and widowers roll up in their blankets every night in a barely roofed shack at the top of the village, but they can't really be said to live there except in cold weather.

The head of the family is the only possible source of information on financial conditions. Needless to say, statistics of the 'average income' are completely misleading, since Shebika has no share in the so-called national wealth. We can find out only by asking around how much money a family really has and how many dinars pass through its hands every year. Various figures are given, but we must note at once the surprise of people to whom we have shown a five-dinar note,* because they have never seen one. This goes for most of the *khammes* and two of the small land-owners. The grocer and the pedlar, of whom we have just spoken (we ran into her three

---

* Ten dollars (according to the official rate of exchange).

times in the course of the first two years and never thereafter), were familiar with this blue note and could even change it for us. Also two land-owners, who have dealings with the Bedouins, and one *khammes*, who goes to sell the pepper crop at Tawzar. This doesn't mean that the sum of five dinars doesn't pass through the average man's hands in the course of a year, but simply that he gets and spends it in one-dinar notes or small change. In any case, the study of the family budget raises strange problems.

'What do you need to live on, you and your family, for a year?' we ask a land-owner whom we have never seen in the oasis but only outside the Mosque.

'A lot. Three hundred dinars or more.'

'Have you got that much money?'

'One can always get it.'

'Do you know what three hundred dinars mean?'

'What I need to live on.'

'How much money do you give your wife?'

'What do you mean, how much do I give her?'

'She needs money doesn't she, every day?'

'I arrange that with the grocer.'

'What if she does need money?'

'She has her jewels.'

'But for an unexpected purchase of food, for the children?'

'Sometimes I give her a hundred millimes, sometimes two hundred.'

'By the day?'

'For one day, occasionally.'

'And after that, nothing more?'

'Why should I give her more?'

'And how much money do you make in all?'

'Sometimes eight hundred millimes. Three dinars, when I sell the peppers, and a little more when I sell the dates.'

'For the whole year?'

'For the whole year.'

'Don't you ever buy clothes?'

'What for? I got these overalls when I was working on the road, a long time ago.'

'And your wife?'

'She has her veils.'

'Then do you have three hundred dinars a year?'

'I don't have them. They're what I need to cover my expenses.'

A *khammes* is even more positive.

'I have what I need every year. I need two hundred dinars, because everything's so expensive.'

'And you really have them?'

'There's couscous and meat and the needs of my son, and school.'

'The school-books are given him, aren't they?'

'Yes, they give them out at the school.'

'Well, then?'

'There's all the rest.'

'What rest?'

'What pleases God.'

'How much do you spend every day?'

'How should I know? Semolina and flour cost fifty millimes. Oil is expensive, too. Everything's expensive.'

'Do you have the two hundred dinars you need?'

'If I borrow them, yes.'

'From whom do you borrow?'

'From Ridha, the grocer.'

'Everyone seems to borrow from Ridha.'

'From Ridha and from the pedlar.'

'So everyone owes Ridha money?'

'Yes, everybody. Soon there won't be any more money. Because no one pays him back all that he owes.' *

Another *khammes*, who works on a piece of land that belonged to his father and which he sold in order to get married, calculates as his both the land and the money that he paid out for his wife. And to this he adds what he needs to go to Tunis in order to consult a doctor about his eyes. Almost all the men we questioned calculate their wealth not by what they have but by what they wish they had. This is not only because their

---

* Ridha is jokingly and flatteringly called '*Al bank el shaabi*', 'the people's bank'.

language permits a looseness of this kind but also because they are unwilling to admit that they have nothing. But is this the only place on earth where words have it over reality? Here, as elsewhere, they serve to cover up an inadmissible situation.

'You, Ridha, you know, don't you, how much they have to live on?'

'Two or three hundred millimes a week, a dinar per month, perhaps two.'

'Then they get all their food from the land?'

'Yes, except for sugar, semolina, tea, and oil.'

'Can a man live off two dinars a month? That's only a little over twenty dinars a year.'

'Some of them do.'

'Not all of them?'

'No, not all.'

'And the others?'

'They eat as well as they can; they help one another.'

'And the women, what do they do?'

'They do the cooking. They cut the dates. They grind the wheat and make flour.'

'And does everyone have two hundred millimes a week? Do you have that much yourself?'

'Something like that, yes.'

'Any more?'

'No, no more.'

But no one can be frank on this point. Centuries of pillage and of gouging tax collectors during the periods of Turkish domination and the rule of the Beys, the threats of a punitive tax or the accusation of usury all further a propensity to dissimulation. But how can one expect to find abstract truth at this level? After all, only Ridha, the grocer, the pedlar woman, and two miserable small land-owners can really count.

'That's it,' says the pedlar. 'Here [pointing to a pile of pebbles at her left] we put what we have, and there [at the right] what we owe. When the left pile is bigger then we can afford to buy something.'

'Do you wish you had more than you do?'

'I have nothing, sister, nothing at all. How should I keep accounts?'

'Where did you learn to count as you do?'

'My husband, when he was alive, was a grocer.'

'And do the people here buy much from you?'

'Not much, no. I come here because it's where I have my house.'

If we push our analysis beyond idle words we can figure out that the average family of Shebika handles about ten dinars from one end of the year to the other, that is, except for Ridha and one or two land-owners who 'do business with the Bedouins', selling them some forty dinars' worth of dates and peppers every year. In short, the domestic economy of Shebika cannot be calculated in money, but rather in terms of exchanges and favours. The discussion of monetary policy heard over the radio has about as much concrete meaning as the daily palaver of the men under the portico.

The economy of the market-place is a subject for theorization on the part of Europeans and the ruling class of Tunisians. The men of Shebika express their desires in terms of money because they have picked up from the radio a certain attitude towards that which is desirable, which the new government has, in its turn, picked up from the West. From this contradiction between an artificially learned terminology and real conditions divorced from any modern concept of economics derives the ambiguity of the language in which money is discussed at Shebika and the flexible character of the family budget. Money, something barely known and then in very limited quantities, is the symbol of a system set up by ingenuous European visitors and government financial experts. The radio is its most effective means of communication. But what of all this the man of Shebika takes unto himself is much more difficult to understand. He grasps the meaning without being able to translate it into substance. These people actually live in a world of words, words which they have elaborated out of the contrast between their poverty and what they hear over the radio. Their words do not correspond to facts, and this accentuates the village's isolation.

How could they, indeed, learn the economy of the market-place? Of the two groceries of Shebika only one, Ridha's, survives, and most of what is 'bought' there is paid for in service. Debts are wiped out by exchanges. The pedlar woman sells her needles and thread in exchange for the food she eats while she is in the village. If she borrows a mule to go and try her luck with the Bedouins she pays for it with trinkets for the children.

Marriage is the only thing that really impels money to circulate. Old Qaddur (no relation to the *Imam* of the same name) has married several times, and every time he had to sell some of his date-palms in order to raise money to take to his future parents-in-law. The parents-in-law themselves, who live at El Hamma, told us that Abdullah had simply turned over the land and added to it five borrowed one-dinar notes for the marriage expenses. Nureddin thought he had a good deal of money when he went to fetch his wife from Tamerza, but it was only passing through his hands. When Ali married off his daughter to a man from Redayif he got from him ten or twelve one-dinar notes, but most of them went into paying off a debt that Ridha had been trying to collect for five years. The money that Muhammad put down for his second wife, Nawa, came from a merchant of Tawzar who owed him the payment of two years' supply of peppers.

The road-building projects (which are in operation no more than twice a year) afford a fortnight of employment to those who are lucky enough to be recruited, and a cash payment of two and a half dinars. Obviously, the sale of agricultural products should bring in money. The peppers, for instance, are bought by middlemen, some for the regional cooperative, others for the city markets. But the buying price is miserably low. In 1965 a pound of the super-fine pimentos, which go into making *harissa*, brought fifty millimes at Shebika and was re-sold in Tunis for over three hundred.

If the people of Shebika know neither the mechanics of buying and selling nor that of wages and salaries, it is not for lack of information. It is simply because they cannot attain the level at which there are laws other than those of the exchange of services or petty borrowing.

'My father never saw any paper money,' old Ali tells us. 'Never. I saw it myself for the first time when the French were here and I worked in a military camp, where I was well paid. Later I worked for the Germans and the Americans. They all pay more than the Tunisians. For a while I had a lot of money.'

'A lot?'

'Yes, fifty or a hundred dinars.'

'And what did you do with it?'

'I took another wife. My first one was old.'

'When was that?'

'Before the Law. Before Independence.'

'And now?'

'My old wife is still around. The young one died. She had a child in her belly that wouldn't come out. First thing I knew, she was dead.'

'And now, have you any money?'

'Yes, plenty.'

Nureddin is more confused.

'Money? We've seen that; yes, we have. But nobody knows where it goes. Perhaps to the Bedouins. Anyhow, God doesn't intend it to stay at Shebika. It travels. They have money in other places. Dinars don't come to Shebika, because there's nothing to buy.'

There is an ancient form of saving or capitalization, represented by the women's jewels, which are their personal property or, in certain cases, go back to their father when they are dead. The jewels are of Bedouin origin: brooches, buckles, arm and ankle bands, plates to be worn on the breast or forehead, all made of beaten silver. The women sell them when they emigrate with their families to the suburbs of the city and suddenly find themselves up against an urban economy. Their husbands do not object, and eventually these often quite beautiful pieces are re-sold at a much higher price to collectors. But at Shebika the women are proud to wear them, and never, in the course of our stay, did they try to sell them to us.

This economic factor is very meaningful. Woman is a centre of real accumulation, the recipient of wealth that is spent and tied up in possessions but at the same time 'socialized'. She causes a man to pay a dowry to her father, and then her parents endow her with jewels which remain in her possession, setting her apart by their obvious value and, in any case, giving her a sort of independence, since she is free to dispose of them as she will and keep the money.

The value of such jewels can be calculated. Nawa has two plates, priced in Tunis at ten dinars each, two five-dinar bracelets, four buckles, and two brooches priced at two and one dinars, respectively. That makes a total of forty dinars. Iimra has even more: five plates, one of them ornamented with a slightly damaged precious stone, ten bracelets, and as many buckles and brooches, representing a value of a hundred dinars in all. The old wife of the *Imam* has about the same amount, and so do the wives of three other *khammes*. This proves that the possession of jewels has nothing to do with the financial status of a family; it is passed down from mother to daughter, with occasional additions. The women of the thirty established families of Shebika, if we calculate the average value of their jewels at forty dinars, have a total capital of twelve hundred dinars, which is neither invested in the community nor enters into the customary exchanges, but is, instead, a woman's glory and the symbol of her financial independence. In this way the women are wealthier than the men, except for those who are in business.

Actually the only stimulant to the circulation of comparatively large sums of money is marriage, which activates apparent financial transactions, with which are mingled traditional exchanges, the latter indicative of an incapacity to progress beyond the ancient tradition of barter. Obviously, under present conditions, the village has no chance of doing things in any other way.

'Economic' relations between groups and individuals are, then, almost exclusively in the form of exchanges – exchanges of goods, of the fruit of the orchards, of services, and irrigation privileges. These make up the living network of village life and the foundation of family. Whether the exchange is a simple *quid pro quo* or part of a system of allegiances, it bears on every possible object and activity at Shebika.

What, then, are the exchanges? On the basis of questions asked of five *khammes* and two land-owners and repeated after an interval of two years, it seems that they are of a wide variety of objects. Among them are women's veils, men's burnouses, a transistor radio, a sieve for semolina flour and couscous, two hoes, one oil-press, bottled oil, sugar, cigarettes and livestock (a chicken, a goat, a mule, cuts of meat and crushed dates). The services exchanged are even more curious: hours of work in the oasis, assistance in childbirth, errands at Tawzar, units of water for irrigation, transportation of an old woman's corpse to the cemetery. The most commonplace object or product or action can enter into the circuit of exchanges. The relative values of the objects or services exchanged are subject to a definite classification. Thus a unit of water is equivalent to an errand at the pharmacy of Tawzar, a certain number of hours' work in the oasis to five or six cigarettes, assistance at childbirth to several measures of oil.

The accounting of these exchanges is far-flung, and every individual is involved in a complex network of credits and debits. Certain men or heads of families are focal points in the circulation system, such as Ridha, the grocer, because of his cash reserves, or Muhammad, because of the transactions attendant upon Nawa's services as a midwife. There are, actually, four focuses of circulation at Shebika: the families of Ridha, Muhammad, Nureddin and Si Qaddur, the *Imam*. These men, rather than the elders of the village, whose age lends them no reputation for wisdom, are called upon for advice as to the best use of seeds, the settlement of a quarrel with the nomads or the illness of a child. Likewise their houses are gathering points. Nureddin and Muhammad know that, during their absence, the women of the village come to visit their wives, and this contributes to their prestige.

Exchanges are the chief subject of the palavering among men and women alike. All day long their minds are occupied with the endless chains of services, with what they have borrowed and lent and the chances of repaying one favour in order to gain advance credit for another. An outsider, of course, is the last person to whom they talk of this preoccupation;

it enters not at all into the picture which they paint of the village.

There are two fundamentally different forms of exchange: one strictly economic, entailing usury and debt, the other based on loyalty to the ties of friendship of family. The first of these dominates the daily life of the village and makes certain holders of wealth into representatives of a monetary economy in disguise. The outstanding example is Ridha, the grocer, to whom absolutely everyone has become indebted during the four years when his business has allowed him to 'help' his fellows. This doesn't mean that Ridha is a rich man. His oil, tea, and sugar, and the money he lends, without usury, bring him no return for a period of years, and the return is always pendant, inasmuch as his customers continue to have the same needs as those for which they have indebted themselves in the past. He is simply the holder of a certain wealth which he can never capitalize, because every repaid debt leads to the formation of a new one. Ridha has acquired a modern mentality, that of a dealer in money, although he handles relatively small sums which we have calculated at two or three hundred dinars a year. He knows that, under the form of work on his land in the oasis or of accumulated services, he is building up reserves which he can eventually spend at Tawzar or Qafsa. For, we may note, he has no intention of investing money in Shebika. Thus amid a 'barter economy' we have a class of rich, or fairly rich, peasants whose holdings stem from their claim upon the services of their poorer fellows and from a dogged determination (rare in the South) to better their lot.

The second form of exchange, based on allegiance and co-operation, is extraordinarily generous in view of the general poverty, but in recent years it has lost much of its vigour. In 1967, at the moment of installing the promised state socialism, the necessary impetus was lacking. In the long period of waiting between stagnation and development, the goodwill of the peasants, baffled by their contact with a monetary economy in which they had no part, was purposeless and thus quickly exhausted.

This cooperation is practised, to a striking extent, among the

women. By its cleavage between the roles of men and women
Islam makes for a strong group loyalty (almost complicity)
among the members of each of the sexes. We may hazard the
hypothesis that, in spite of its apparent humility, the role of
woman is actually more important than that of man. Because
woman profits from man's dependence on her for food, sexual
gratification and children, she is a powerful, even if hidden
and unacknowledged, factor in the public life of Tunisia.

At Shebika this secret strength is not so obvious, but it rules
over the psychological life of the village. The women, while
they are left to themselves during the day, jointly make decisions which they suggest and even impose upon their husbands.
They discuss not only food, illness, and the birth or absence of
children, but also prospective marriages. In only one out of
seventeen cases within the family of Nureddin did a husband
oppose his wife's decision about a child's marriage, and that
only because he had to repay a personal obligation. Cooperation among the women is essentially based upon mutual aid and
services which benefit sometimes the whole family (when
Nawa serves as midwife to the wife of Ridha her whole household shares the oil and sugar she receives in payment), sometimes the women alone. The network of exchanges among
families is paralleled by another, more subtle, among women.

'When a woman has a baby,' Iimra tells us, 'we all take her
tea, sugar, and other gifts.'

The young woman who has given birth sits amid old rags.
The tattooing stands out against her wan skin and the end of
the umbilical cord, tied up in a ribbon, rises up grotesquely on
the baby's belly. Childbirth is a form of illness and its care
includes not only tea and sugar, but magic words and incanta-
tions. The presence of the other women is a gift which the
young mother will eventually repay in kind. Even Nawa's
singing is the rendition of a service and, like any gesture made
in public, it calls for acknowledgement. Did not the women
propose to Naïma and the girl of our party whom they call
'Christ' to come to Tunis to help them through childbirth
when their time came? They themselves go occasionally to
render this service to their cousins at El Hamma and Tamerza.

One particular example of cooperation among the women is in the realm of handicraft, namely pottery. Some of the women (usually the young ones) go up into the mountains towards Redayif – a whole day's walk – and bring back clay, in sacks suspended by a string from their shoulders. Sometimes they exchange it for tea, but more often, so Nawa and Iimra told us – they give it to other women who know how to model and bake it. Usually these are the three Qadduri women, who live not far from the portico, who make them into the pots (*tajin*) which serve for cooking. This specialized work is free, in return for the free porterage of the clay. And afterwards the pots are distributed free, to anyone else that wants them.

'If they want eggs or chickens, they come to me,' says Iimra, the wife of Nureddin.

When the pedlar arrives from Redayif the women lend her a mule to carry her wares down to the Bedouin encampment and El Hamma. Their husbands tacitly approve, and the compensation is the gift of some ribbons. A blind old woman, a Qadduri, who has no immediate kin, has been taken in by another family, unrelated to the Qadduri, which feeds her and invites her to all its celebrations. Similarly, Ibrahim Imami, an old bachelor whose mind is failing, lives with a family and is given a full share of its food. Many other less important favours are done as well. A woman pierces the ears of her neighbour's daughter, because the mother cannot do it herself. Or, on the occasion of a marriage, Ridha's wife lends the bride the silver jewellery which, as we have seen, is her own personal property.

In the realm of food these friendly exchanges are the most intense. Hardly a day goes by but one family asks another for eggs or a chicken, so that, quite beyond ties of relationship, the whole village is affected. This is a matter not just of holiday celebrations but of everyday living.

Since food enters into the influence which the women exercise upon the men it is one of the firmest foundations of the family circle, the bond which links man to nature and to his very existence. It is the object of the most frequent exchanges and, in view of the general poverty and under-nourishment (which formerly amounted to periods of near-starvation), the domain where we see the most striking examples of group loyalty and cooperation among the women.

'If anyone needs bread or flour he is sure to find someone who will give it to him,' says the wife of the *Imam*. 'He has only to ask.'

In this case the act is a simple one. But cooperation extends further, to the joint cooking, a ritual which all over the South women learn, already in childhood, from other women, just as they learn to make the gestures that favour fecundation. These two form a single activity which brings all the women of the village together and is far more continuous than any activity of the men.

The harvested wheat is pounded and ground into flour in first one house and then another, with a complete sharing of tools and utensils, whose individual ownership is forgotten. The emotion engendered by this action often leads to verbal invention and to profoundly erotic dance motions,* in which hips swing in time to the blows of the pounder and the undulation of the breasts accompanies the stretching out of the arms that hold it. While she is dancing a woman often strips off her clothes, revealing her tattooing, and the others respond with the *zaghret*, a harsh, throaty sound. It is as if the gestures and signs of sensual pleasure, often lacking in concrete sexual acts, were shorn of their original purpose and sublimated into the symbolic gestures of the dance and of exhibition.

These dances heighten the feeling of participation in the cooking process, the mounting of the couscous, and then its drying-out, during which the women share the clothes and covers which serve these purposes. When they roll the soaked grains of wheat, every woman has a wooden plate, a sieve, and the basket in which she makes the mixture. Young girls – almost children – carry the baskets up to the solid parts of the crumbling roofs or else put them out in the courtyard, after shooing the chickens away. If a man comes along they playfully throw a handful of grain at him in order to keep him at a distance.

* For certain of these ceremonies see the amusing description by W. Marcais and Abdel Rahman Guiga in *Textes arabes de Takrouna* (actually from a more northerly region).

There is little built-up reserve and the quantities involved are very small, but they make for an intensive form of collaboration. The same tender attention is brought to bear upon the preparation of the daily foods, stews made of chick-peas and kid or mutton boiled for so long that it separates into ribbons, assortments of cooked vegetables, all of them seasoned with red pimentos whose sharpness is said by some to serve as an aphrodisiac, by others to balance the body functions during the height of the heat or to cut thirst. Probably all three together.

We may note that among all these boiled meat and vegetable dishes, there is never any question of frying. This not for any logical reason, but simply because the act of collective cooking and its erotic character go with long-drawn-out processes of ripening, mixing, stirring and heating. Frying is an essentially solitary process, one proper to isolated shepherds or mountaineers.* The lengthy preparation of boiled dishes suggests, on the contrary, an intense and communal woman's task of making food for the males. The man of Shebika is never less alone than when he appears to be so. When he goes down to the oasis or out over the steppe he carries with him in a vessel or basket the fruit of the pious and erotic collective effort of the women-folk of the village, taking with him, as it were, a symbol of the family life whose allegiance is stronger than any other.

Cooperation among the men is effective in their work and in the satisfaction of such personal needs as tea and tobacco. Down in the oasis it is voluntary and disinterested, whereas up under the portico or at the grocery it has the form of a calculated exchange. Of course, in case of disaster (a flood caused by a sudden storm or a plague of locusts) both land-owners and *khammes* aid the victims without any thought of return. Likewise if a man suffers an accident, one of his fellows will always take him to a clinic in the nearest town or fetch the necessary

* Cooking is not a language, it is not the mere observance of rules. Eating and sex are *acts* before they are transposed into a system or language.

medicine, even if it means losing precious working time during the harvest season.

Masculine cooperation assumes a less active form, in terms not of deeds but of words, in the palavering that goes on on the square during the leisure hours which, as we shall see, form the essence of the life of Shebika.

Whether spontaneous or calculated, the system of exchanges dominates not only the family circle but the entire life of the community. The fact that any object or action may circulate in this system, completely alien to an economy based on money, gives a particular colour to the reality of daily life. Men and women are thus involved in a network of loans and repayments which underly the whole social fabric, although *they are not necessarily expressed in everyday speech*. Because the national government knows that it will not be able for five or ten years to change the life of the South, to draw the people into a monetary economy where wages are the rule, it insists, over the radio and through the intermediary of its local administrators, on the necessity of cooperation. In this case government propaganda serves to justify the man of the village.

'They said so on the radio,' says a young *khammes* called Ahmad. 'They said that everyone must help his brother and neighbour. We've always done that; it's God's will, and we don't need to be told. Since the government says so, we say so too. When somebody wants to borrow my hoe I lend it to him, when it's not in use. If someone needs eggs I give them to him, and I ask him when I need them myself. That's the way we are ...'

And so the system of exchanges of Shebika makes up a closed, monolithic unit. The cousins of El Hamma or Tamerza enter into it occasionally, but to a very small degree. The system is Shebika's own, and it is inside the home, where the man spends so little of his time, but where he finds the substructure of his psychic existence, that the group life develops. Nothing comes out of this warm intimacy, this continuous sharing; it simply accentuates the all-embracing relationship among the villagers as contrasted to the *abstract* separation into families, often at odds with each other where a marriage is concerned. Cooperation and exchange are at a different level of experience and do not make for the integration of the single units or give them a structure. They achieve the identification and affirmation of a unity of their own which comes out in the interplay of reciprocities, complicated by the tangle of relationships not only of the present but of the past as well.

Cooperation and exchange have a curious function. Instead of pushing Shebika into a new form of experience they freeze it in its present mediocre situation. In a different kind of society exchange multiplies human contacts and creates prestige. Here it isolates Shebika from the rest of the South. By virtue of a whole section of its social experience the village undoes that which is brought about by marriages; it separates and underlines the solitude of the group by closing it in on itself, occupying it to the exclusion of all else and shutting it off from the rest of the world. Mutual aid becomes an element of deterioration when it makes the group which practises it into a ghetto.

Three Lives

In the course of our long progression into the labyrinth of the collective life of Shebika three persons spontaneously told us their life stories, a long one in the case of Ahmad and old Qaddur, a shorter one in the case of Fatimah. With all the anecdotes that they bear in their train they show up the tangle of cycles and clans which give the village its shifting physiognomy.

Ahmad bin Ali bin Ibrahim Qaddur calculated in 1962, when we first met him, that he was seventy years old, since he was born when the 'Frankawi' first entered the Regency. He is a tall, gaunt old man with a heavy black moustache which contrasts with his bald head. His ears, pierced for long-since lost ear-rings, are covered with yellow scabs. All day long he sprawls in the dust either near the portico or in front of the Mosque, never in the neighbourhood of the grocery, because 'it takes money to go there, and I haven't any'.

When he raises himself up to talk he barely shakes off the

dust from his bare legs and his burnous. He looks at us almost mockingly, knowing what we are after and hoping that we will talk about him. He attaches considerable importance to the notes we make and the photographs we take. Perhaps he hopes, through them, to escape his inevitable death.

'My grandfather was the biggest land-owner of Shebika. He had many palm-trees and eleven parcels of his own in the oasis. All the water went to him. The *khammes* were his associates in his work and he divided everything with them.'

Everyone envied his grandfather's wealth and importance and asked his advice. He was a staunch believer, but was never able to make the pilgrimage to Mecca because the 'Frankawi' arrived when he was just of an age to go. He himself, Si Ahmad, was born in a no longer existent house above the *wadi* and lived the same way as the other children of his age. He remembers that at this time children died much more frequently than they do today, and he has lost most of his former friends, except for one or two who have lived to be as old as he.

When he was twenty years old Si Ahmad went to see his cousins at El Hamma and then as far as Tawzar, where there was then no railway, only a French post and soldiers who travelled about by camel. Then the railway was built and, like most of the other natives, he worked at laying the rails across the desert, then at building the road from Qafsa to Tawzar and Naftah. He worked very hard, while his father stayed with his grandfather at the oasis. When the railway was finished he saw the train, the first train of the Sahara. The Bedouins walked for hours to see it arrive at Tawzar, preceded by a squadron of red-uniformed soldiers.

'That was a celebration! They gave out food, and people camped near the train. The officers ordered the drums and bugles to play.'

They said then that life was going to change, that the advent of the train marked the end of an era. But nothing really happened. The caravans came to the station, and the soldiers arrived and so did some specialists in tree blights and camel diseases.

'Everyone thought there would be a big difference, and then life went on just as before.'

There was more work, to be sure, at places like Tawzar, but only for young men who could learn to wait at table or prepare food in European style. Ahmad went on to take a look at Qafsa, the city that is so much talked about in the South.

'Markets, everywhere markets. Camels and oranges, anything you wanted to buy or sell. And people buying, 'Frankawi' and people from Tunis. A city of markets.'

'You've never been back to Qafsa since then?'

'No, never.'

'And that was before the war?'

'The war? *Ya awlad* [child], I've seen plenty of wars. In the South people are always fighting. People have come from all over to fight here, and then they've gone away.'

'The Second World War, for instance?'

'A war. . . . Yes, that's what they called it. In a village near Tawzar I saw the flags change between one end of the day and the other. We woke up with the Frankawi, and in the evening there were the Italians or the Germans. Then the next morning they hauled down the German flag and raised another. How can a man know what's going on? You say *"Mabruk"*, Welcome, to them all, and then they're happy. You have to get along, that's all. But all that's over now, with Habib.'

'But it was before the first war that you went to Qafsa, was it?'

'Yes.'

'And you never went back?'

'Never, I returned to Shebika, and I've never been away since. My father was there but my grandfather was dead. We had our big house then. Yes, we were the richest family and, please God, the most just.'

'Did the palm-trees produce many dates?'

'Yes, they produced more than they do now. And the dates were very much in demand. We ate what we wanted, and then we went to the market at Tawzar. "You want dates, and I want oil." Now they're sold for money. My grandfather and father were very rich. My father was the Sheikh, the Sheikh of Shebika.'

'Under the French . . . ?'

'Yes, the French were there.'

'And how did you like them?'

'The Frankawi? When I was young they were all right. But as I got older they were bad. The older I got the worse they were.'

'But originally they were all right, were they?'

'Yes. There was a doctor and an agricultural expert. The soldiers spent money and so did the tourists. It seems that up North they bought land. But there's no land they'd want to buy here.'

When Ahmad's grandfather died his son seems to have been one of the richest land-owners of the village. Then something sad happened. It's impossible to say whether it took place when Ahmad was very young or when his father was very old and about to give him his land, that is around 1938. This second date is based on the fact that Ahmad's father was let out of jail during the war, that they went once to see him at Tawzar before he was transferred to a jail in the North, from which he returned to live as miserably as his son does now. But none of this is very clear, and Ahmad can bring no light to bear on it.

'There was a fellow called Grombi, a sergeant with the gendarmes under the Protectorate, who wanted to do my father in and become Sheikh. He'd been looking for a chance for a long time. He buried some pots with charges of dynamite in the oasis and then exploded them and said my father was concealing weapons.'

'When was that?'

'I don't remember. But that's what he did. I married for the first time when I came back from Qafsa, and that's when it all began.'

'I've heard a story of the same kind that led to a man from Tamerza becoming the Sheikh. It wasn't so long ago, in the years just before Independence.'

'The men of Tamerza have always done things like that in order to take away our land. Even our cousins have done it.'

'But if it was only ten or twenty years ago, then it wasn't when you got married for the first time. That was much earlier.'

'There was always trouble with that fellow Grombi. He had

Shebika, seen from the rocks above

Shebika

Shebika : the retaining wall

Si Tijani

Under the portico of the *qaddus*

The *qaddus*, or water-clock

By the postern of the grocer

Nawa

Another view of Shebika
To the right, the pile of stones hewn by the men of Shebika
(see Chapter 5)

Old Ali

The waterfall above the village

In the oasis

my father thrown into jail and let him out only when I paid a ransom. The ransom was part of my father's land, the land he'd cultivated.'

'You mean that your father and you became *khammes* and worked for Grombi?'

'That's it.'

'And your father was willing to work for a fellow who'd turned him in for something he hadn't done?'

'Exactly.'

'Wasn't there something else to it? Hadn't Grombi perhaps suffered some injustice at the hands of your father or grandfather?'

'Grombi was the son of a local *khammes*. He was an Imami from Tamerza, with relatives at Shebika.'

'He had land here, did he?'

'Yes.'

'And you lost yours, did you?'

'He was a heavy drinker.'

'A drinker, at Shebika?'

'Yes, a heavy drinker.'

It seems that Ahmad's father was twice arrested, the first time only briefly, when he gave some land for bail, the second for longer, because he was sentenced to imprisonment, at about the time of Ahmad's second marriage, 'during the Germans'. It is possible that Grombi had it in for him or that the Sheikh of the period immediately preceding Independence, a man of Tamerza, entered the picture and reported Ahmad to the French for hiding or stocking arms (for what purpose we cannot know), so that he was brought up before a military court. It is almost certain that the old man was freed when the Axis invaded Tunisia, but again there is no telling for what reason. In any case, when he came out of jail he was landless and had to become a *khammes*. And yet it was just then that Ahmad contracted his second marriage.

'Where did you find dowry money?'

'I had it.'

'And you chose to marry at this particular time?'

'Yes.'

After his father's death Ahmad became the *khammes* that he remained until fifteen or twenty years ago. His father lived to a ripe old age, and now Ahmad too is very old. He has sold all the jewels of his deceased wives. His sons died too, one of them during the last war. Now he lives with one of his daughters, Hafziyya, at the foot of the hills at the edge of the village. All day long he stays in the sun, moving in winter from the Mosque to the portico during the few hours that it is shining. Most of the time he sleeps.

When we came back to Shebika in 1965 we saw a body, wrapped in the dirty sheet from the Mosque, being carried to the cemetery. Si Tijani was able to tell at once, from the people who were accompanying it, that the body was that of Ahmad. And he added, laughing – because here death is not such a great tragedy – that old Ahmad had had plenty of time to prepare himself for meeting God.

'A great liar! He told tall stories all his life!'

Fatimah is the wife of the owner of a parcel of land in the oasis. She is between forty-five and fifty years old, and her face is brown and hardened. The tattooing stands out clearly on her cheek-bones: a circle on one side and the palm-tree of Tanit on the other.

'I don't work, like a man. Women don't do men's work.'

She shows her jewels: a beaten-silver buckle in the shape of a circle with an arrow going through it, and a round plate bearing the same motifs as those of her tattooing. These two motifs sum up the past of North Africa, as if the Bedouins who for thousands of years have engraved them found here the symbols of their multiple spiritual adventures, their rapid conversions and equally rapid apostasies: Judaism, Christianity and Islam, and even before these the Roman and Punic religions. The survival of these symbols does not mean that they are archetypes transmitted by some 'collective unconsciousness', the spiritual equivalents of the mechanism of heredity in the body. It means that people with no writing and with a language fragmented by dispersion and the confused and degrading life of the steppe make out of familiar signs a sort of lingo completed from generation to generation, a single form gradually created in obedience to a continuous desire to perfect it, whose finality time and chance alone will reveal. The key to this continuous process, which is illustrated in the shape of the jewels and the association of Punic, Roman, Christian, Berber and Arab symbols, is to be found in the *graffiti* haphazardly traced on the walls of the cities of the Maghrib and notably in the Medina of Tunis. These *graffiti* are quite unlike those of Europe, which are finished and evocative. They obey a curious law of synchronic composition, as if a succession of strollers before these stone or cement walls had, one after the other, completed the sketches of their predecessors, filling a certain space and discovering outlines of a constellation, of a figure unknown to the individual and yet achieved by the collectivity. This, of course, with no over-all intention. In the superposition of hasty, unfinished strokes we decipher the elements of a game played with the shape of a fish or a bird which seems to balance a face and the orderly pattern of mathematical figures.

The decoration of a Bedouin plate is similar, inasmuch as it restores to immediacy a composition elaborated in the course of centuries, a unique figure whose achievement is pursued by one generation of engravers after another. It is as if popular expression (to which some people still give the outmoded name of folklore) were the progressive constitution of an image equivalent to a hidden internal logic, independent of personal or historical events, to the necessarily slow and approximative crystallization of a language of symbols distributed in space (that of a silver plate or a tattooing), which picture the collective mentality of a group or collection of groups long since dispersed and fragmented.

'I sold most of my jewels,' Fatimah tells us, 'when my first husband died. I went back, then, to my uncle, at Tamerza. My oldest daughter had married here at Shebika and she took her younger brother into the house where she lives, beside the grocery.'

Fatimah comes of a family of nomads. Although her first husband was an Imami, she was classified with the Yussufiya, who are still called awlad Ali and are not considered true inhabitants of Shebika. Her uncle, obviously, belonged to the same family and it was he who took her in when she was left a widow. But this state of affairs did not last for long. A man of her own age from Shebika, also an awlad Ali, but the owner of a dozen palm-trees, came to take her for his wife. He had never been married before.

'He's a good man and a hard worker. He goes often to Tawzar to buy medicine when it is needed. He found a wife for my son.'

'The son of your first husband?'

'Yes.'

'Where did he marry?'

'Here at Shebika. He married another awlad Ali.'

'And have you any children by your second husband?'

'Yes, a daughter. She's ill.'

The relation of cousinship between husband and wife and their relatively advanced age were not favourable to little Latifa. She is twelve years old, half-blind (from a remotely inherited trachoma) and can barely speak. Most of the time she is sleeping.*

Fatimah is what, elsewhere, might be called 'popular'. Her house is one of those where the women meet in the afternoons, when they come up from the *wadi*. Not all the women, but a dozen of them, who are either Imami or Qadduri. The segregation of the awlad Ali (Yussufiya) is enforced when it comes to marriages, but not in everyday life or exchanges.

'The women come to my house, and we talk about what's going on in the village.'

Fatimah has gone fairly often on mule-back to Tawzar, with both her first and second husband, and also across the mountains, which she climbs as nimbly as a goat, to Tamerza. Wherever she goes she is accompanied by a big white dog with its ears clipped in order to protect it from the wolves of the steppe and other dogs. At home the dog always sleeps at the foot of her bed. We tried to find out if Fatimah, with her active and smiling good nature, is what we should call 'happy'. Of course the word *saïdah* would have no meaning for her other than a

* This little girl died in 1966.

mystical beatitude. We asked, rather, if she envied any of the other women (which she does not) and whether she wished she had lived any differently from the way she has. But all she could say was that God had willed it so. We asked her further whether God had been good to her, and to this she had an answer:

'God gives something to everyone. He gives to those who ask. Some people ask Sidi Sultan, but I don't. Sidi Sultan is not for me.'

And she added this sentence, which explains the role of magic and of the marabout:

'Sidi Sultan is for the unhappy, the disinherited ...'

'But what about your daughter, Latifa?'

'There's the doctor at Tawzar.'

Herein lies Fatimah's superiority over the other women – and many of the men – of Shebika. She thinks that medicine is more efficacious than the magic attached to the marabout. Where did she pick up this idea? She claims to have had it as long as she can remember. Si Tijani, who has been made an army nurse and knows her well, gave us an explanation. Fatimah's first husband worked with him as an attendant in the clinic at Tawzar. In any case, Fatimah is readier than anyone else in Shebika to embrace a more modern form of existence. And, strangely enough, she is not drawn to the cities. She seems to know, intuitively, that emigrating to the shanty-town of Tunis would not enable her to live better than she does here.

The man we call Old Qaddur is a very distant cousin of the Qaddur who is the Mosque *wakeel* or attendant, and some-times the attendant at Sidi Sultan as well. He too died during our inquiry; he belonged to the generation that lived through the beginnings of the French occupation and also the first years of Independence.

Old Qaddur's real name is Si Mahmud bin Ali. His first name is of Turkish origin and comes out of the period of the domina-tion of the Sublime Porte which, two hundred years before the arrival of the French, was the colonial power that left the greatest mark on Tunisia. He remembers neither where he was born (in a tent, not far from Shebika) nor when, but we calculate that he is about eighty.

'My father had a tent somewhere, and lived there with his family. He lived there for a long time. At that time caravans came to Shebika, and my father came with one of them. But my father was a Qadduri who left El Hamma because there was no more room in the part of El Hamma where the Qadduri like to live. He came here to join some cousins. There was no house, but he found work and became the *khammes* of Nureddin's father, who at that time owned a large number of date-palms.' Old Qaddur is also the uncle of the younger man we call 'the skinny soldier', who served in the Congo with the Tunisian contingent of the troops of the United Nations.

It seems that he married, when he was very young, a Qadduri girl from El Hamma, for whom his father gave ten palm-trees. She was a good wife and bore him six children, of whom only one, also a *khammes*, and in his turn a father and grandfather, still lives and works at El Hamma. The others died, along with their mother, in an epidemic, before the First World War. The surviving son deserves a special mention. His name is Abdullah and his father says that as a young man he was 'as handsome as a gazelle'. He worked for five or six years, between the ages of fifteen and twenty, in the hotel run by the Compagnie Transatlantique at Tawzar, on the left side of the street leading from the railway station to the local government office (at that time the seat of the French military commander). The hotel is a one-storey brick building, which couldn't have been very comfortable, but it was there that André Gide and Isabella Eberhardt, who were then exploring the Jerid from Naftah to Tawzar and Al Wad, were staying. The young man, 'whom everybody liked', his father tells us, had an opportunity to guide the hotel guests around. Now Abdullah is sixty, almost an old man himself; indeed, it was he that helped us to calculate the age of Old Qaddur, his father.

'I married again and had four children.'

'No girls?'

'Yes, two. They're married here at Shebika.'

'That makes six, then.'

But Old Qaddur is interested in showing us the wall, which he built with his own hands, at the custodian's request, around the marabout of Sidi Sultan in order to protect it during the summer pilgrimages which at one time attracted a great many Bedouins and people from the villages near by.

'Is Sidi Sultan so very important?' asks Salah, our researcher, who for some months seems to have lost his interest in Shebika.

Old Qaddur looks at him and smiles and says that Sidi Sultan is 'the treasure of Shebika'. Does he mean that Sidi Sultan is the most important thing in the place, Salah asks him. And Old Qaddur assures him that there is nothing more important, that everything centres about Sidi Sultan. This it was that aroused Salah's idea of conducting an investigation into Sidi Sultan, which for a whole year was to lead us down a blind alley.

For the moment, however, Salah is silent and the old man continues to talk. He tells us of the time when caravans came to Shebika, at least for the annual feast-day of Sidi Sultan, the healer.

'The old folks, unlike the people of today, cultivated patience. Once upon a time there was a shortage of dates and we had to eat the grass of the steppe while no one dreamed of selling his sheep. Now, if a man goes two days without food he'll sell everything he has to get it.'

But such talk does not allow us to date the events of the past or lead to any notion of 'history'. Every answer of Si Qaddur is a general statement, often gnomic in character.

'There are things that lead men to hell and things that lead them to God. Nowadays there are many things that lead them to hell.'

Once upon a time exchanges were even more widely practised and there was no recourse to money. This Qaddur expresses in moralistic terms from the Quran.

'If three or four persons come together and discuss things in a spirit of honesty, God is with them. But if it's to lie and to deceive one another, they are blinded by Satan. And today men tell one another lies.'

He remembers, quite definitely, that when he married for

the second time he had to give up some of his palms, 'fifteen, to be exact, because my second wife was more expensive than the first'.

Qaddur claims that his second wife was not as good as the first one, but he does not tell us why. He says only that he married for yet a third time, that is, he went to El Hamma to get a younger woman whom he installed in his house, at first in the capacity of a servant. The fate of such supplementary wives was far from happy. Often the cause of polygamy was an old woman's desire to have a servant or slave to do her work, even if the newcomer had with her husband the sexual relations of which she herself was no longer capable. In this case, the third wife died when she was still young, and the cousins of El Hamma refused to give back the ten date-palms which he had given for her.

'Men have turned bad. We owe God obedience, and he owes us our daily bread. God never abandons his creation. But today there are twenty "bad" men to one "good" one.'

After this third marriage Qaddur worked as a *khammes* on what had formerly been his own land. He had five palms left, and he gave them up for a fourth wife, during the war. At this point his second wife went back to her own family, and is still living at El Hamma.

'She wouldn't do anything. She was lazy and wouldn't make couscous.'

Qaddur insists that he didn't repudiate her, that she left of her own free will, but we have no way of judging the truth of this assertion. The fourth wife seems to have been good enough, although she bore him no child. She kept his house during all the years that he worked, for the benefit of his cousins, in the oasis. During the struggle for Independence Qaddur went with the men who took to the mountains to fight a guerrilla war against the French. But the war as he fought it was not a very bloody affair.

'Nobody got killed. We took up arms and marched all night. Finally they signalled to us to come to lay down our arms. There was a friend of Habib with the French soldiers, because they had made peace.'

When Qaddur returned to the village he got a cash award for his services. With this he bought five palm-trees and set a *khammes* to work on them. This way he is assured of his daily bread and doesn't have to depend on anyone. The award convinced him that it was worthwhile to be in the good graces of the new government. But it is far from clear how genuinely grateful he is to Habib Bourguiba:

'With the colonists there was violence. Now there's Bourguiba, and his reforms, and Independence. ... And yet people are so ungrateful that they don't thank God for the good things – liberty and peace – that he has allowed us to acquire. . . . Today men are lacking in patience.'

Of patience Si Qaddur has plenty, the patience of the old men who no longer work, but sit or lie near the two vital centres of the village – the grocery and the portico. He has a certain sense of humour, and is always joking with his fellows. We have questioned him on every possible subject. One day, when we were speaking again of his life story, he burst out laughing and said:

'I've nothing left. Thanks be to God, all is well. I ruined myself for women.'

At the Living Heart of Shebika

The men are there, on and around the square. At the foot of the Mosque some of them have drawn a checkerboard in the dust and are playing a game, with bits of camel dung and pebbles from the *wadi* for checkers. Others are clustered around the grocery where the 'skinny soldier', Abdelqadir, is working the sewing-machine, others are still under the portico. The heat of noon weighs down upon the village. A wind, slowly blowing from the desert, sweeps up clouds of dust, which rise into the air and fall again.

Here in the centre of the village the men may linger for hours, from morning to evening and into the night. At certain seasons they neither go down to the oasis nor do they go home.

Lazy? Overtired? Nothing to do? All these things together, perhaps, and none of them. The 'dead time', the non-working time is probably the true focus, the hard core of the village. The labyrinth of levels of experience ends here, where men talk, now very fast, now very slowly (one word every thirty or forty seconds), in this palaver, which is the matrix of most decisions.

Over five years, during every trip we made to Shebika, we took our place in one group or the other, either under the portico or at the grocery. (The spaces at the foot of the Mosque and in front of the storehouse of the former grocer are re-served for napping and sleeping.) We know what the talking is about, and the differences between the conversations at the grocery and under the portico.

At the grocery they talk of dealings with the Bedouins, of the price of oil and tea, of the goings and comings visible from the village, of the quality of the materials which 'the skinny soldier' makes into clothes on his machine, of the scores of checker games and the trails of wild animals. Before Independence French army officers and better-class Tunisians camped at Shebika when they came to hunt the wild sheep of the moun-tains, and often Si Tijani served as their guide. Here, where there was not yet a grocery but a seed store, the locally hired beaters laid plans for the hunt.

Under the portico they talk of working hours, of the distribu-tion of seeds, of possible marriages, of the latest news (since around the radio at the grocery they simply listen to the news without comment) and, above all, of the allotment of water. There is not at Shebika, as in larger oases, a regular 'market' in which irrigation time is put up at auction (thereby allowing the big land-owners to bid for the most, even if through an agent), but there is discussion of the exchange of hours and of 'shares' of the water from the *wadi*.

The talk under the portico is definitely more important than that at the grocery. From time to time Ridha comes to sit with the others and take part in the conversation, either as a land-owner or as the money-lender and 'banker' to the village. The talk is literally 'palaver', inasmuch as the words do not necessarily lead to action but build up according to an intrinsic logic. It is as if an imaginary space were set out before the participants and it were up to them to organize its various parts the way one fills the squares of a lotto board, without taking the practicability of the whole into consideration. From a tape-recording of one of these talks under the portico one can follow its interminable ramifications, even if the living quality of the palaver is lost in transcription.

'There's too much water for Nureddin,' says Ali.

'God's water,' retorts Nureddin.

'Bugs are causing the peppers and tomatoes to rot,' says Qaddur. 'God causes bugs to kill the plants so that He won't have so many to nourish.'

'If you have money you can buy seed and plant tomatoes,' says Ali.

'If you plant a hundred, two hundred, three hundred toma-toes,' says Muhammad (counting on the fingers of his left hand, beginning with the thumb), 'then you can harvest enough to buy a camel.'

'When the water runs towards Nureddin then it doesn't run on the other side,' says Ali. 'On the side where there's the dry land that has to be irrigated. If I had water, you'd see what a harvest I'd get.'

'God gives the rain,' says Muhammad.

'There's going to be a storm. The sand wind is blowing, and after the sand wind comes the storm,' says Qaddur.

'When the Frankawi were here there were heavy rains,' says Old Ahmad. 'Everything was covered with water. Wherever you looked there was water. We were floating. That was a rain. It lasted for days.'

'There are no heavy rains,' says Ali.

'There are the rains that God sends,' says Ahmad.

'The rain reduced the seeds to pulp and they had to give out more seeds,' says Ahmad.

And the man from Tunis (a sort of beggar who was drawn to Shebika by his admiration for Sidi Sultan and has stayed here for the thirty years since) says that at Tunis there are droughts, while Shebika has water.

'Haven't you heard? At Tunis there are only two ponds that attract all the water. It's a permanent drought.'

They can go on this way for hours, around and around the same subject. Finally they get up and go away. The conversation evaporates into thin air; as a matter of fact it was never intended to leave any trace behind it.

In front of the talkers, in a cavity dug out of the rock, there hangs the *qaddus*, or water-clock. This is a jar, about twenty inches high, hung from a hook, which is filled at regular intervals with water from a basin. This water drips back into the basin, through a hole whose size is calculated in such a way that the jar empties within about ten minutes. Around the neck of the jar is wound a stalk of grass, which is knotted every time that the jar is filled. When the jar has been emptied the number of times, counted by knots, which corresponds to the share of irrigation due to a parcel of land, an owner or *khammes* picks up his hoe, goes down to the oasis and shifts the sluices in such a way that his land is irrigated. Thus the measurement of time is also a measurement of water, and the measurement of water a measurement of property, since irrigation rights are more precious than the possession of land. All these things – time, irrigation and property – are concentrated in the interminable palavering, under the portico.

This concentration is a form of the social density which is at the heart of the collective life of the village; everything has here the focus of its centripetal and centrifugal flow. The only men who have wrist-watches are Ridha, the grocer, and two young fellows who bought theirs when they were doing their military service, and they never use them except when they are going off on a trip. Time is measured primarily by the *qaddus*, by adding up the units of water, since everyone knows the exact number of knots in the stalk of grass that represents them.

At noon, of course, and again at sunset, the Mosque attendant tosses his cap into the air and counts the number of steps that separates the Mosque from the shade in order to check on the fact that it is time for a prayer. But this is another quality of time, the time of religion, which is rigid and subject to no discussion, although actually it varies in length between winter and summer. The time measured by the *qaddus* is, on the contrary, one that can be discussed, exchanged and even modified by the transactions of which it is the object, by the loans and gifts which constantly manipulate it. This is the fundamental time of the village, since it measures work, property and the progress of the day. We observed the functioning of the water-clock every day, that is, every summer day, since in winter, when the *wadi* is swollen, there is no need to measure the water.

'Some people say that our patron, Sidi Sultan, invented the *qaddus* and set up the quotas of water for irrigation.'

'At Tawzar they say the same thing of Sidi Shaban.'

'That's because he too was a holy man. He said: "Divide the land of the oasis and distribute the water in such and such a way", and that is how we distribute the water.'

'A fellow from the tents once bought a watch with him to calculate the amount of water to which he was entitled. A watch isn't the same thing, and we objected. You can't measure water with the *qaddus* and with a watch at the same time. Finally he put away his watch and left it to the *qaddus*.'

'The French, too, wanted to give us a clock. But what was the use of that? Sidi Sultan made water to be water, and to serve for the allotment of irrigation time.'

While the men are gathered around the water-clock, the total irrigation time down in the oasis is running away. But the group above lives apart from any concrete measurement.

'We like being near the *qaddus*,' Nureddin tells us. 'Not only to divide the water, but also just because we're all there together. Even the old men come.'

'Sidi Sultan started the whole thing,' says the man from Tunis, always wrapped up in his dogmatic devotion to the marabout. 'Sidi Sultan made the oasis into thirty parcels, one for each of the thirty families. And he said to each one: "Go and measure the water that God owes you by the *qaddus*, and take care, along with the others, of its division."'

'It's our way of life,' says old Ahmad. 'The *qaddus* has been here as long as I can remember. The jars used to be made at my house. Now there's not enough good clay.'

'There's clay, all right, up there beyond the "narrows", in a gully.'

'It isn't good clay, though. Everything you make out of it breaks.'

Most of the time the men lie or sit on the stone steps rubbed smooth by generations of peasants. Those that find no place on the steps crouch on the ground in the typical nomad position, with their weight on their right heel, which leans against the left leg, held at a right angle. For hours on end nothing happens. Some of them smoke, others chant a vague song. Often the dripping of the water is the only sound. Since the portico faces east a light breeze keeps it relatively cool. Here, in this atmosphere of idleness, which somehow reduces the village to its bare essentials, mingling the web of language and that of collective existence, the concept of 'we, the people of Shebika' takes shape. At the grocery there is talk of business and goings-on; here, at the meeting-place of time and property and the distribution of water, there is the original expression of Shebika. The very essence of the village is manifest in the gathering of relaxed men who find in their numbers and the sight of one another the social reality of the group which they form.

Yet the hard core of the village is not all in the talk which accompanies but inadequately represents it. The palaver which takes shape in the portico does not represent the village's collective life; it disguises it. Let us look back at what we have said of the different circles of its existence: the circle of marriages, which impoverishes the village, ruins the oasis and points up its deterioration, the ingrown loyalties of family life which close the village in upon itself in a ghetto; the system of work, which year by year increases the poverty of the *khammes* and the ruin of the landowners. The talk around the water-clock takes into account and respects these traditions; at the same time it retains their element of corrosion and destruction. When they are thus gathered together the men achieve a momentary balance between the negative forces which tend to dissolve the group and the far-away environment of Tunisian society as a whole. All their relations with the outside world pass through the discussion around the *qaddus*, because here they attempt, in words, to maintain an ever more threatened equilibrium.

Some observers have been struck by the 'death instinct' or 'power of destruction' which seems to dominate the life of the various groups (and sometimes entire nations) of the Maghrib. The urge to destroy that which has so painfully been built up is, indeed, frequent, especially among the peoples of the steppe. We may say, stretching the point too far, that this derives from the far-away times of the wandering and pillaging Hilali. Actually, things are more complex. *What in Europe we call traditions and structures are, here, elements of permanence or continuity which tend to the slow but inevitable destruction of the groups which they underpin.* Certain Western observers are particularly ingenuous in thinking that they have put their finger on a living reality, when they have really touched that which is impelling the groups under observation towards death. There are societies which sentence themselves to suicide. Plunged into an ungrateful cosmos which they have never been able to master, drawn into a succession of dispersive events in a land whose morphology is itself dispersed, where they cannot build themselves a history, they shut themselves up in a microcosm which prevents them from reestablishing a link with nature such as would restore their creative dynamism. Many groups of the Maghrib, isolated one from the other by the fluid immensity of desert and steppe, staked out on the rare spots of fertile land, have closed in upon themselves and have no contact with humanity in general except through the universal but abstract faith of Islam. In the life of Shebika it is as if the system of protection had become, with time, an instrument of auto-degradation. The structures, traditions and rules that govern daily existence, no longer turned towards nature nor caught up in a process of historical development, function in a void, with no outlet other than repetition. In the measure in which, at this dead end, Shebika preserves itself, it destroys itself as well.

The 'palaver' of the idlers gathered around the water-clock masks this interior destruction, or at least tries, by verbal means, to limit it. It is an attempt, also, to link Shebika to what is going on outside, to the economic and social changes reported on the radio. It pushes the village towards the other world in which there is a possibility of restoring the lost contact with nature, a nature without which man is only a wraith, decked out in empty social regulations.

Shebika as seen by the Tent-dwellers

Impelled by the stubborn blast of the wind the sand courses over the desert, at times like a caravan moving along the stony crests, at others like a wing hovering over the banks of salt. Ismaïl's big, grey, female camel gracefully raises her neck and sniffs the opiate, heat-laden air. Then she lowers it to the ground where, beside her spongy feet, the baby camel with the damp hair is slowly dying.

The other members of the herd are filing along the side of a hill made of crumbling rock, which the sudden darkening of the sky by the sand-storm has drained of its yellowish colour and left like a face from which the blood has faded away. The painstaking slowness of the camels' steps stands out in indecipherable hieroglyphs. The body of the dying baby sinks into the sand, while the mother lowers her sensitive nose to touch him. She slept all night on her feet, while a current of icy air swept over the dead land, as if the vast orbit of the horizonless horizon belonged already to the far-away future time when man will no longer inhabit it.

All night long the hard breathing of the baby camel was added to the pounding of the wind. Now there is only the crackling palpitation of a great wing of sand which hovers over the stony ground where the mother is kneeling. Leaning her head to one side, in the attentively and tenderly self-contained manner of a camel, with her front legs already folded under her and her rear legs starting to bend, she licks the pallid hairs of the baby. At least she is careful not to let herself dissolve into the mass of sand whose impermanent configuration the wind never leaves the same as it was before. She clings to what is left of the motion and sounds of the night: the hard breathing of the baby, the clattering footsteps of the herd, which marks time in the early morning before setting out to search for fresher clumps of pallid esparto.

During the night, before the arrival of the gusty, hot breath of the south wind, the profiles of the other animals stood out in the darkness, rimmed by a vague halo made out of the natural phosphorescence of the air. But there was no halo around the baby camel. He had collapsed first on to his knees and then on to his side, the way animals do when they are fatally short of breath. His mother knew what was happening to him; although animals are not really aware of death they feel its presence, especially in the desert, from far away, and give it a wide berth.

Now the mother camel is reclining with all four feet tucked under her and her chin resting on the little one, who ceases, little by little, to be a mass of fever and starts to melt into the stones and whatever there is of earth, stuck together with sand and salt. Soon scorpions and dung beetles will fasten on to the flesh, softened by the heat. A week or a month later the herd will pass by a white skeleton, stripped of its last remnants of skin by persistent swarms of insects, sharp-toothed jackals, and birds of prey. In the sky overhead birds are already gathering.

The grey wing, which dulls all colour, overlies the steppe. Through it there pours the tireless, burning breath of the great desert to the south, from Tassili and perhaps from Timbuctoo, incandescent from its passage over stones burned by the sun and from the shimmering sand which it has picked up along the way. The wind comes from the heart of Africa and the people of the steppe look, as we know, towards Asia. Here the two cardinal points of East and South, which are the focuses of every steppe-dweller's life, come together. The sand arrives in waves, covering the track of the road and effacing the sign-posts. In the distance the village of Shebika is still lit up by a bright but morbid light, like that of a tomb illuminated by a storm. Little by little this fades, until the flank of the mountain melts away into an impalpable cloud of dust.

Through this haze made up of infinitesimal particles, driven by the wind, there comes, in his brown burnous Aamr bin Sidi Abid, the son of Ismaïl, who has been sent to see what has become of the big female camel. As in the month of Ramadan, when the inside of the body must be pure in order to serve as a receptacle of God, Aamr holds his mouth tightly closed and the hood of his burnous over his face. But no barrier can resist the sand, and he walks backwards or sideways in an attempt to avoid its impact. There, at last, is the corpse of the baby camel and the mother, heavy with milk, crouching with her chin resting upon it. But there is no use trying to lead her away to-day. In the evening, or the next day, she will move on of her own accord, when the odour of life has left her little one and he has become alien to the order of things that she can measure during the course of her rumination. Then it will be time for her to rejoin the herd, which outlines a sort of alphabet along the side of the far-away mountain.

As Aamr starts back, bent over double to fight against the wind, which has by now deposited a thicker and thicker blanket of sand, he moves sideways towards the obliterated road, which can be known only by guesswork to lead to Shebika. Here we have halted, in uncertainty, amid the tide of swirling grey sand.

Aamr comes over to the car, disclosing a clean-shaven, almost beardless face and a pair of incredibly beady eyes. Khalil calls out through the canvas side-curtains of the jeep and motions to him to get in. Can he help us rediscover the road-track and guide us, so that we shall not fall into a crevasse or ravine? Aamr points to the tents, climbs into the car and squeezes on to the back seat, instructing the driver with clipped words as to how he should proceed. Khalil, who has seen him before, at Ridha's grocery, asks him some questions.

'I'm Aamr, of the awlad Sidi Abid. We live in the desert, below Shebika. You can make out the tents, over there. I was born not far from here, and I'm twenty-seven years old. We settled in this particular place years ago, because there's water at Shebika and we can cultivate the land on the edge of the oasis.'

He points again towards the tents, three dark, low shapes, motionless and half lost from view amid the sand-storm swirling around them. Then he accepts a cigarette and lights it, bouncing up and down on the back seat like the rest of us.

'We live on the desert.'

'About how far from Shebika?'

'A couple of miles.'

'And how do you happen to live here?'

'I've lived here as long as I can remember.'

'You were born in a tent?'

'Yes.'

'Are there many of you?'

'Before I was born my parents lived less than a mile from Shebika. When I came back from my military service we dug a well over there, where we are now, and planted a few palms. When the garden was ready, we moved, and we've been there ever since, that is, since 1960.'

'Do you have sheep or goats?'

'Yes.'

'And do you have a shepherd?'

'We pasture the animals ourselves.'

'So you never go very far from the tents, is that it?'

'We go a quarter or half a mile, to where there's some grass.'

'And you go back home every evening?'

'Yes. But when it's dry we go farther, taking provisions, and spend the night out.'

'How many nights would you say you spend away from home in the dry season?'

'That depends. When it's rainy, the grass grows, and we stay in our tents. If it isn't raining, we stay out.'

'And when it's dry, where do you take the animals?'

'Near here, on the desert.'

'How far from the tents?'

'About a mile and a half from where we are now.'

'When does it stop raining?'

'That varies. I can't say exactly.'

'When it's dry, do you all go at once, or does each one set out separately with his own herd?'

'That depends. If a family is big and occupies three or four tents, they all go together. If it's in just one tent, they go alone. Then again, twenty tents go at one time.'

'Aside from the herds do you have some other source of income?'

'Yes. We work the land.'

'Do you own land, then?'

'We don't have definite areas of land. The land belongs to all of us, to any one who can and wants to work it. On the other side, towards Tamerza, there's a dam. The water comes from Algeria. If the government keeps up the dam, we have water, and we can plant and work the land, but if the government doesn't keep it up, then the water goes to Algeria and there's nothing we can do. All of us are losers, those that worked and those that didn't. Without water we're helpless. Just now things are going badly.'

'Haven't you asked the government to give you back the water?'

'We've asked and asked, but. . . . The stones to fix the dam have been assembled since 1959, but the work still isn't done.'

'Who assembled the stones?'

'The government and the men from the work-camps for the unemployed.'

'Then why hasn't the work been done?'

'How should I know? The government had the stones assembled, and people were happy to think that the water would stay here instead of going to Algeria. They hoped to have a better life. But the stones are still there.'

'And you've never asked why the government didn't finish the job.'

'No, we haven't asked. That's the way it is.'

'So how do you raise anything? Suppose there's rain, but not enough to make anything grow, what do you do?'

'There's a little stream that flows from time to time.'

'And if it doesn't flow?'

'If it doesn't flow? . . . Well it doesn't flow, that's all. If we have a chance, we go to work in the road-building camps, for 200 millimes and three pounds of flour . . .'

'And if there's no work-camp?'

'We sell some of our land, or some sheep, or some wheat.'

'Have you any date-palms?'

'Some people have them, not all.'

'Do the people who live in the tents over there have palms?'

'Not all of them, no. About two families.'

'Do they have many?'

'No, very few.'

'How do you count the palms?'

'We count them by *huwaiza*.'

'And how many palms are there to a *huwaiza*?'

'Ten or eleven, or a hundred. It depends on the soil.'

'And how do you buy the palms? By the tree or by the *huwaiza*?'

'By the *huwaiza*. After that you can sell "half a *huwaiza*" or a "quarter of a *huwaiza*".'

'If you are somebody's partner on a piece of land and you want to sell part of it, do you divide it by *huwaiza*?'

'No, but when the harvest is taken in each one claims his share.'

'And you, do you own any land?'

'No.'

'And does your father, Ismaïl, own any land?'

'No. My brother wants to cultivate some land. But my father's against it.'

'Do you all live together?'

'Yes, in one tent. We all eat out of the same dish.'

'You haven't yet divided your possessions?'

'I've just told you no. We haven't divided anything.'

'Isn't such a division frequent among you?'

'Yes, of course.'

'When do you divide your possessions and why?'

'When Satan gets into it.'

'And when does Satan get into it?'

'He doesn't have any schedule, that one.'

'When you quarrel, for instance?'

'Yes, exactly. That's just it.'

'And what causes you to quarrel? Do you know anyone who has separated his possessions from those of his father?'

'When a man does that it's usually because he's married. He has children, or his wife is pregnant. Satan steps into it, and his wife makes a row. If the man loves his wife and wants to keep her, then he asks for a division. He calls in some older friends and they tell his father that he wants to keep her, then he asks for a division. He calls in some older friends and they tell his father that he wants a separation and that he is giving up his right to his father's home. His father gives him a tent, and he sets it up some distance away. Beginning that same day he works for himself, separately from his father.'

'After the separation does the son go to see his parents?'

'Oh, yes. They visit one another. After his father's death, if he has brothers he divides the inheritance with them. If he has no brothers then he keeps it all until his own death, when his children inherit.'

'Is there any man among you who preferred his wife to his parents?'

'If a man doesn't care for his wife and prefers to stay with his parents and work for them, then he sends his wife home. When he's older he can remarry.'

'Are the men you know whose wives don't get along with their parents-in-law more apt to choose their wives or their parents?'

'The parents don't hold them back, if they want to give up their blessing. Usually the man chooses not to anger his parents. That is, unless he's a coward, and then he follows his wife.'

'What do you mean by a coward?'

'A man who prefers his wife to his parents.'

At this point Salah, who has been listening silently as he struggles to keep his seat in the jolting jeep, enters the conversation.

'So a man who prefers his wife to his parents is no good, is that it?'

'No good, for sure.'

'Do you want to get married?'

'No. I'm a bachelor.'

'If you were married and your wife didn't get along with your parents, whom would you follow?'

'They say that the woman with whom a man shares his bed has more influence than his mother.' *

'Why should she? A wife can't call down the blessings of heaven upon a man; only parents can do that. And if a wife asks God to punish her husband, God doesn't listen. But a mother can draw down God's wrath upon her son.'

'Sometimes a wife can draw down God's anger upon her husband. That may lead to their sleeping apart.'

'How should I know? I'm not yet married. If I got into any such trouble, I think I'd choose my parents, when you come down to it.'

'You say that because you're not yet married.'

When we look ahead the tents seem to be just as far away as ever amid the sand. Shebika has disappeared from view. Every now and then Aamr addresses a brief word to the driver, who veers to the right or left, slows up because the front wheels have struck a rock, loses the direction of the tents and finds it again. Naïma, the girl student from Tunis, who has been sitting beside the driver and concentrating on the road, turns round to interject:

'Among the Bedouins of the North if a wife and mother-in-law fall out, the husband breaks a stick over the back of his wife without even stopping to find out who's right and who's wrong.'

'That's as it should be. A man must side with his mother. Otherwise he's considered a rebel and he must go away with his wife.'

'You've spoken of a wife pitted against her mother-in-law,' says Naïma. 'What if they get along perfectly well, but the wife can't tolerate her father-in-law? In this case whom would you choose?'

* *Al-hasida taghlib al-walida*, a current proverb. (Literally, 'The jealous woman overpowers the mother'.)

'A father-in-law has just as much right as a husband to beat her.'

'Why should he beat her? Would you look on without saying anything?'

'What should I say? He has a right to beat her if she won't obey.'

'And if you choose to object?'

'Then I have to separate my goods from those of my parents and leave their tent.'

'Whose imprecations are more effective, the father's or the mother's?'

'The mother's, because she has carried the child for nine months in her belly, and nursed and washed and brought him up.'

Silence. After a moment Khalil points to Shebika.

'Would you like to live at Shebika?' he asks Aamr.

'If I had an income there, yes, I'd like it. Otherwise there wouldn't be any point.'

'As far as we've seen the people of Shebika don't have incomes.'

'Exactly. So why should I want to live there?'

'What do you think of the people of Shebika? Have you relatives among them?'

'No; they're strangers.'

'Are you on good terms with them? Are they friendly?'

'Yes, they're friendly, and we're on good terms.'

'Are there never misunderstandings between you? Have they ever insulted you, or anything like that?'

'No, never. We don't insult them and they don't insult us. Neighbours are apt to squabble over one thing or another; that's the way of the world. But we've never had any trouble.'

'Are there no marriages between you and the people of Shebika?'

'No, they don't marry among us and we don't marry among them.'

'How do you explain that? You're neighbours; both of you have unmarried girls and unmarried men. Why are there no marriages?'

'Such is God's will.'

'Sometimes it's more man's will than God's. I marry my cousin because I like her and refuse to marry a stranger because I don't like her. But there has to be a reason. Give me one now.'

'We're Bedouins and there are points on which we don't agree with the villagers – on burnouses, for instance. And then their women aren't good at weaving.'

When we arrive at the tents two white desert dogs bark at us convulsively. Aamr jumps down from the jeep and chases them away with stones before going to tell old Ismaïl of our arrival. The wind is still crackling around us. Now we see why the tents seemed to be so low. They are set up in a sort of bowl which protects them from the wind. There are three of them surrounded by a fence of woven reeds, which keeps out both dogs and jackals and affords protection to a flock of chickens inside.

We walk towards the old man who is emerging from one of the tents of the enclosure. He is leaning on the arm of a man older than Aamr, probably his brother. The two men advance slowly, because the son is treating his father with enormous gentleness, which does not seem to be at all related to the difficulty of moving through the storm. As they come closer, we can see by the way the old man gazes up at the sky and holds out his hands shakily before him that he is blind. The wind bellies out his ghandurah and blows up the ends of the scarf knotted about his head as he greets us with the appropriate blessings. We pause in obedience to laws of etiquette which must be followed even on the desert, even in the midst of a storm. Each member of our party bears his hand to his lips and touches the tips of Ismaïl's fingers with his own, and Ismaïl himself repeats the same gesture.

As we stand in silence, a turbaned, tattooed oldish woman, with a tense expression on her face, wearing a plum-red dress, comes out of the tent to the left. Her head is lowered against the wind, but she does not bat an eyelash, almost as if she were unaware of it. She too calls down a welcoming benediction upon us and leads us towards her tent, while the old man, guided by his son, continues to say how glad he is to see us and that we have brought with us God's blessing.

Once inside the tent, the sudden calm and the absence of wind have an immediately relaxing effect. We have entered, as it were, into a shelter, where time has a different rhythm from that of the steppe. The tent is mounted on poles and held down by stakes driven into the stony ground. It is divided in two by a partition made of sacks of grain and rolled-up rugs. At the right side – forbidden to us – two half-hidden girls are weaving on a high-warp loom; at the left we take our seats on rugs spread out on the floor. Outside wind and sand beat against the tent, setting it apart as a place of calm and of almost maternal protection. In spite of the darkening of the sky, it is light inside.

Old Ismaïl has come in behind us.* His older son has left him in order to stack up some rugs and make more room, and he stands alone, leaning on his cane, with his head wobbling from side to side as he stares out of sightless eyes at the sides of the tent, the loom, the woman and girls on the other side of the partition. Now he tries to tell us apart by our voices. Salah and Khalil have told him what we are after. The mention of Shebika causes him to laugh, we don't know why, whether because of the northern accents or because he doesn't think Shebika is much of a place.

The older son is called Nureddin; he is the one to seat the guests and bring more cushions. Finally, clearing his throat, he sits down beside Khalil. Aamr comes in with a single glass and a pot of boiling tea. The glass is filled and passed from one hand to another with a shake in between. From the conversation between Si Tijani and Ismaïl there emerges a long complaint about the difficulties of obtaining supplies and the disadvantages of having settled in a limited area.

'Once upon a time we moved every season, and there were markets where we could always make exchanges. In those days settled people were usually rich; most of them were land-

* 'Usually strangers aren't received in a tent where there are women,' he tells us. 'But times are changing, and we're happy to do you a favour.'

owners who were ready to buy rugs, perfumes, other transportable objects, and even camels from the Bedouins.'

Ismaïl talks uninterruptedly. His white, wide-open eyes are looking at the wall of the tent, as if they did not see us but were fixed on some other reality, far away. Si Tijani is very fond of old Ismaïl whom he has known since childhood, at the caravan gatherings of Naftah and Tamerza, which went out of existence during the war of 1914–18 and the advent of the automobile and train.

Old Ismaïl speaks his mind freely. He is possessed of 'old men's wisdom', that is, he has acquired something which the younger men, shut up in obedience to rules and prescriptions, do not possess: ideas of his own which do not wait upon the approval of his fellows. Thus he says that 'very deep is the hole in which are piled up the events of the past, the things experienced by men who are not "sessile", or settled, like those of Tawzar and Shebika, by men who pick up their tents and follow the rains'. Once upon a time the man who shepherded the ten or twenty families never stopped more than once in the same part of the steppe. He knew that pasturing camels and sheep scatter the grains that should sprout again in order to re-establish the order willed by God for plants, even on the desert. Nowadays, although this knowledge does in some places endure, it is mostly discarded. He, Ismaïl, remembers the big French trucks with ten pairs of wheels, which moved slowly over the desert tracks, with frequent break-downs, during the First World War. The Bedouin men watched them pass by, and the children ran away. His father's father, who had practised *jaiysh*, the almost ritualistic form of pillage, would have known better what to do. In the days before the automobile he and his companions surrounded a broken-down camel caravan and politely asked the travellers to hand over weapons and money.

Ismaïl is given to laughter. When someone talks to him he squeezes the speaker's hand in the affectionate manner of an old man and a tent-dweller. At intervals he sips his tea, and there is a moment of silence, just long enough to make it apparent that the wind has fallen and the light has returned, while the great cloud of sand has passed on to the north, to Qafsa and the section of the steppe rising towards Qassireen and the dorsal chain of mountains. When he has finished drinking Ismaïl laughs again, to himself, staring at a fixed point beyond us. Then he says that he likes us because we brought back his son, Aamr. This proves that we are God-fearing people, and he considers us friends. More silence, broken only by the hum of the loom, run by the two diligent girls, and the sounds made by their mother in the preparation of a chicken and eggs which we are to take away. Khalil has begun to question Nureddin.

'Your brother tells us that the people of Shebika are no good to marry. Why so?'

'We're nomads, and they're settled. I'll make you another cup of tea; after that I have to go, as it happens, to Shebika.'

'Are you bored with our company already, that you want to go away?'

'No, I'm not bored.'

'You've just said that you don't marry among the people of Shebika because they're settled. But we understand that you've been in this same spot for ten years. You're not exactly a nomad.'

'The women of Shebika can't work like ours. No city woman knows how to work like a nomad.'

'If Shebika's your idea of a "city"! ... What is it that your women do?'

'They weave the *qleem*, the blankets, the tenting; they replace old ropes with new and do all sorts of other things that a city woman could never do.'

'Can't the women of Shebika do them at all?'

'No, they can only work in a house. They can't endure the hard work of life in the desert.'

'Aren't there other reasons besides? Apart from the fact that you lead a different sort of life, what else prevents you from intermarrying?'

'There's only one reason, and that's work, why we can't marry a city woman. To do that a man needs to have a house and to be settled at Shebika or some other town.'

'But you're pretty settled, yourself.'

'Yes, I'm settled, if you like, but I'd never take a wife from

Shebika. I don't want a woman that can't work in the fields and carry water.'

'The women of Shebika carry water. . . . Isn't there really some other reason? A feud, for instance? I've heard that there were quarrels between you.'

'No quarrels, no.'

'Since you've been here haven't you ever heard of quarrels between Shebika and, say, Tamerza?'

'Oh, Tamerza! One city's about like another! But I've never heard of a quarrel between the people of Shebika and the nomads.'

'Do you really expect me to believe there's never been a quarrel of some kind?'

'No big fight, anyhow, no bloodshed.'

'What do you call a big fight?'

'A fight with guns or sticks or razors. I've never heard tell of anything of the kind.'

'Just fist-fights, then?'

'Fist-fights? Yes, there've been those.'

'Just minor fights that never led to anything serious, is that it?'

'Exactly.'

This is all he's willing to say. He shrugs his shoulders and looks over at the other side of the tent, whence his mother calls out something we fail to understand. He gets up and goes away, and Aamr takes his place. Si Tijani has thrown back the entrance to the tent. The sun is shining harder and more brightly than before, in a sky washed clear by the sand. The clarity is so great that Shebika suddenly appears very near. We can make out children running across the square, old Qaddur moving slowly along the wall and Ridha, the grocer, walking briskly towards the Mosque. The light-coloured ghandurahs of the Bedouins and their dark-ochre rugs frame this miniature view of Shebika.

Aamr tells us that his brother, Nureddin, will probably go to get married on the other side of the highway between Qafsa and Tawzar and live there with his wife's family, which owns some palm-trees in the oasis of Dakash. His marriage will be celebrated at the same time as that of his sister, Latifa, who is to marry a man called Hassan, from a neighbouring tent. The two tents will be thrown together and perhaps, eventually, a house will be built, out of stone, here on the desert.

'And what about your other sister?'

The other sister's name is Fatimah, but Aamr is unwilling to talk about her. It seems that she's different, but nobody wants to explain. Si Tijani whispers that Fatimah can't get married because she's 'sick with fevers'.

'And you, Aamr, what are your plans?'

Aamr turns his head to one side.

'Your father says that you want to work in the mines at Redayif.'

'Yes, I may do that. I like the city. I'd like to work there.'

'You don't like your life here?'

'Yes. That's not it. But I've done my military service.'

We are supposed to understand. Aamr is proud of his military service, because it took him to Susa, which he still remembers. But he won't go anywhere until Nureddin and his sister are married. Even then, when Hassan becomes the head of the family, he'll have to work with him. He is unwilling to say anything further.

Nureddin returns, and old Ismaïl, whose senses of hearing and smell make up for the loss of his sight, begins to tell us that he is happy to share with us the couscous which is about to be served. The dishes are laid on the rugs, and Khalil asks Aamr:

'Is this what you eat every day? It's better than what they have at Shebika.'

'Here on the desert we eat couscous, bread, soup and meat.'

'All the time?'

'All the time. Bread during the day and couscous at night.'

'How does it happen that people around here don't eat more meat? Didn't they used to eat more of it than they do now?'

'People that have livestock kill and eat it.'

'Do they eat meat so often?'

'Whenever they feel like it; above all on the big feast-day. On that day the people of Shebika either slaughter some of their own animals or buy meat outside. And the nomads likewise.'

'Do the people of Shebika buy meat from you for the feast-day of Sidi Sultan?'

'Yes, for that feast they buy meat from us.'

'And don't you celebrate that feast too? We've been told that it was celebrated even outside of Shebika.'

'Only by people who promised something – say, a sheep – in return for some favour they've asked and received from Sidi Sultan. We nomads have no set date for celebration.'

The couscous is strongly spiced and in it there are bits of meat, no doubt kid. Through the entrance of the tent we look out at Shebika. Someone mentions the village by name, and old Ismaïl stops eating in order to talk about it.

'I knew Shebika when it was a prosperous village, when all the families owned land and were well off, and bought things from the steppe-dwellers. At that time we used to go to the celebration of Sidi Sultan, a highly venerated holy man. Certain brotherhoods came from very far away and danced all night around the marabout. Then Shebika wasn't the mass of ruins and the nest of scorpions that it is today. The people were proud, and they'd never have worked for Bedouins or for the inhabitants of other towns and villages. Why haven't they continued to prosper, you ask, and how did they become day-labourers for land-owners from El Hamma and other such places? Here, on the desert, when a man marries, the two families are drawn closer together and strengthen each other by mutual aid. At Shebika they give up pieces of land in return for a wife. Obviously they're not wise about what to do and what not to do. Nomads like us learn their way around, without getting in trouble or asking advice. You never can tell what is forbidden, not to mention what is the law and what the aim of the new government. Meanwhile the people of Shebika stay cooped up in their hole, without knowing how to live in such a way as to honour God.'

This does not mean merely that life is a sort of prayer. Among the peoples of the South the phrase has a secondary meaning: the life that honours God is one of material happiness and success. But the subject which we discuss most frequently – just because it is one on which Ismaïl is more definitely at odds with the people of Shebika – is that of families and genealogy.

'We come from farther down,' says Ismaïl, 'from below She-bika and Tamerza. Nowadays it's called Algeria, but in the time of my grandfather and great-grandfather, it was a place in-habited only by ourselves and our families. We used to come up to the markets of Naftah and Tawzar. Now there's no passage because of the war [1961] and before that there were French customs posts. But we used to get over the border at night, through the *shatt*. We smuggled salt and tobacco, because prices were higher here than there. Now there's no more smuggling, and no more going to and fro.'

'Do you miss the time when you used to travel, Ismaïl?'

'There's a time for travelling as there is for everything else. Now I'm too old. A man has to travel to increase the number of his friends. Not like those benighted souls of Shebika, who've become poor because they never wanted to budge. We go to one place or another, sometimes with our families and our tents, sometimes alone.'

'Have you travelled much alone?'

'Yes, on horseback, because I was always on the go. My father didn't want me to be listed for military service, and so I went from one place to another.'

'And you, do you come from here?'

'No, I'm from Al Wad.'

'And you, do you come from there, too?'

'No, I'm from Tawzar.'

There is a pause, while Ismaïl chews his cigarette.

'The army. There are men like Si Tijani here, who've been in the army and learned something from it. It was good for Tijani; he's told me his story. The French took him all the way to near Mecca, to Lebanon, where there are Arabs like ourselves, who are tent-dwellers. He learned to be a nurse and to build a road. He's been not only to Tunis but to Marseille as well ...'

'And your father lived the way you do, with camels and a tent?'

'Yes, he didn't have as many camels as I do, but he had more horses, because at that time there was no road. We are of the

Sidi Abid, the largest family of the desert, and we have cousins everywhere, because in the old days there was more division of property than there is now, when it leads to poverty. Of course, if our children want to strike out on their own, let them go, taking their share of goats and camels with them! The Sidi Abid of this part of the country descend from Ali, and Ali had five married brothers, Muhammad, Bashir, Murad, Salah and Muhsin. They're all Sidi Abid, and before Ali and his brothers (he was the oldest) there was Muhammad, who was a tent-dweller, and further back there was the original Sidi Abid, a cousin of the Prophet, who came here with the Hilali.'

'Then you're Hilali?'

'We come from over there [pointing to Mecca], like them. The Sidi Abid married into the Sidi Abid of the Sahara, but Muhammad had uncles who married in Libya ...'

Again we run into these long genealogies, these heavy verbal constructions, transmitted from generation to generation, which link the miserable individual of today to the pillaging tribes expelled in the twelfth century by the Sultan of Egypt, both to deliver his own territory and to harass his rebellious vassal of 'Ifriqiya'. What grain of truth is there to be found? We are dealing with systems of classification worked out with the same resolution and logic as the customs which govern transhumance, the choice of pastures, all the natural events which must be codified and comprehended in order that a family may survive and maintain its social position amid the confusion and fluidity of the desert and of the Maghrib in general. We have seen that 'Sidi Abid' is a simple name which the Bedouins of the steppe and the desert take unto themselves, not because they are actually descended from such a family but merely in order to attach themselves to a known denomination and to take out some sort of insurance against the anarchy of the South.

Words – particularly those concerned with genealogy – seek to create a reality, by dint of rationalization, by the apparent coherence of a chain of marriages and connexions and inheritances. We need not recall that the people of the South are never content with succession in time but insist on involving the individual in the web of simultaneous relationships.

How could it be otherwise? The Sidi Abid endure only through the construction of this system, which has no real foundation. For years and perhaps for centuries, this *arsh* or family has not actually existed. In this region – both in the tents of the nomads and at Shebika – the logical construction is purely verbal. Here on the desert it does not serve the purpose of attaching one village to another and strengthening topographical connexions or economic exchanges. It simply aids a fragmented group, implicitly aware of its weaknesses and isolation, to find in some logical form a confirmation of its existence and protection against annihilation and dissolution in the time and space which are without history. Unlike the degenerate genealogy of the people of Shebika, the genealogy of the nomads is not an effort to find some stable ground. As old Ismaïl told us: 'Our relations, even those whom we've never seen and shall never see, these are our fortune.'

There are cases in which a man can buy or exchange a genealogy, where the family tree is negotiable or negotiated. A young man may wander from family to family; then, suddenly, he exhibits a long chain of genealogies which he has acquired from an elderly protector or from the group with which he has integrated himself.

The genealogies recited under the tent are words or, etymologically speaking, myths. They are spoken not in order to pin down and understand a reality but rather to fill in the emptiness that otherwise would exist among men. If the women of the steppe wear tattooing it is as a sort of passport. They attach themselves, thus, to the widespread family name of which it is the sign, securing for themselves both protection and identification. Tattooing is a language, a means of communication, bespeaking family connexions and a sense of belonging and allegiance which actually no longer exist. In the intermediary world of today, where there is as yet nothing new, these are pegs on which men hang a theory of the change for which they are preparing.

There are other means, besides, of re-creating a sense of continuity and solidarity which has no roots in real life. Along with the myth of genealogy there are the myths of adventure, as told by poets who travel, even today, from village to village, from encampment to encampment, staying for some days and singing long narratives which they often do not even understand, because they have been passed on from one 'minstrel' to another simply as a way of making a living. These poets relate to the myth of genealogy the myth of 'an epoch of glory', or, more simply, they furnish the group with a language to which it can attach its present sensations, giving them a name and feeling them through the words which describe the glorious deeds of the past. The art of the epic, in nomad or settled patriarchal societies, is the perpetually renewed support, by recital, of a verbal context upon which man projects his existence in order to live it and to express himself. Degenerate as this form of poetry and song is in modern Tunisia, it still has an importance not yet destroyed by the radio, which, however, has taken up some of the songs and poems in stylized form, that is in a form worked over and deformed by pedants.

Ismaïl explained one of these epics to us. In his cracked, nasal voice he even sang the first few lines :

> '*I spurred her on and she outran the other horses;*
> *I hurt her, unfortunate man that I am;*
> *Her sweat wet the saddle and the dust of the road . . .*

'It's a story they tell about the nomads. Once upon a time, when a man fell in love with a woman from another tribe or another region he couldn't marry her, because her parents preferred to give her to one of her cousins or at least to a tribesman. And so the lover arranged with his beloved to see her by night, in secret. When everyone was asleep he approached her tent; silently she came out and they stole away together to some far-away place where they could make love beyond the stare of curious eyes.

'The author of the song which I have just begun was a great horseman. One evening when he came to see his beloved her tribesmen caught sight of him and pursued him on horseback. His mare ran so fast that they were not able to overtake him, but they swore that they would have his blood. His beloved, hearing them vow his death, charged a friend with taking him a message of warning. On the way the friend came across an old man and asked where the horseman could be found. This old man happened to be the lover's father. He told the messenger that his son was nowhere near and promised to convey the message to him. When his son came back the old man gave him to understand, in the course of a conversation, the danger which was overhanging. Then the son told him, in song, his romantic adventure.

I spurred her on (that is, the mare) *and she outran the other horses;*
Her sweat wet the saddle and the dust of the road . . .

This means that her sweat, in wetting the dust, made it like *bessissa,** and *bessissa* is very sweet. Do you get the play on words? This sweetness recalls that of his beloved. There are three elements in this story: the horseman, the woman, the earth (which represents the woman and also works for the lovers). This song is sung at night on the desert, to the accompaniment of a *nay* or reed flute.'

Ismaïl talked to us again about Shebika, when we came back, months later, to see him, this time during the summer, when his sons were beating the wheat, not far from the oasis. While his brother assembled bundles of wheat Aamr drove a waggon equipped with rollers to crush the grain, round and round in a circle. Old Ismaïl had had himself brought to the scene, in order that he might hear the voices of the workers. The site, outside the oasis, was a piece of apparently desert land, which no one thought could produce anything. But Ismaïl, when he could still see, had insisted upon sowing it with wheat. He had realized that the water of the *wadi*, after going through the oasis, was still near the surface of the land and would render it fertile.

On this day, then, he took one of us by the arm and pointed with his stick in the direction of Shebika. Up there, he told us, they hadn't yet understood, as he had, that you could grow

* An oriental sweetmeat, made of semolina, butter, sugar and water.

anything you wanted in the desert if you had the nerve to step outside the oasis. Those people! ... They had forgotten everything they ever knew and hadn't even the knack of cultivating the land. But the government, if it helped anyone, would help the people of Shebika. Nobody trusted the nomads, even when, like himself, they had been installed for a long time in one place.

He promised to take us into the desert, towards the *shatt*, where years ago he had discovered a stretch of damp, black earth which might indicate the presence of the oil that everyone was talking about. He had spoken of it to foreigners before, but no one had ever taken any interest.

We have come back at regular intervals to see Ismaïl, inasmuch as we have had dealings with him. He gave us a white Kabyl dog with a mane like that of an Eskimo husky, 'in order that we should remember him when we were back in Tunis'. We brought him oil and sugar, and he gave us a sheep and eggs in return. These exchanges are not mere courtesies. They create a bond, engage us in a reciprocal action and allow us to communicate on a deeper level. A relationship which it is very hard to create between two groups of strangers has here come into being.

The men of Shebika laugh, and say Ismaïl has found a way of getting foreigners to supply him. This is a weak point, however, since we have brought oil and sugar to them as well. The fact is that they don't care for the 'tent-dwellers'. When they have heard that on our way back to Tawzar we intend to stop off to see old Ismaïl they have often tried to detain us. It was at about this time that Ismaïl invited us to the marriages of his son and daughter.

Upon another visit, some months later, old Ali of Shebika told Si Tijani that Ismaïl had died and everything was changed in the Bedouin encampment. We went down at once to see while our Shebika friends shrugged their shoulders because, in their opinion, we attached importance to people that didn't deserve it.

We found that Ismaïl's tent had been moved a short way to the east. No one was in sight, and we had started to call out when his widow appeared at the entrance. It was very hot that day and even the dogs were sleeping, overcome by the sun. The old woman beckoned to us to come in.

To linger in a tent is to create a parenthesis in everyday living. The porosity of the canvas lets in air and even stimulates a sort of ventilation. The way to be comfortable is to relax on two or three layers of rugs and let one's body follow the configuration of the ground below. The old woman spoke excitedly; she told how one morning old Ismaïl had failed to wake up and how he was buried at Shebika. Her elder son had gone to live with his wife's family, at Dakash, and her son-in-law, Hassan, the husband of Latifa, was now the head of the family and had even built a house.

We had seen, as we approached the site, a new, square, low building with a wooden door. The stones are joined by a cement made of sand and the roof is made of corrugated tin. Soon Hassan came to take us on a tour of inspection.

With him we made no polite exchanges. Hassan is a busy man and an important one, engaged in building up a capital from the price he gets for livestock and wheat. We saw him at work, concentrating his whole attention on the job at hand, that of stacking up straw. A quite different type from old Ismaïl and his two sons. Hassan told us that Aamr had gone, as he hoped, to work in the mines but that he came occasionally to lend a hand at home. Since a storm was impending we all pitched in, gathering the straw into bundles and storing it in a covered shed. The old woman watched us from the entrance of her tent. Beside her stood her unmarried daughter, Fatimah.

On this occasion Hassan gave us half a sheep, but it was in payment for our work rather than as a gift; he simply had it put, quite unceremoniously, into our jeep. We returned to sit down in the new stone house, and Hassan spoke of Shebika and its people. He feels much more strongly about them than did old Ismaïl.

'If the people of Shebika want to live better, do you think they should wait for government aid or go to live somewhere else?'

'They'll never leave Shebika.'

'Why not?'

'They wouldn't like it anywhere else.'

'You mean that, in spite of their poverty, they're attached to the place?'

'They wouldn't want to go away.'

'Have they ever had a chance to go to work elsewhere?'

'No.'

'Then how can you be sure they wouldn't want to go?'

'Even if they were to have a chance they wouldn't go.'

'If they had brothers or cousins at Tunis, wouldn't they go to join them?'

'They have no kin at Tunis ... yes, perhaps one or two of them ...'

'But what do you think: would they do better to go away, or to wait for government aid and contribute to the betterment of the region? Should they go to Qassireen or Redayif or Bizerta or simply stay here?'

'I think they should go somewhere else and make money. But they'll never go!'

'Is this laziness on their part, or incapacity?'

'They come to the same thing.'

'Here you are, within a couple of miles of Shebika. Wouldn't you be glad if it were to be better off than it is today?'

'Well, when someone lives in a place he quite naturally wants it to be better than any other. Perhaps if Shebika becomes more prosperous we shall have some benefit as well.'

'You're an unprejudiced outsider. What if someone said to you: "We don't know what to do; the village is very poor. What do you say should be done to improve it?" '

'The people ought to work.'

'Why? Don't they work already?'

'Yes, but ...'

'If, for instance, the governor were to come to you and say: "They don't live well at Shebika. ... It's a known fact that there are many poor ..." '

'Many, many, yes; they're all poor.'

'If you were asked: "What can be done to better the situation of the oasis?" '

'The government will give them a subvention!'

'What's that, a subvention?'

'Money . . . a loan. The government ought to help them, but they ought to work, too.'

'And how do you say they should use the government money?'

'To buy food and equipment.'

'What kind of equipment?'

'Food, mostly.'

'If they buy food will they improve their situation?'

'Food, I say. But they must work, also.'

At bottom he isn't interested in Shebika. He may, like so many other outsiders, buy land in the oasis and have the men of the village work it for him. But this would be simply because the possession of some date-palms is a status symbol.

'It's true, true, you know,' says Khalil; 'they've colonized Shebika.'

The tent-dwellers do, indeed, own, either directly or through an intermediary, a large number of parcels of land in the oasis. Little by little they are displacing the land-owners from Tamerza. Over the last two years the men of Tamerza have been alarmed by rumours of 'socialization' and the announcement that land in the Sahil and the North has been transformed into cooperatives. They have decided to get rid of any land they own outside their own town, and in most cases this has been bought up by the Bedouins.

Among the four petty land-owners of Shebika itself, the only ones to have held on to some part of their formerly larger possessions, two have become dependent on nomads by accepting seeds and plants from them in return for the right to half the yield of the land and an option to purchase the rest. There are still parcels called the 'Garden of Bashir' or the 'Paradise of Nureddin', but these two men are no longer working for themselves. The nomads pick up this land not by the methods of the indebted money-lender, Ridha, but by supplying mutton for a marriage or some other celebration, by accepting a camel or a goat for pasturage along with their own livestock, or by sowing some wheat on a villager's behalf, in the land which they have cultivated outside the oasis. Obviously the villager can make no direct return for these services, and he gradually loses the actual possession of land which, for reasons of prestige, he still pretends to own and on which he pays taxes, thereby indebting himself further. On the day when, because of a marriage or a funeral, the Bedouin sees fit to exact his full rights, the land will definitely become the property of strangers.

'Even ten palms belonging to Ridha have fallen into Ismaïl's hands,' says Khalil, 'simply because the grocer prefers all sorts of wheeling and dealing to a clear-cut settlement of accounts. He asks Ismaïl for some wheat which he re-sells in the village, partly as it is, partly in the form of bread. But for three or four years he has been unwilling to make a monetary payment, in part because he doesn't want the extent of his business known, in part because that's the way of Shebika. And so some of his land has gone over to Ismaïl. The only difference is that Ridha, who has other resources, keeps a man of Shebika, who incidentally owes him money for groceries, at work on it.'

Such relationships, as we know, are complex, with an endless chain of links joining one to another. Are not their complexity and wilful confusion (which some economists consider indicative of a primitive mind) a purposefully organized hedge against the encroachment of the new market-place economy? The lack of technical preparation and of even the groundwork of a modern social set-up threatens the peasants with even greater poverty, of the type found in the slum environs of a big town or city.

In any case, the men of Shebika, who affect disdain towards the Bedouin encampment, are in many cases actually working for it. Everyone pretends, as usual, not to notice, but there is a new social set-up based on the exchange of debts and services between the nomads and the 'sedentaries'. The nomad has ceased to be a long-distance wanderer, but mobility gives his life a dynamic quality such as is shown in his cultivation of the desert. The settled villager, in spite of his pride and pretension, is no longer self-sufficient; indeed, the Bedouin is taking his property away. This is not only because the nomads' heritage has given them the advantage of greater energy and initiative but also because Shebika submits to them passively, having lost faith in its own existence.

One might think that the exchange of services, even if it is weighed down more heavily on one side than on the other, would lead to matrimonial relations. Not so. The Bedouin's disdain for Shebika stands in the way. For the absence of already established 'cousinships' is only a secondary obstacle. Where they do not exist these are easily invented, in the course of long genealogical discussions.

Two bachelors of Shebika (one Imami and one Qadduri) have put out feelers for a marriage with Fatimah, the girl 'sick with fevers'. Old Ismaïl had already turned away these two suitors and Hassan, his son-in-law and successor, is, although for different reasons, equally dead set against them.

Hassan is not very communicative. When old Ismaïl was alive we sat around in the tent, discoursing on family connexions. The hum of the loom was conducive to sleep, and only the voices of Khalil and the old man filled the silence or, rather, the emptiness. But when we tried to engage Hassan in conversation he asked if the governor had sent us, as if only an official inquiry would win from him any reply. His only interest is in work. When he has put together a certain amount of money he will go to Qabes or perhaps even to Tunis, where his children can receive a good education. 'Life can't always go on as it used to, and the money a man puts into educating his children is sure to bring a good return.' He'll keep his newly built house on the desert; his brother or the husband of Fatimah – should she marry – will be left to cultivate the land. But he doesn't intend to spend the rest of his days looking at Shebika.

One of us did manage to ask about the girl 'sick with the fevers', as Si Tijani had put it. There had been some idea of marrying her off, we were told; a suitor (a cousin, of course) had come from an encampment not too far away. He had not seen Fatimah herself, but he had talked with her brother. 'What's one to do, with an ailing arm, *in sha Allah*, and no doctor? Is one to go to town or to address prayers and promises to Sidi Sultan, like the women? Going to town is expensive, and who is to look after the livestock? The trip to Tawzar is difficult. On foot it takes two days, and if one isn't lucky enough to be admitted at once to the dispensary, there may be a day or two more of waiting. As for going by car, one doesn't pass by very often, and usually it doesn't have room. Of course, there's the medical truck, but it doesn't come more than once a year. Yes, it's difficult to get taken care of when one's ill.'

The cousin made the gift of a sheep and also of a rug with a flower design, which was spread out on the gravel in front of the tents for the family's admiration, while Aamr galloped up and down excitedly on a small horse, as if exhibiting his prowess, a short distance away. The suitor went off, without ever speaking of his suit again, either to Ismaïl or to Hassan, whom he ran into a few days later.

After this came the two suitors from Shebika. Apparently Hassan made short shrift of them. He spoke to us, as if it were an insult, of the fact that they came 'to talk about a marriage', and that he told them at once that he wasn't interested.

As for Fatimah, she continues to kneel, quite peacefully, before her high-warp loom. Whenever we have caught sight of her it is to admire her calm, smiling, handsome face, with tattooing on the right cheek. There is no trace of the sudden crises, during which she rolls on the ground, making strange sounds.

Now, when Hassan, the new head of the family, comes in, she makes a slight movement of her shoulders and goes on with her work, taking the thread with her left hand and then, with her right, passing it in front of the vertical web and subsequently pushing it down with an iron comb. Doubtless she saw the suitors, when they came, but she said nothing. She is waiting, that too we know. That is, her every gesture is directed towards that which should happen some day, towards the crowning acts of a Bedouin woman's life; the preparation of her husband's couscous, the bearing of a man-child and the talk, on an equal footing, with the other married women.

When old Ismaïl was alive he spoke quite freely of Fatimah. She was a good cook and a good weaver, he told us; only from time to time she had the 'fevers'. Once upon a time, here in the South, girls so afflicted were a source of good fortune; they foretold the future and took care of the ill. They were called soothsayers, not witches, for witches cannot see God, whereas soothsayers are always in his confidence. They stayed single, but people came from afar to consult them, not about trivialities but about such important matters as an inheritance, the division of land, or a marriage. 'But everything has changed, even if life hasn't', old Ismaïl told us. 'The girl can't be what she might once have been, because the government won't tolerate the practice of medicine by anyone that isn't a doctor, even if there aren't enough doctors to go around.'

Fatimah continues to weave and to prepare couscous for the women and children. She has not the right to call down God's blessing on the brothers who support and protect her. Unconsciously they detest her, but if she were to be insulted they would be ready to die in her defence. As a person, she does not count. Here everyone obeys secret rules, unformulated but unbreakable.

Are not societies without a writing more formalistic and rigorous than any others? Here no one dreams of attributing any importance to personal feelings and emotions. Even more directly than the man of the village, the man of the steppe lives under God's eye and lives uncompromisingly. The fixity of this unimaginable stare, concentrated upon his every gesture, accentuates the abstract quality of the rules of everyday living. A man acts, not on the basis of the attraction or repulsion he feels for one of his fellows, but rather according to what his role demands of him. This role is definite and eternal, determined by a plot which seems to have been elaborated with no regard for individual existences. Here, more than in any other place, life is a play whose characters are governed by rules which brook not the slightest transgression or even hesitation. This because the rules are never clearly set forth and nobody seems to want an explanation. Between the demands of real life and those of the role he is called upon to play, a man will always choose the latter. His existence is predicated upon submission rather than upon the shifting situations and 'chiaroscuro anarchy' of daily existence.

Fatimah, hemmed in by her role of expectation, the expectation of another role which she may never play, changed over the two years since we first saw her. Her features hardened and we found her most often lying down. The women of our group, who have the easiest access to the tent, told us that she barely spoke, and stared constantly at her older sister's children. A woman who was taught since childhood that her woman's role called for bearing male children could not be annihilated by this sterility. Hassan, intent upon the expansion of the limitless property he had unexpectedly begun to develop on the steppe, gradually discovered that his sister-in-law's marriage would be a hindrance. He said, quite frankly, to Si Tijani, that the necessity of dividing property and setting up a separate household would require money which he could not spare.

Gradually, it seems, Hassan took up the idea of Ismaïl. Talking to his mother-in-law (who repeated his words to Si Tijani, in whom she has great confidence), he suggested that it might be worthwhile to encourage Fatimah to exercise the gifts which she possessed by very virtue of her 'fevers'. As old Ismaïl had said : 'If a girl like Fatimah is "sick with fevers", it means that God has chosen her to interpret His will, to tell us what we should and shouldn't do. Since she has been chosen, she must develop her natural prophetic ability.'

We don't know exactly how it came about, how Fatimah accepted the role thrust upon her by her malady, by the particularity which set her aside from the crowd and at the same time endowed her with special powers. Was it by dint of being looked at in a certain, purposeful way, of feeling the expectations of those around her, that she spontaneously acquired the ways of a soothsayer or witch, both so common in the Maghrib? Did her mother and brother-in-law bring about a meeting with some already initiated old woman of the mountains or the Jerid? Then did Hassan, in the course of his frequent travels, let it be known that Fatimah was ready to hold consultations about the future? Be this as it may, upon one of our returns to the encampment we met two women coming out of the tent and setting out across the steppe to another encampment some distance away. The man of Shebika whom we were bringing back from Tawzar told us that here there was a girl to whom everyone came for advice, about business matters, the likelihood of the birth of a male child, the choice between taking an old man to the doctor or attempting to cure him by offerings to Sidi Sultan.

'Yes,' a Bedouin told us, 'people go to see Ismaïl's daughter because she knows things that they would like to know. Mostly women.'

'You don't ever go to her yourself?'

'I should say not.'

'And if your wife were to go, what would you say?'

'That's her own affair.'

And other people told us approximately the same thing.

When we returned, most recently, to the encampment, we were received as we had been at the beginning. On the women's side of the tent there was a hum, not of the loom but of voices. An old woman was crouching beside Fatimah and her mother. Fatimah had not changed; she was stouter, but she had still, when unobserved, the same absent, distracted expression. A few minutes later Hassan came to sit down beside us. After some beating about the bush we asked him why, in the last analysis, none of the Bedouins cared to marry a man or woman from Shebika.

'Shebika ... you're always talking about Shebika! They're a bunch of paupers, who never go anywhere. Only a man that moves around can make money. The people of Shebika don't know how to do anything. God hasn't willed that they should know how to use what they possess. They drift along, all of them, waiting for the government to help them. We count on God. What should we hope to obtain from Shebika?'

3
THE 'KERNEL OF BEING'

Salah

'Our researchers,' says Khalil, 'in particular Salah, come from the very environment which we are studying. The two factors which have changed their lives are the city and their education. When we go into things a little more deeply we see that, for all of us students, the inhabitant of Shebika or the Bedouin is, genealogically, quite close: for most of us a grandfather or great-grandfather; for Salah, his father. Salah himself was a shepherd in the region of Qassireen. His father went off to Tunis, but remained in the outskirts of the city while Salah got all the way in ...

These facts have a bearing on our inquiry and, above all, on the relationships between the researcher and the individual who is the object of his research.

'Students usually behave,' Khalil says further, 'as if they did not know what is meant by a backward peasantry, or as if they had long since forgotten it. They may study the ethnology of Black Africans or Red Indians. There are North African scholars in the Musée de l'Homme in Paris who feel as remote from the groups they are studying as if they were Frenchmen or Americans. And yet, among us, this feeling of remoteness is misleading; at best it is overlarded with the notions we have learned at school. Even in our own countries we often become foreigners "observing" customs, as if they were not very close to those which we ourselves have known. But all this we hide from ourselves and refuse to admit. Actually, the more deeply the researcher is involved in the research the more difficult it is for him. I find proof of this every day. Involvement means that we go straight to the point, without error, because we know in advance, even if not consciously, the significance of the familiar signs or symptoms which we perceive. We risk not only understanding but also shocking the individuals whom we question, far more than do you Europeans ...'

This involvement is what determined the relationship between Salah and the village of Shebika. As Khalil tells it :

'On the very first day, up at the mountainous end of the village, he came upon three men engaged in the sacrificial killing of a young camel. They had cut his throat and were waiting for the blood to drain away.

' "What are you doing?" shouted Salah. "It's wasteful and wrong to kill so young an animal!"

'The three men stared at Salah, at his bony, typically Bedouin face, just like their own, at the notebook he was holding awkwardly in his hand, at his steel-rimmed glasses, above all at the glasses. For months and months, until he had become the most passionate of our researchers, they would not answer his questions or even speak to him. On this first encounter, one of them, whom Salah had addressed as "brother", raised his head and said simply, as if he were talking to a stranger :

' "Leave us alone!"

'Salah ran down the mountain and back to the jeep.

' "These people are savages," he told me. "We're wasting our time. I know the sort of fellows who cut the throats of young camels; they need to be eliminated, that's all. And who are these people of Shebika, after all? Lazy beggars that haven't the guts to go to look for work in the city ..." '

The two of them, Khalil and Salah, lingered for a few moments beside the jeep, in the hot sun; then they walked down the path through the gorge to the rocky area where we had pitched camp, just above the spring, the sound of whose constant trickle was magnified by the surrounding mountains. For a whole year Salah was unwilling to take part in our investigation, except by reading background material and, when necessary, serving, quite mechanically, as an interpreter.

Salah's totally committed life, when we first met him, was this. In order to pay for his studies he was working in the library of the University of Tunis, where he spent considerable time reading the books around him. In the evening, when he left the university, he went to the Avenue Bourguiba, whose dense, many-coloured trees throw a blue shadow in summer. He entered one of the small European cafés, where Tunisians never used to go before Independence, and there sat down with friends, particularly Ali, a self-educated man, bald and thin, with a short beard, on account of which he liked to be called 'Lenin'.

They drank coffee, never alcohol. Salah had no money with which to pay, but he did various favours – the outline of a thesis, a translation from classical Arabic – for anyone that treated him. He was one of the university's prize students, and knew it.

The evenings usually ended in Ali's tiny room, hung with crazy-quilt draperies, made out of many-coloured rags all sewn together, and filled with books borrowed from various libraries, and musical instruments. In twos or fours the men hummed snatches of nasal Bedouin songs, or else Ali turned on the record-player which he had bought at the flea-market of Bil Suwayqa. Sometimes he played a record made by Salitha, a truly remarkable Bedouin singer, who came to Tunis during one month of Ramadan and stayed there until her death, shortly after Independence, composing her own songs, inspired by the poetry of the nomad peoples. The young men swayed to and fro, chanting the verses of *maalaf*, a type of song supposed to echo the nostalgia of the Andalusian Arabs driven out of Spain when it was 'reconquered' from them. The *maalaf* is an interminable love song, a sort of erotic psalm.

Late at night Salah left Ali's room, making his way through the narrow alleys of the old city, where everything was long since closed and the only light was that of the *turbeh* or tombs. From time to time a policeman, wearing springy, silent rubber-soled shoes and swinging a long rubber truncheon, went by. After he had circled the modern building of the university Salah encountered the odours of brine and marshes characteristic of the slum area of Melasseen. Today these slums have been partly torn down and some of their tenants moved to better housing on the road to Bizerta, behind the Bardo. Many of the slum dwellings, however, are still standing, because new arrivals continually come to take the place of those who have gone.

In Salah's house everybody is sleeping. He has only to lift the latch, enter the small, smoke-filled room, lie down on a mat with some army blankets rolled up under it and listen to the snoring of the other members of the family before he too goes to sleep. The only difference between Salah and a young man of Shebika is that Salah knows he has the brains to make himself equal or even superior to the average city-dweller, and that in a few years he will cash in on the advantages of his education.

It is understandable that Salah should be repelled by anything which recalls his early years in a village near Qassireen (long before the construction of the cellulose factory). His thoughts are all directed towards the future. When we came back for the first time from Shebika to Tunis he did not conceal his hostility. This village represented a part of his life that he wanted to banish from his mind, and we had plunged him back into it. However, he did not go so far as to say that he wanted no part of the investigation. He followed us around, even if he stayed in a corner, reading a book or talking to the driver. Si Tijani took a liking to him, and he began to 'think about the South', about the 'Bedouinity' from which he had sprung and now wished to escape in order to become, by virtue of his studies, a member of the new ruling class.

Salah said over and over to Ali and Khalil that he came along with us simply for a look at the country and a breath of fresh air. Actually he was busy reading up on the South, chiefly the books of Berque and Massignon. One day he remarked that we should never understand Shebika if we didn't take into account the fact that, in a Muslim country, religion is just as important as everyday life. Here was where we should look for the village's real centre of gravity. This remark was surprising, inasmuch as Salah claimed himself to be totally emancipated and, indeed, scornful of the past. He respected none of the prescriptions of Ramadan, and indeed smoked all during this holy month in the *suq* of the old city, where most people are respectful of tradition. This contradiction did not bother him in the least.

Meanwhile his interest in our project grew. He wanted to prove to us that the structure of the village rested on a sacred substructure, a religious or magical centre embodied in Sidi Sultan. He asked himself why this little lost place, scorned by politicians and administrators, exercised such a fascination upon his friends and a small group of Europeans. One day he heard Jacques Berque say in one of his university lectures that the new independent nations of the Maghrib could not, without the risk of corruption, do without the 'Bedouinity' which was the foundation and source of their essential, individual spirit, that which is called in classical Arabic *as-sala*. He thought this over for some time, and we gradually talked him into coming back to Shebika in order to establish the importance of Sidi Sultan.

'Yes, my parents were poor peasants from the central and eastern part of the country. When I was born they had settled down to till the land, but before that they were nomads, based in villages, but migrating, with their flocks, during the dry season. Half settled and half wandering, perhaps that is their similarity to the people of Shebika. But there is one big difference. They and their fellows emigrated in large numbers to look for work in the big city.'

'Have you kept up with those that stayed behind?'

'My relatives come to visit us in Tunis, especially when they need medical attention. Yes, we do keep up a certain relationship.'

'And the first time you went to Shebika?'

'What struck me first was the shape and colour of the houses, the way they harmonized with the surrounding sand. What touched me most was the mixture of mistrust and cordiality which they showed us. And the complete idleness of the older people ...'

'It seems that your first contact was difficult ...'

'Yes, because they mistrusted us.'

'And you mistrusted them, too, didn't you?'

'Yes and no. Because they were mistrustful I didn't know what subject to broach and how to lead up to it. It was equally hard to skim over commonplaces and to go deeper into their beliefs. Before asking them anything it was necessary to penetrate their mentality. But they reacted either by laughing or refusing to answer. One day I finally got to talking with a twenty-four-

year-old man. It started because I happened to be questioning
him, for the purposes of our study, about his forthcoming marriage. The interest I showed in his problems caused him to open
himself up quite freely. This young man lives and works with
his father. He was employed for a while on a road-building
project, and now he hopes to marry one of his cousins.'

'But didn't you already know, implicitly, everything that he
told you?'

'Implicitly, perhaps. . . . Then I made a friend of the old
Bedouin, Ismaïl, and also of another old man, Rasheed, the one
who has built a sort of store-house across from the Mosque. He
is a former grocer, who was ruined during the struggle for independence, and now he earns a living by organizing the women's
basket-making and sending their handiwork by the National
Guards or chance visitors, to be sold in the city.'

'But did you, more than the rest of us, encounter resistance
to your questioning?'

'Yes, and that's how I came to take an interest in Sidi Sultan.
At first, every time I mentioned it, they changed the subject.
Anyone asking them questions is necessarily a stranger, particularly people like ourselves who come from the city and are
associated, in their eyes, with the government, with city-based
authority. These are two things at which they automatically
baulk, both here at Shebika and in the region where I was born.
This attitude doesn't date from independence or even from the
colonial period; it goes much further back, to the time of the
Beys and, before them, of the Turks. For centuries the countryside has been administered and watched over by the city. Then
certain questions probe into hard facts which incite the
peasants to change some of their ritualistic, pre-conceived attitudes, to question *themselves*, and that is something to which
they are not accustomed.'

'And how did the people of Shebika, in general, seem to regard
you?'

'As a city-dweller, as a representative of the government.'

'But they knew that you came from a part of the country
like their own.'

'Yes, they knew; I told them. But for them I am still a city-dweller, and a city-dweller represents governmental authority. And to be "observed" has for them the connotation of being laughed at. Then again, they may have a feeling of envy, in spite of the fact that, unlike the peasants from my part of the country, they have no desire to go away. They know, at bottom, that their children will be emancipated like us. Perhaps that's what finally made them open up. But I know that they're holding something back, something they keep for themselves alone, like the only treasure left to them in their state of disinheritance and deprivation. That's how I came to take an interest in the marabout of Sidi Sultan. There, I felt, was where they were resisting us. There is what's called, in theological terms, the *halq*, the "hard kernel of creation and being".'

The Custodian of the Tomb

Salah went down to the tomb of Sidi Sultan with Qaddur, the *Imam*, who keeps it clean and is apparently in charge. Qaddur knocked several times with his stick against the outside wall; then they went in through the low door in the smaller wall of the shrine itself. Both of them stooped to catch a glimpse of the holy man's platform, the draperies, the faded green flag and the scattered empty vases.

'Why is the door so low?' Salah asked.

'It's better that way, on account of the wind and the dust.'

'How long has Sidi Sultan been here?'

'Over a hundred years. My uncle Ibrahim, who lived to be a hundred and ten, remembered him from his childhood.'

'What do you know about him? About the offerings that are made to him, about the people who want to be buried inside the wall and bequeath to him the income from their palm-trees?'

'Palm-trees in the oasis of Shebika?'

'Yes. When a man wants to be buried inside the wall, doesn't he say: "I dedicate such-and-such a parcel of land to Sidi Sultan"?'

'Yes ...'

'Then who collects the income from the parcel and sees that it is used for this purpose?'

'It used to be the man who led prayers at the Mosque; now the "Habus" office * has taken the whole thing over. It has sold lots to those that want them and manages the rest.'

'If someone makes an offering to Sidi Sultan, do you take it?'

'Yes. If a visitor offers a hundred or fifty or even twenty millimes, I take them, and I provide him with lunch and dinner. You know, of course, that visitors no longer offer a ram or a camel.'

'Used people to offer more than they do now?'

'Ever since I've been here they've offered a hundred or fifty or twenty millimes.'

'And who receives this money?'

'I do. And it's up to me to provide the donor with lunch and dinner.'

'Suppose a visitor comes to make an offering, where does he go to eat? Are you obliged to give him lunch and dinner?'

'If you come to visit Sidi Sultan and bring nothing with you, I provide you with food.'

'In old times, if a man brought a ram or a camel, but didn't stay all day and had no occasion to eat a meal ...'

'Then he gave his offering to whoever was in charge. The man in charge welcomes everyone that comes along, and provides whatever meals are needed. There's no set rule. One visitor provides an offering, another comes empty-handed. Both are entitled to a meal or meals.'

'Where do the visitors come from?'

'From the various tribes of the region, from Sidi Obeid, from Tamerza ...'

'And from Redayif?'

'No, never.'

'From El Hamma?'

'A woman came the other day from El Hamma, with the offering of a lamb.'

'What did she ask of Sidi Sultan?'

*A government agency which manages all the funds donated to religious shrines.

'She didn't say.'

'What do women usually ask of him?'

'They want to have a child. Or to have a sick child made well.'

'If a woman's child is sick what does she ask of Sidi Sultan?'

'She says: "If my child is cured I'll give you this and that." Or else she may want a husband, or want the husband she has to love her more. "Sidi Sultan, make my husband love me, and I'll bring you a ram." Or: "Sidi Sultan, give me a child and I'll bring you a goat."'

'What good things has Sidi Sultan accomplished? What stories do they tell about him?'

'He wasn't alive in my lifetime or in that of my parents.'

'That's true. We haven't, any of us, known the Prophet, either, but we know the good things he did.'

'That's not the same thing. The Prophet performed miracles. Here they pass on from one generation to another the story that such-and-such a one asked Sidi Sultan to heal her son, that she brought him a sheep when her son was healed; that another woman asked for a child, and when she had one she brought bread to Sidi Sultan. That's the kind of story they tell.'

'But what are the greatest things he ever did? For instance, in another part of the country there's a well-known holy man called Sidi El Bashir. He's known above all for having lessened the value of the dowry. In my village he's famous on this account. If a parent demands a dowry of more than sixty-nine millimes, Sidi El Bashir curses and punishes him. Isn't Sidi Sultan famous for something of the same kind?'

'I've told you all I know about him. I can't tell you any more.'

Salah is quite aware that Qaddur knows more than he wants to tell. Muhammad had told him that Qaddur took in the offerings to Sidi Sultan, but not in the capacity of custodian, only as an intermediary. Muhammad said that even he himself did not know the identity of the other man. 'There are things that are said and things that remain unspoken.' After which he muttered something about the *jinn* or evil spirits, which flee from the salt-beds into the mountains. Against them Sidi Sultan provides effective protection. The plainsmen, below, are less fortunate and at certain seasons their herds are attacked by the spirits. 'We're safe, here at Shebika.'

Other villagers were no more communicative. Salah caught one of them watching over the *qaddus* alone one hot afternoon and smoking one cigarette after another. He seemed to regard the answers to Salah's questions as obvious.

'Is Sidi Sultan really known as a great holy man in the whole region?'

'Yes, there's none other like him.'

'And do you know his story?'

'No.'

'Why not?'

'I don't, that's all, and I don't want to be bothered.'

'Tell me something about his life, about the miraculous accomplishments which won him the reputation of being holy.'

'I've always heard that Sidi Sultan is precious to us, that's all.'

'They say that Sidi Sultan is "the man of proof". Do you know where he got that name?'

'Because he had great faith. If someone obeys him and visits his tomb he grants his requests.'

'What exactly does "man of proof" mean?'

'He is a good spirit and grants the requests made to him.'

'Have you ever asked him for anything, you or your father?'

'No neither of us.'

'Why not?'

'People say: "Protect me against everything bad. Keep illness away." If he does so, then they bring him what they promised: couscous, a lamb or a sheep. The women cook them, and then all the neighbours are called in to eat. That's the *waada*, the vow to Sidi Sultan.'

'Sidi Sultan's story is known. A little old man told it to us.'

'If he's old he ought to know.'

'Everyone knows. The old man told me that on the day of his death Sidi Sultan asked that he be put on a camel and that the camel be allowed to go where it would. Wherever the camel stopped, there he was to be buried. And the camel stopped at Shebika.'

'Perhaps so. An old man might well know about such things. Not I.'

'How does it happen that you don't know?'

'I never heard the story, that's all.'

'Why?'

'No one ever told me. Most people don't even wonder why Sidi Sultan came to Shebika or how he got here ...'

But Sidi Sultan was gradually taking shape, as his image was tossed back and forth among the inhabitants of Shebika. Some people said that he was an Algerian from Tabissa. Others that he lived much longer ago and did things that cannot be told today. Everything pointed to a hidden and mysterious person. Connected with him are also gestures of which no one wanted to speak, the dancing of women and children dedicated to the holy man's veneration. And so the women were questioned about him, and they were quite willing to talk to Naïma and Munira, our women researchers.

'Sidi Sultan belongs to us,' said one of them. 'He is a women's saint, and he comes, not from Morocco or Mecca (like most holy men, who originate in the former and pass through the latter), but from the mountains in the centre of the country.'

'When women come to Shebika for the great religious holiday, can they enter the shrine?'

'Yes, indeed.'

'Do they recite verses from the Quran, like the men?'

'No. They go "yoo-hoo-hoo" and call upon Sidi Sultan.'

'And can children go into the shrine?'

'Children, yes, but not adolescents.'

'When do they begin to be adolescents?'

'When they are ten years old.'

'And after their adolescence, when can they once more go in?'

'When they are bigger.'

'After a young man is married, can he be admitted?'

'Not at the same time as the women.'

'And if a young boy makes an offering, can he go in?'

'Anyone who makes an offering can go in.'

'Even young girls?'

'Young girls especially.'

'Do you know anything about the life of Sidi Sultan, about his accomplishments?'

'No, I don't. I've never heard a thing about him.'

'Why is he called a holy man?'

'I don't know.'

'Could the custodian of the tomb give us some information?'

'Certainly he could.'

But when she was asked to name the custodian, she laughed, held her hand up to her mouth and ran away. Salah tried again, with the men lying under the portico. He stretched out with them in the dust, for he no longer cares, as he did in the city, for the cleanliness of his clothes. Tall and thin, with his long teeth and wandering eyes he talked to the men in their ghandurahs in a manner quite different from that in which we are accustomed to hear him. And his interlocutors scratched their ears and noses and stared at this young fellow not so very different from themselves, who was questioning them about things that everyone knows. Only what everyone knows is so simple that it defies expression. And this very simplicity may be the sign of a secret.

As Muhammad was to tell us one day: 'When we answer your questions we end up by saying to ourselves that we know something.' Salah repeated his questions over and over, until they became statements which everybody approved, and thus there could be an unending discussion which helped him to track down Sidi Sultan, the holy man beloved of women.

'Did he ask to be buried here or did you – or rather your ancestors – bury him?'

'I don't know. How came he to be buried here? I can't tell you.'

Another man intervened, without moving:

'We've heard nothing about him. And read nothing. You know we can't read or write. All we know is that he passed by on his way from Mecca. He died here and was buried, and since then everyone calls him Sidi Sultan. The people who were living when he came saw him, with their own eyes, perform things that caused them to consider him "holy".'

'What did they see him do?'

'You'll have to ask them that! But they must have had their reasons. Take me, I never knew my grandfather; he died before I was born. But he told all sorts of things to my father, my father told them to me and I'll be telling them to my son. That's the way a legend gets passed on.'

'Are you sure they saw Sidi Sultan accomplish great things?'

'Yes, otherwise they wouldn't have called him "holy".'

'Why did he never marry and have children?'

'He was coming from Mecca, and he wasn't thinking about marriage. He found himself at Shebika and so he stayed there.'

Other men had gathered around Salah. When they heard that the talk was of Sidi Sultan they wanted to go away, but he held them back and eventually they weren't sorry they had stayed.

'We hope to come back for the next feast-day of Sidi Sultan,' Salah told them. 'Do you celebrate it every year?'

'Yes, every year.'

'And do people come from far away on that day?'

'Only from the neighbourhood. They come for dinner and that's all. They come, cook and eat their couscous and meat, and then go home.'

'Everyone brings his own food, is that it?'

'You'll dine with us, whether or not there's a celebration, and whether or not you bring provisions.'

This, Salah knew, was no empty promise. The hospitality of Shebika is something very real. He knew, too, that one shouldn't talk about it, that one should confine oneself to a formal thank-you.

'Is the festive meal eaten at Sidi Sultan?'

'No. Everyone takes his share and goes to eat it at home. He takes it in a pot of just the right size for the number of people there are in his family. Families are all different; there are those of eight, ten or even just two people. In short, everything is cooked together and then taken home separately.'

'Do you kill only sheep? No goats?'

'Only male sheep. No ewes, and no goats.'

'Why not?'

'Sidi Sultan doesn't like them. He likes only male sheep.'

'How many animals do you slaughter?'

'That depends on their size; seven, eight, or ten; it all depends. If they're very large, then five are enough.'

'Who usually does the slaughtering?'

'Abdel Aziz, or Moqqadim, or Abdel Majeed. All the older men know how to butcher. The young ones don't know and don't want to.'

'Does the celebration begin early in the day?'

'Yes, at dawn.'

'And what does it consist of?'

'Nothing special. We kill the animals, call everyone to come, and distribute the meat. That's all there is to it.'

From time to time the conversation lags. Then one of the villagers – not Salah – is the one to revive it. Obviously no one has ever talked about Sidi Sultan before, except in terms of rules and proscriptions of long standing. To discuss it on a commonplace, everyday level is new and exciting. Salah puffs at his cigarette and looks at the deeply lined, smiling faces, the bright eyes, where there is a gleam of mistrust. One or two other men join the group. Ridha, the grocer, passes by and, learning that Sidi Sultan is the subject of the conversation, goes his way. Not, however, before murmuring a word to a little old man lying in the dust with most of his body exposed to the sun. Salah doesn't know what Ridha said, but another one of our group did overhear the words: 'They're beyond the influence of God's will.' The men have started talking again. The subject of Sidi Sultan affects them all, although they have never explained why.

'You know,' one of them says to Salah, 'in a way Sidi Sultan has been a source of wealth to Shebika, but a long time ago, when there were caravans. Now only poor people visit the shrine.'

'Men, are they?'

'No, mostly women. They come in, go "yoo-hoo-hoo", burn incense and walk around the tomb. Meanwhile, outside, the meat is cooking. When a woman has finished her cooking she goes home.'

'Does none of the women cook at home?'

'No, they cook at the shrine and take the food home to be eaten.'

'And what do you do after the meal? Do you men, for instance, get together and recite the Quran?'

'No, the men no longer get together. During the celebration we have lunch, say prayers at the Mosque, then go to the tomb, reciting the *Burda* [a religious text] on our way. Then we go home.'

'Who recites the *Burda*, the older men?'

'Everyone that knows it. Those who don't know it join in as best they can. Then, at the shrine, we recite *Al Fatiha* [the opening prayer of the Quran]. Then we go home.'

'And who makes offerings to Sidi Sultan?'

'Everyone that needs to.'

'Do the nomads bring offerings?'

'Yes, those who promised Sidi Sultan a pot of something, come here, cook it, distribute it to the people of the village and then go home.'

'Is that the way things are done on the feast-day also?'

'No, for the feast-day a man promises a *qilba* * of something or other and a sheep; two *qilba* and two sheep; one, two or even five dinars. . . . If your son is about to be called up for military service, then you say: "Sidi Sultan, keep him from going, and I'll give you a millime, or six or seven millimes." Or else, if your son is sick, then you say: "Cure him, Sidi Sultan, and I'll give you this-and-that." Or else: "Bring my children back safe and sound", or: "Inspire me", or: "Open the gates".'

'What does "open the gates" mean exactly?'

'When you have a project of any kind, or when you're looking for a wife, or when your children are away . . .'

'Did you promise anything to Sidi Sultan when your children were away?'

'Yes I promised him some *aalaam* [pieces of cloth, or small flags]. One man promises *aalaam*, another the money with which to buy incense. The petitioner may repair the wall of the shrine, or else he may purchase new draperies.'

* A *qilba* is a measure of weight equal to several pounds.

'Where did you buy your *aalaam* and how much did you pay for them?'

'At Redayif, for six dinars.'

The man who has just spoken gets up, beckons to Salah and leads him across the empty square and down to the marabout. He opens the low door and shows him the flags, the silks, the bits of cloth.

'There are many things. These are the holy man's riches.'

'Are all these *aalaam* thank-offerings?'

'Yes.'

'From people at Shebika or from other places as well?'

'From all over. There, that's an old bowl. And there's a cracked ostrich egg.'

'Did the son for whom you made a vow ever come home?'

'Yes. He was in the Congo, down there along the ocean, in the direction of America. I missed him, and so I made a vow. Some people said he must be dead, and I struck my face, like this and like this. Then I made the vow, and God sent him home. He brought back money, and with that I found him a wife. He lives with me now and is in good health, thank God.'

'Is that the only vow you've ever made?'

'I promised Sidi Sultan a full pot and a sheep for the return of my son. I killed two sheep, which I bought for two dinars each, and invited the people of the village to come and eat them.'

'You didn't kill them here, at the shrine?'

'No, at my own house. And that's where people came to eat them.'

'When people have a request to make, what do they do when they get here?'

'They roll on the ground or fall on to the columns. Those who know any, recite *suras* from the Quran.'

'Standing up or sitting down?'

'Either; it doesn't matter.'

'Outside the door or inside? Which is better?'

'They say inside.'

'Do you go home before or after you've killed the sheep?'

'First I kill the sheep, then I give out the meat, then I come here to the shrine.'

'And then what do you do?'

'I finish what I have to say to Sidi Sultan.'

'And what sort of thing do you say?'

'"Sidi Sultan, keep my children safe, and you shall have this and that."'

'When you make a vow, do you tell other people about it?'

'In this case I spoke of it only after my son came home.'

'Before that you didn't mention it to anyone, not even to your other children?'

'No, I didn't. But silence isn't obligatory. I could have spoken of it if I'd wanted to.'

'If you come here after a holiday celebration, exactly what do you do?'

'I come in, I recite the first *sura* of the Quran and then I say: "Sidi Sultan, I have come to you as a petitioner; send me away as a debtor. Sidi Sultan, grant me what I wish!" Then I recite the first *sura* again and go home.'

'You don't stay here overnight?'

'No, but anybody can that wants to.'

'What are all these pieces of pottery?'

'They're thank-offerings. Here you have candle-holders, which the custodian lights every Thursday and Friday. Over there are pots for burning incense.'

'In order to visit the tomb does one have to give notice in advance, or can one just drop in?'

'You come, leave some incense, and go away. The custodian is the only one to know. If you like you can leave a dinar, or fifty or a hundred dinars, or else just the incense, as I said.'

'Someone else may hear of the visit, however.'

'No, no one but the custodian.'

'No one can come in without an offering, isn't that so?'

'No one but the custodian.'

They raise themselves from the leaning position in which they had looked into the shrine. The man is proud of Sidi Sultan for having granted the wish for his son. He touches the stone of the marabout as if it were the neck of a horse or dog. Once more they walk around the tomb, looking at the partially effaced inscriptions on the door and walls. Salah knows that his guide cannot read and that he will answer with something he learned in his childhood to the request:

'Read me that!'

'I know it by heart. I don't have to read it.'

'Did you learn the *Burda* when you were a child?'

'Yes.'

'Who inscribed it here?'

'Kittani, the fellow who sells our cloth at Tawzar and Qafsa.'

'What's this red and white here?'

'Just decoration.'

'The door seems to be very old.'

'It's fallen down several times and been put back in place. That's one way of making a vow, to say: "I'll pay for the holy man's new door." '

'What's written here?'

'Another prayer.'

'The door needs repairing right now.'

'Yes, but the custodian hasn't enough money and lately there haven't been any offerings.'

'Is this column made of palm wood?'

'No, of the wood of a fruit-tree in the oasis. A carpenter from Tamerza made it.'

'And does no one else know anything about Sidi Sultan?'

'Perhaps old Qaddur. Or Sidi Bashir, who comes from Tunis, but has lived with us since my father was a young man. A bachelor, a wise and honest man, who has no worldly possessions and came here in order to be near Sidi Sultan. But he doesn't like you, on account of your questions.'

They had started to walk back up to the portico, where the water-clock was running.

'A bachelor, yes. . . . He's not very talkative. He likes to be alone and talks, even to us, very rarely.'

'How does he live?'

'He lives with Sidi Amin, who provides him with food, even although he has a family of his own.'

'Don't Sidi Bashir's relatives send him anything?'

'They're at Tunis, if they're still alive. He has no one here.'

'And when did he come?'

'Eighteen or twenty years ago.'

'And he's never married? I suppose you refuse to give him a wife.'

'He's never asked for one.'

'If he did, you'd give her to him?'

'Certainly. Why not?'

'But he has no money, I suppose.'

'True. He's a wise man who came here to live in the company of Sidi Sultan.'

'He has no land, no trees?'

'Nothing at all.'

Sidi Bashir was there, a little to one side, as he had been a short time ago when he spoke with the grocer. Salah's guide went his way, because Salah was stopped by the Mosque attendant, who asked him for a cigarette. Salah paused in front of the Mosque. From a distance Sidi Bashir, the man from Tunis, was staring at him. Down the hill, behind the school-house animals could be heard moving in the direction of the Bedouin encampment. Otherwise all was still under the hot sun.

'Qaddur,' Salah was saying, 'I don't see how you can be the Mosque attendant and the custodian of Sidi Sultan as well.'

'I'm not the custodian. I simply replace him.'

'Why should there be two custodians?'

'I don't know.'

'You know something about Sidi Sultan that no one so far has told me. Try to believe me when I tell you I'm not prying. I simply want to know whether this Sidi Sultan whom you call a holy man, a marabout, was born around here or far away, whether he means a great deal to you, whether he played a great role in your past.'

'He came from far away, like the rest of them. He was returning from Mecca when he died.'

'In some places they've made saints out of men who were from their own village but had been to Mecca. In other places, out of perfect strangers, some of them women.'

'I know nothing about that. In any case, he's not our ancestor.'

'One older man told me that he was.'

'He must have meant another holy man, Sidi bu Ali, who's buried to the west, over the Algerian border. Before the war one could go to visit his tomb at Tabissa. Now that can no longer be done. It seems that many families of Shebika come from over there.'

Qaddur puffed at his cigarette and looked at Salah with amusement.

'Only one man here can tell you more, if he wants to. You've been told already who he is. Sidi Bashir, the bachelor from Tunis. He knows.'

'Did he belong to a brotherhood?'

From the way Qaddur turned his head away, it was plain that this aspect of religious life is a forbidden subject. All through the Maghrib, and particularly in the South, mystical associations, resembling secret societies, long played an important role. In this dispersed world, where there is no 'social density' whatsoever, religious allegiances take the place of integration with homogeneous social surroundings. In some cases they are remnants of the religious past of a land whose historians – from Gauthier to Charles A. Julien – have remarked upon its unorthodox attitude ('the Maghrib, home of heresies'). In others they were a reaction to the Turks and to the anarchical situation under the Beys, whose power extended barely beyond the cities and the *henshir* (great estates given to loyal vassals). By the beginning of the European penetration they were perhaps equivalent to the 'mutual aid' groups which Georges Balandier found serving in Black Africa as refuges of the natives. Intelligent French colonial administrators were able to manipulate them in such a way that they became elements of stabilization. Sometimes, but not always, for many of the 'brotherhoods', especially in the South, were not integrated with the French administration, in spite of the fact that the marabout movement in the rest of the country innocently compromised itself.

The brotherhoods, in any event, were groups which held a certain fascination for the men of Tunisia. In the mystical celebrations centred around the tombs of holy men they found a moral and spiritual unity lacking in the sordid life of both city and country. Isabella Eberhardt, the Russian anarchist who came, for mystical motives, to North Africa at the end of the last century, became a member of one of these brotherhoods, the Qadiriya and frequented its *zawiya* (cloisters) near Al Wad, around 1900–1901.* This membership was doubtless the cause of the very nearly fatal attempt on her life which took place in the village of Bashima, on the road between Al Wad and Naftah, and of her subsequent expulsion by the French government. The man who tried, with a rusty sword, to kill her, was a member of the rival brotherhood of the Tijaniya. It is to this latter widespread association that our friend Si Tijani owes his name and perhaps the prestige that he enjoys all over the Jerid, although we have never fathomed the exact extent of his relations with it. There are many other less spectacular stories of the rivalry between the two great mystical brotherhoods.

When the young lay leader, Habib Bourguiba, undertook to spread his political movement, the 'Neo-Destour', beyond the cities and into the countryside, where hitherto no political party had ever made a dent, he quite naturally came up against the brotherhoods and other cults of the marabouts. The brotherhoods opposed his new political organization with mystical ideas of sacred fatherhood. This struggle between the two still endures, ten years after Independence. The man of the Maghrib, living in isolation on an often ungrateful land, looks beyond weakened family life to new forms of meaningful association. The political movement which led to liberation was one of these, but because of the inevitable let-down after victory and also because socialist ideals and slogans appealed chiefly to the already uprooted, there has been a certain revival of the old brotherhoods. Even though this is limited to no more than an exchange of signs of recognition and 'common memories of the past', the government views it with suspicion.

* Isabella Eberhardt, in an article for *La Dépêche algérienne*, 4 June 1901, reproduced as an appendix to Victor Barrucand's posthumous edition of her book, *Dans l'Ombre chaude de l'Islam* (Paris: Charpentier et Fasquelle, 1917), pp. 334–7.

Radio broadcasts and the admonitions of the National Guards and local administrators have created a feeling of guilt on this score among the people of Shebika. They are unnecessarily secretive and reluctant to talk about the local shrine.

This explains the silence of Qaddur, who knew all along that on the feast-day of Sidi Sultan (as a young girl called Rima was to tell us) members of the brotherhoods gather and dance together. The silence would never have been broken if Salah had not seen, at this moment, a woman enveloped in a great black *bawta* go towards the tomb of Sidi Sultan and disappear through the door in the inside wall. This gave him an excuse to ask:

'What do women make vows for?'

'The same things as men, exactly.'

'Has your wife made vows?'

'No, she's never had any reason. She had a son who went off to Tunis and died in an automobile accident. But he wasn't my son. His father was a man from Tamerza.'

'And who took over his affairs?'

'He died in an accident, as I told you. There was an insurance payment of 1,200 dinars.'

'That's a lot! Who got it?'

'His father was dead, but he had brothers.'

'And how much did his mother – your wife – get?'

'170 dinars.'

'Did she give them to you?'

'Not all of them. She kept some for her children.'

'And what did she buy with them?'

'Nothing, so far.'

'Is she saving them up?'

'She hasn't got them with her. They're kept by her brothers at Tamerza.'

'Why didn't she give them to you?'

'She isn't holding them out on me. When I need money I have only to ask.'

'Have you bought anything with the money?'

'She gave me ten dinars for the marriage of my son, and later ten more. I spent them. Whenever I have need she gives me something.'

'She didn't buy any palm-trees?'

'No, she didn't.'

Now the two men saw the woman's head reappear near the shrine. Qaddur shrugged his shoulders. Turning towards Salah he resumed, of his own accord, the conversation.

'Sidi Sultan may be of Algerian origin. That's what they say.'

'How long ago was he around?'

'People over a hundred years old remember him from when they were very little.'

'What do they say about him?'

'They call him Sidi Sultan bin Slimi, a descendant of Slim.'

'Where did the descendants of Slim come from?'

'I don't know. I know him only as a *waali*, a holy man, buried in this shrine.'

'Did he leave any family at Shebika?'

'No.'

'Did he live alone?'

'Yes, alone.'

'When do you celebrate his feast-day?'

'During the summer.'

'When during the summer?'

'When we have time. When the harvest is in; when we have found animals and can buy them.'

'Who does the buying?'

'Anyone. Whoever buys buys for us all. We kill the animals and then divide the meat. But we don't pay until autumn.'

'You buy on credit?'

'Yes.'

'From whom do you buy?'

'From Obeid, or the *lahhameen*, the men who have livestock. May God or Sidi Sultan inspire them to grant us credit!'

'Do they wait for the date-harvest?'

'We always have something at harvest-time. We sell the dates and pay for the animals. Sometimes they ask for dates instead of money; sometimes for both.'

'On what day of the week do you hold the celebration?'

'Generally on Friday.'

'Do many people come from outside?'

'Only those whose path leads them here.'

Qaddur and Salah laugh, like accomplices. Qaddur tugs at Salah's sleeve and points to Sidi Bashir, who is sprawling in the dust.

'He knows more than anyone else.'

Together Salah and Qaddur cross the square, meeting Nawa, the wife of Muhammad, on the way. She is scurrying along in her black dress, with two or three naked children behind her, and a moment later pushes open the gate into her courtyard. Old Ali, Muhammad's friend, comes down from the grocery, smoking a cigarette. He looks at the jeep, parked in the sun. The driver is asleep, stretched out on the front seat with his feet sticking out over the door.

'You keep coming to Shebika,' says Qaddur. 'And you stay just long enough to get us to talk. As if there were anything going on here that you couldn't see in Tunis. There's not much difference, really, except that we're poor, very poor.'

'Exactly. That's our purpose, to show that you're Tunisians, just like the city people, and that you need more help than they do because you really want a change for the better.'

Salah points to the crumbling houses, baked by the sun. Qaddur laughs, shrugs his shoulders and leads him over to Sidi Bashir. Salah sits down beside him, leaning his back against the wall.

'What brought you to Shebika, Si Bashir?'

'God's will.'

'Did you come for a visit or with the intention of staying?'

'I came for a visit, and then stayed.'

'Had you heard about Shebika before you came?'

'I had a friend who worked here. He's dead now.'

'And why did he come?'

'He was a land-owner. He returned, every now and then, to the section of Tunis where I lived, near the Rue du Pacha.'

'And you, have you bought some land?'

'No.'

'Then why do you stay here, Si Bashir?'

'It was God's will that I should come.'

'Is it the place that you like, or the people?'

'God's will brought me here in spite of myself.'

'You mean you really wish you hadn't stayed?'

'Yes, I'd have liked to go away, but something keeps me here.'

'What keeps you here?'

'The Mosque and my patron saint, Sidi Sultan.'

'You mean that if it weren't for these you'd have gone away?'

'Yes. We are people that recognize only the will of God. In the cities you go by reason and opinion, but for us there is only God's will, which rules over land and sea.'

'Perhaps God's will brought us here.'

'No, you came here for your studies.'

'You mean that we're beyond the influence of God's will?'

'You fall, inevitably, under God's will. But you are destroying yourselves with your own reason.'

'How do you know?'

'By the way you talk and the way you act. I've been watching you for some time.'

'Do these things prove that we don't recognize the will of God? Don't you know that one Muslim shouldn't suspect another, that he must be quite sure before he condemns him? How can you know that we have no faith?'

'By listening to your conversation.'

Salah is at a loss for what to say. Finally he makes another stab:

'Do you know many people around the Rue du Pacha in Tunis?'

'Yes, I do.'

'Who are they?'

'The ones I know best are no longer there: the Almatari, the Almassiri ...'

'What did your father do?'

'He was a peasant.'

'Did you come here when you were very young?'

'No, I was forty years old.'

'Have you any children?'

'I'm not married.'

'You weren't married when you were in Tunis?'

'No, I didn't have anybody. ... Look here, these questions of yours are more than I can take. You're digging into my soul . . .

'That's perfectly natural, isn't it? When you go to a strange place, you ask questions. If you were to go to Tawzar, wouldn't you question the people you met?'

'Yes, but not the way you're questioning me.'

After a short pause Sidi Bashir goes on to say that during the two years of our visits to Shebika our questions have been highly disturbing. Previously people went to the marabout without asking themselves whether it was right or wrong. Now they have begun to think that there's something more to it, which only the city-dwellers can teach them. And yet the city-dwellers' questions are always about what happened to this one and that, never about what they do with their hands and feet when they work or walk. He, Bashir, came to Shebika because he wanted to be near Sidi Sultan. But ever since people like himself have no longer been permitted to live the way they want to but have to account for themselves to people who don't understand he has wanted to go away. When he first came, people gathered together and did what was pleasing to the holy man, with no questions asked. Now this is impossible. But since Salah was so keen to know, he would tell him how to meet the custodian of the tomb.

'Who is he, anyhow?'

'A certain Omar Ibn Ramadan. Just now he isn't here. You can meet him next month, if you are here again then.'

'Is it possible to talk to him?'

Sidi Bashir laughed and rolled over in the dust.

'He's a very old man. He has a piece of land, where he lives all alone, near the "White Spring".'

The Rebellion of Rima

The *wadi* water flowing into Rima's bucket is clear, and rippled by the wind that blows down the rocky ravine from the spring to the oasis. The bucket is made of darkened yellow plastic; her uncle brought it a year ago from Tawzar. It mustn't be set down anywhere near a fire, he told her, but it can fall any distance, even from the top of the village into the ravine, without breaking.

Rima is standing with both feet in the water, watching tiny fish knock up against her ankles. The soles of her feet are already calloused because, like the other women, she walks without shoes over the stony ground, but the toes are well-formed and the ankles shapely. On the feet of Iimra the aunt with whom she lives, the calloused sole comes almost up to the level of the instep, forming a sort of shoe, in which the toes are embedded. Rima's eyes are following a leech which has just attached itself to her left foot. When she feels the tiny creature's bite, she plucks it away with her fingers and tosses it, suddenly coiled up, upon the sand.

On the other side of her straddling legs the bucket, lying on its side, fills with water, according to the speed of the current. From the banks of the narrow *wadi* frogs stare at her out of their globulous eyes, so much like the glasses worn by strangers. No one in Shebika owns a gadget of this kind. When somebody can no longer see enough to go to the Mosque or the oasis, to know his way around the village or to make out the arrangement of the beds inside the house, then, even if he does have some sight left, he is 'blind'. There is nothing to do about it, because the condition bears this name, and has been accepted under it for generations. A fellow becomes 'the blind man', and around him there forms something like a hollow, just like that which is dug out by a stone in the river-bed, as it turns upon itself and continues to turn indefinitely. Because he is 'the blind man', someone takes him by the arm and guides him through the alleys leading to the grocery, and someone divides with him everything that is to be divided.

In the same way Rima is 'the orphan', the only one, for the moment, in Shebika, and very young. When the other girls were seven or eight years old they went out, under the protection of their brothers. Rima, having no brother, did not go out. Now the other girls talk about their eventual marriage. On this subject Rima has nothing to say. She does what she is allowed to do, and for the rest Iimra has told her to make offerings and vows to Sidi Sultan, who is the patron of women. Iimra has further told her that Sidi Sultan was, in reality, a woman, that she came from the mountains to the west, that her name had been changed years ago and she was not a 'sidi'.

Rima does what is expected of her and of all women. She sleeps in Iimra's house, grinds the wheat and puts together the ingredients of a couscous or a stew. She does not cook them completely, because only a married woman can put the finishing touches on a dish and bring it to her husband. But she washes clothes in the *wadi* and spreads them out on the rocks to dry.

The bucket has toppled over. Rima picks it up and starts up towards the village. Soon her feet are covered with dust. Above her, to the right, is the steep spur of the mountain, on which is built Shebika. The mountainside is honeycombed with caves, and in them live the donkeys which go to work down on the oasis. Above these are the stone blocks, reinforced with wire and iron staves, which the villagers put in place after Independence, with the co-operation of workers and other men from the city. At this time Rima and the other children chased the trucks, watched the boiling pots of food and ran all over the place. You can never tell what you are going to remember from your childhood and why. This memory, in any case, retained its vividness because of the bustle which the temporary 'construction job' brought to the village. When the workers went away, no one really believed it, and ever since they have been expected to return.

Rima comes up on to the square, lowers her head so that the men will not look at her, turns to the right, passes behind the portico where the water-clock is hanging, crosses the smaller square, where a donkey is always looking for some stray fodder, follows a narrow alley which winds upward between tumble-down walls with weatherbeaten palm-wood reinforcements, and finally pushes open the door of Iimra's house.

She goes first through a sort of shed, containing the tools used in the oasis, the donkey's harness and a loom, no longer in use because the price of wool is so high. Beyond, in the courtyard, five or six women are sitting on the dusty ground, among the pecking chickens. In the group are two women who are obviously outsiders. They wear, not the *haïk*, a black or purplish veil, but dresses. One of them has blonde hair such as could never be obtained from a henna dye. At this particular moment the women are all talking about her blondeness. How does nature come to create this colour?

Rima sets down her bucket and sits with the others, in this courtyard that separates the tool-shed from the main part of the house.* She too pulls the blonde hair of the foreign woman, and laughs when the hair doesn't come out. The woman who is with the blonde talks Arabic, but she cannot be recognized at first glance as a Tunisian. She calls them 'sisters', but it is hard to believe that she is a fellow-countrywoman. From time to time she jots something down in a notebook. She has come, she says, to get acquainted with the life of the people of Shebika and to talk about it in the city. She picks up the familiar household objects, which they have all known since they were children, and asks their names. As she does so the women pat and press her belly to see if she has had a child (as a girl her age should). But she pays no attention, continuing to examine the various objects as if they were precious things. How strange that they should astound her when they are so necessary for everyday living and she is supposedly a Tunisian!

Of course any woman who listens to the radio (Iimra's husband has bought one and wrapped it in a piece of violet cloth with pompoms) knows that the women of Tunis and Sfax ride in private cars or public buses and that when they work in an office or a factory they don't wear veils. After all, Bedouin women don't wear veils, either; even in Shebika they are not always worn, and a tattooing may replace them. An unmarried girl doesn't show her face, or tries to make it appear that she is not showing it. Veils are fundamentally for rich city women who walk out on the streets. Even in Tawzar, where she has been twice, Rima has never seen a white city-style veil. The fact

* 'We soon noticed,' reported both Naïma and her French companion, 'a girl called Rima, who made frequent visits to Sidi Sultan and lived in the house of the awlad Imami. She was an orphan, who worked like the others but did not really share their life. This was doubtless because she was not related to anyone in the village.'

that the women of Tunis don't wear veils doesn't surprise her. What is more remarkable is that they should drive about in cars or go to see a moving-picture.

Once upon a time a moving-picture was shown at Shebika. Some doctors came with a truck and attached a big rectangle of white cloth to the wall of the Mosque. Then they waited until night, so that the picture would show up clearly. Many men of the village had seen a moving-picture, but none of the women. And so it was explained that in the city there are houses which contain nothing but chairs and a big white screen. The women listened. They are quite willing to admit and understand anything. For years now they have known that anything is possible and that, with sufficient explanation, anything can be understood. At nightfall they all went to see the big, animated figures on the white cloth and to hear a loud voice explain how to combat diseases of the eye by keeping away flies and by taking drops. The picture didn't last very long. The following night everybody hoped there would be a sequel. But the doctors had packed everything on to the truck and driven the truck away into the darkness.

Yes, moving-pictures are not difficult to understand. But there are other things in the city. While the other women are touching – much to her amusement – the European woman's belly, to see if she will have children, Rima questions Naïma. Naïma says that city life is hard, and you have to work, even when you don't feel like it. Above all, you can't ever be late; time is time. Rima wants to know everything about the life of a city woman and how she spends her day. Naïma tells her that a city woman works in a different way from that of the woman of Shebika. She cooks or washes for rich people and manages to put together a little money. Do the women see one another? Can they go where they want to? Naïma says that, if they have money, they can go shopping and even without it they can go to look at things in the shop windows.

When the women have finished patting the European's hair and belly they make tea, and then go to collect some eggs to offer the visitors as a present. They offer eggs, because a chicken is a woman's personal property and eggs go into all her cooking.

Meanwhile Naïma and her companion photograph and draw an enormous stone, which has always been there and serves to press oil from the olives. They have given candies to the children and asked what use is made out of the plates attached to the palm-wood pillar. Flies cluster around the visitors as they do around their jeep. They seem to prefer them to the village women, perhaps because they are attracted by their perfume.

When the city women stand up and walk, they take long steps, without swinging either their hips or their shoulders. It seems as if their bones were glued together, and they could never balance a pitcher on top of their heads. Whether it is necessary or not, they are always on the go. They talk very fast between themselves, and in Arabic as well as in French, when the young Tunisian speaks to her 'sisters'.

Naïma and her European colleague, whom the village women call 'Christ', will soon be going away.* Tomorrow morning Rima will go down to fetch water and to wash the linen, of which she is in charge, then return to the courtyard to feed the chickens and wash the dishes in which Iimra prepares the men's food. In the afternoon she sits, cross-legged, in the courtyard watching over the small children, who crawl in the ashes around the fire, knock pots and pans against the stones, whine and generally make a racket. The members of the family roll up in a blanket or stretch out in the shade to rest, but it is understood that Rima will stay awake and take care of the children.

Calm, so thick you could cut it with a knife, descends upon Shebika. Even the chickens stop cackling and running aimlessly about; they squat in the ashes, turning their tiny snakelike heads from side to side. Rima waits, but nothing ever happens. Her role is to be an orphan just as the role of the blind man is to be blind. She hopes that a man, who is also an orphan, will come to take her away. But all the men belong

*'Rima is a pretty but nervous young girl,' Naïma told us. 'Her condition of orphan excludes her from everything that goes on at Shebika : weddings and other celebrations, where she always occupies the lowest place. She seems to feel that she is being treated unjustly.'

to families, and the cousins always intermarry. She is nobody's cousin; the surviving members of her family went to work in the mines or somewhere even farther away and there is no news of them. Of course an isolated single man might arrive in the village, but the place is so poor that this is unlikely. And why should he take an interest in her, when she is the poorest of the poor and has no connexions? All day long, just like other girls, for that matter, she dreams of these things.

But something did happen during the afternoon siesta some months ago. Iimra's son goes to the school, down near the cemetery. Usually he spends the afternoon with the other children, lying on his belly with his books in a bag beside him. But on this particular day he showed the books to Rima and taught her to recognize the signs that serve for reading. She was surprised that the boy of the family should speak to her for any purpose except to give orders. Later she learned that school was not a privilege but an obligation and that the children were told they should try to teach reading and writing to those around them. (Actually only little Bashir had ever carried out such an idea.)

Reading was something that didn't fit in at all with her everyday activities. Who, in Shebika, knew how to read, and what good would it do? Only school-children. . . . Reading belongs to another world, which none of the living will ever see, a world of the distant future. Ridha, the grocer, needs to read and write in order to keep his accounts, one or two older men learned to read when they were in the French army, and the National Guards, of course, were taught in the city. Reading and writing are typically city activities. In the country communication is simpler and more rapid. A tattooing, a gesture of the hand, a roll of the hip, and everything is understood. School, in short, leads to everything that is not Shebika.

Gradually Rima learned the signs. She pored, in secret, over Bashir's school-books and, with some slight help from him, she mastered them. She learned to read whole sentences and to count with numbers. Rima was the only woman in the village to possess this knowledge. But what, beyond the books that Bashir brought home from school, was she to read? The newspaper? She would have had to penetrate a place reserved for men, like the grocery, and then everyone would have asked her what she wanted with it. She did obtain some fragments of newspaper that had served to wrap a package of sugar or tea and read them in hiding. Little Bashir didn't tell on her. Perhaps he doubted that she really knew how.

From Bashir's books she learned that Tunisia is a country, but that it hadn't always been the same as it is today. This she could never have imagined, since she thought that to be related to someone from El Hamma or Redayif was all that one could hope to be. She learned, also, that the people from whom she was descended had come, centuries ago, in caravans from the East, and that since this time daily prayers, accompanied by prostration, were made in this direction. That there were other believers, called Turks, and unbelievers, called infidels. But all this made for a certain confusion. Later on in the book she read, not without difficulty, that the *raïs*, President Bourguiba, whom here they called Habib, wanted to change Tunisia. She didn't know what this meant except having money, being able to go 'shopping' without anyone's permission and driving about in a car.

Si Habib had spoken of 'becoming a country as modern as any other'. There Rima was stuck and could not go any further. She knew something of the nature of a city, since she had been to Tawzar and imagined Tunis as the same thing, only larger. But the houses at Tawzar were low, and in larger cities people were said to live several storeys above the ground. This, too, she could vaguely imagine. But other countries, what and where were they?

Rima carries the *haïks* to be washed in a bag woven by Iimra. She dips them in the water and rubs them hard to get off the spots, which actually never stay in the material. Other women kneel down to wash beside her and she hears their gossip. The grocer has bought a new donkey and gone to fetch oil and sugar from Tawzar. The wife of Qaddur, the assistant custodian of Sidi Sultan, tells how a Bedouin who came to make an offering at the shrine had to be fed by her husband and herself for two days. His wife is sterile, and he had come once before to ask

Sidi Sultan for a son. Qaddur told him to come back another time, with his wife. What can Sidi Sultan do at a distance, especially for a woman?

Another woman speaks of the strangers who are now making regular visits to Shebika. The girl from Tunis must be unhappy to be alone with foreigners and to travel in a jeep with so many men. To leave one's own and make a long journey, that's a real hardship. And just to see the people of Shebika! . . . The countryside, that's understandable, but the people? This couldn't be the real reason. They must be recruiting for a road-building or other project and questioning families to find out the number of their children. Another woman thinks that people simply like Shebika and that more and more of them will be coming there. They'll open cafés, like those at Tawzar, and tourists will follow. Hasn't the radio said that more and more foreigners are coming to admire the country and to present their respects to the *raïs* Habib? Everywhere in the world Tunis is admired, so the radio tells them. The radio says also that everyone must be agreeable to the visitors and let them go where they wish without being disturbed. Everyone can understand that this is advantageous. And the woman goes on to say that Shebika could profit from tourist money.

Another woman voices the opinion that the group of foreigners and Tunisians who have come in the jeep heard about Shebika in Tunis and conceived a spontaneous desire to know its people. Just the way one goes to visit relatives whom one has not seen for some time, simply in order to find out how they have been doing.

Rima never talks while she is washing. She listens to the other women talk about what has happened at their houses or down in the oasis. It would take a really important bit of news to extend their interest to the city or even the desert. Only the men speak of these.

And what could Rima say? What weight would the words of an orphan carry? For words to command attention they must have a certain authority behind them. When Murad, Iimra's husband, speaks, everyone listens, even if he talks unintelligibly about the boundaries between one parcel of land

and another. He speaks very slowly; the words seem to roll about in his mouth like pieces of candy. Iimra, on the contrary, when her husband's absence emboldens her to open her mouth, issues rapid-fire commands to do things that must not be forgotten. But what words could Rima draw upon? In the first place, there are many people to whom she is not entitled to speak: men, of course, in general, and then certain women of families other than that with which she lives. Except when they are all together, doing their washing, and even then a young girl cannot speak unless she is spoken to, unless she is encouraged to join the joking about the state of the grocer's wife's pregnancy and the stratagems of Nawa.

Only little Bashir's school-books have altered her perspective. She knows now that there exist, somewhere, conditions different from what they are here, where one can do things that here are forbidden or else simply inconceivable. In her dreams she has distinctly pronounced the words *Dar el Islam*, the 'House of Islam', which, according to the book, designate, or used to designate, the whole area defended against the Infidels by a series of coast-line fortresses. The word *muraabiteen*, meaning the knightly monks, who lived and fought in these fortresses, equally intrigues her, for the written word is far more fascinating than the spoken one. Around these words, when she is half-asleep, there is a vague light and then a big white building with a domed roof. She imagines herself walking the length of this building. In her dreams she has more than once made this walk; she has an idea, now, what it is to walk in the city, to pass an unending succession of houses, with no country in between, and to wear shoes, like a man.

Other words are more difficult. But she returns, over and over, to the white-domed building and to the knightly monks, whom she imagines to be like the National Guards, with their big pistols, but on horseback, or rather, since horses are commonplace on the desert, in great, shiny cars. The great, calm, white wall of the building, however, is the image which most often haunts her dreams, when she lies down to sleep on her mat, with the dog of the house snoring peacefully beside her.

The school-children do not only have books. They talk quite

freely, boys and girls together, and it is strange that, in so doing, they should transgress with impunity a long-established custom. They speak of Tunis as if they had been there, because their teacher has told them about it. And of other cities, even farther away.

Sometimes the grocer's eldest daughter comes to the house to help Bashir with his homework. The family keeps out of it, unable to understand what they are talking about. Soon enough the children return to their games, but meanwhile a whole area of life to which they and their teacher alone have access has come into being. The amazing thing is that boys and girls, when they talk together, have the same concerns, something out of the question between the grown men and women of Shebika. Sometimes the children seem faraway or superior; in any case very different from their parents. Rima can't think it out any further. At a certain point something closes down before her, like a door shutting off the light from a windowless room.

Thus a year went by. The succession of days and nights is barely perceptible; no event marks the transition from one day to the next. Every act entails the one that follows, and their repetition makes up the chain of events that are taken for granted and which, for this very reason, are not subject to discussion.

A few days before the feast-day of Sidi Sultan, which is celebrated in summer, after the harvest is in, the *wadi* was almost dry, and Rima went, with Leila, to the spring at the foot of the circle of mountains, where wild goats often come to play. In order to reach it they had to wade through an area of purplish clay mud, and as always, they took off their clothes and bathed in the basin. The water is warm, but where it is running it seems comparatively cool, and frogs are jumping all around. The two girls sprawl, with outspread arms and legs, in the water. Some of the village girls arrange for the young men whom they are pledged to marry to loiter somewhere near by.

After a few minutes they crawl out on their hands and knees, for if they stood upright they might slip on the slimy bottom. They shake themselves in the sun, wash their scarves and wait for their bodies to dry off, which they soon do, although there is a prickly coating of sticky mud on the skin. Then they put on their dresses, made of pieces of cloth rolled around them, giggle because they are spattered with mud and return to the village.

The celebration of Sidi Sultan's feast-day will have more to it this year because four Bedouin families from the plain are bringing sheep, which will be cooked and divided at the festive meal. They are said to be petitioning for children. The custodian of the tomb is said to have come up one evening from the White Spring and to have dropped in at Iimra's house. Rima did not see him because the women had gone to bed and he stayed in the courtyard with the men. In his harsh, monotonous voice he said Sidi Sultan couldn't accomplish the miracles he once did, because people no longer had the same faith in him. In any case he particularly favoured the petitions of women, when they brought him an offering. There had been a man, once, who insisted that Sidi Sultan was a woman, a queen from the West. This seemed remote and unlikely, but the statement was made by a venerable old man. Rima imagined that the custodian of the tomb must be very old too, judging by his sluggish speech and perpetual cough. His last word was: 'Perhaps Sidi Sultan will give children to those who ask for them, and perhaps he won't. There's no telling.'

The next day, over the washing, when there was mention of the feast-day, Rima suddenly raised her head and said:

'Perhaps Sidi Sultan will give children to those who ask for them, and perhaps he won't. There's no telling.'

Leila and Nawa shrugged their shoulders and the other women stared at her with astonishment. Never had a young girl been known to emit a judgement of this kind. An old woman – under certain conditions – was permitted to do so. But Rima was a mere orphan. They returned to their work, paying her no atten-tion.

The ceremony actually consists of a prayer and an offering. When the women have taken their place around the outer wall of the marabout they slap their mouths and go 'yoo-hoo-hoo' in a throaty way expressive of both joy and petition. Rima's place is behind them. On the other side, Qaddur slits the throats of the four sheep which have been consigned to him. The custodian is standing in a place where Rima cannot see him.

The blood of the sheep is quickly dried by the sun and absorbed into the ground. When the sheep are stretched out, side by side, Qaddur wipes the blade with which he has killed them on their white wool. Then he sits back during their prolonged death agony, the shudders and the more and more rapid gasping sounds which they emit until, at last, immobility takes over and flattens them out like a hand. By this time all the blood has run out of their bodies.

After this the women chant a prayer which Rima has heard every time she has been present at the celebration, even when there were no sheep to be divided. As they pray the women sway to and fro, and Rima feels obliged to join them, although she says to herself that there must be places where one can simply express one's desire to a marabout without so many goings-on. As for herself, she wishes for and expects nothing. It is this 'nothing' that blocks her thoughts and gives her a feeling of discomfort, as if there were a blood-clot in her head. But then she feels the same discomfort in the accomplishment of her daily tasks. Now, sitting back on her heels, she sways to and fro, with the other women, when once more they strike up their long chant.

Closer to the marabout proper, in the narrow open space circling it inside the wall, a couple of men are beating rhythmically on the skin of a rough terracotta drum in the shape of an hour-glass. The beats point up the contractions of the back and neck necessary to throwing the upper part of the body forward, or else just outlining the movement in an abbreviated form, tossing it, as it were, to the others and waiting for it to be returned. The women kneeling farthest from the marabout barely raise themselves from their heels, while those closer go through the motions more and more completely. One in the very front row rises to a half-standing position and sways back, twisting the upper part of her body and closing her eyes.

The smell of the meat, which is being cooked on the other side of the marabout, where the fire is protected from the desert wind, sweeps heavily, in intermittent gusts, over the intervening ground. Every year at this same time two or three unknown men, led by the custodian, emerge from the tomb, waving their arms. They are clad in white ghandurahs and each one carries a lighted candle. Going around the marabout they pass so close to the women as almost to trip over those in the front row. On the other side they start to chant, and then to go back to where they came from. They seem to be feeling their way, as if they were not sure what they really wanted to do; finally they form a line and move backwards, throwing back the upper part of their bodies at the same time, but always holding the candles upright. Rima can't say how long this goes on, but it is for some time. Soon the men's intentions become less and less clear; they seem to be turning in a circle on one spot. At this moment Rima has a feeling which has deepened from year to year and become so important that she speaks of it to one of our researchers. She is sure she has known and seen the whole ceremony, not a year but just a moment before; the whole 365 days in between are suddenly eclipsed in her imagination.

As long as she remains in the same position among the women, as they repeat some of the words of the men's chant, Rima is aware that nothing ever happens and that she might as well be one of the old crones swaying to and fro before her. She feels 'as dizzy as if she had fallen from the village into the *wadi*', although she is still just where she was before. But now she no longer wishes to remain, either among the swaying women or at Shebika, where she knows that nothing will ever happen, and that next year things will repeat themselves just as they have been repeated for years, long before she ever knelt in front of the marabout for a *zarda*, or celebration. Now, inevitably, she receives the usual piece of mutton, with sauce, and leans forward to eat it, in order not to dirty her dress. Around her other women are making the same chewing sound. But most of the meat is wrapped in old newspapers and carried home. As every year, Rima attributes to Sidi Sultan the inspiration of her idea that nothing ever changes at Shebika and that she must go away.*

When Rima said, in front of the other women, that she didn't want to stay in Shebika but wanted to go with us to

*'She seems to feel that hers is an unjust fate,' notes our researcher, 'that the Bedouin girls are much better off. Apparently her parents were employed in some capacity by the Bedouins, for she seems to be acquainted with their way of life. She asks for nothing; she only says that everything she sees now she has seen before, and that every celebration of the feast of Sidi Sultan strengthens this conviction. Because of this she now wants to leave the village. It must be noted that, with some help from the son of the house, who goes to school, she has learned to read. She has a remarkable intelligence and doubtless suffers from being unable to put it to use. She says that the ability to read has caused her to dream, and that everything that goes on at Shebika is like what she has dreamed during the night. She has, of course, listened to the radio and heard that people, especially women, live quite differently in the city. She says that the people of Shebika would never change their ways, not even if there were factories, as at Metlawi, that they consider their ways the only possible ones and refuse to envisage the future life of their children, even although they suppose that it will be very different from their own. She says also that the people of Shebika consider their life less good than that of their parents; they say the village isn't what it used to be, that there is great poverty and no real respect for God and the marabouts. Their parents held much more elaborate celebrations. We spoke to Rima both alone and with the other women. Alone, she told us that she hated Sidi Sultan, because he had never granted any of her wishes or in any way helped her. Of course she had offered him very little: some pieces of cloth and bits of bread, the offerings of the poor, which obviously he does not welcome. And then it was at the marabout that she first realized that everything repeats itself and she would never escape unless she went away. She wanted us to know that she could read, but that this would never do her any good if she stayed on here, among the women. She wanted to go to Tunis, but how could she? No one would take her; she had no money and she couldn't travel alone over the twenty miles or so of desert to even the nearest city. What would she do when she got there? Beg? She would need the protection of a man, an older brother, for instance, but she had no older brother ...'

Tunis and live like a city girl, they were very angry. They stuck their elbows into her sides, and this must have been painful, because they have very pointed bones. All together they shouted that such a thing was out of the question, that a girl like Rima couldn't leave Shebika, that she belonged to them and couldn't go away. To us they said, more quietly, that this would be an insult to the village which had given us such a friendly reception. We had no right to let her go with us; we were guests, and we couldn't take a woman away. Besides, everyone knew that Rima wasn't well and that she didn't know what she was saying or doing.

Rima crouched in a corner of the courtyard, while the women threatened to call the men. If we started to take Rima away, the men, particularly Iimra's brother, would halt our jeep, smash it and throw it in the ravine. Iimra had housed and fed the girl for years in order that she work for her until such time as she found a husband. She was ready to shave her head in order to prevent her from going away.* Moreover, if we tried to take her, bad luck would pursue us. The women would ask Sidi Sultan to punish us, and we should never get so far as even Tawzar. Rima would not escape, for Sidi Sultan had always granted the wishes of the women of Shebika. Then, in order further to dissuade us – in case we had made Rima any promise – they began to try more conciliatory methods, to offer us eggs and sweetmeats and to make music for our benefit. Rima remained immobile in one corner, with her face quite expressionless, like that of any sad or disappointed Bedouin woman. We did not look in her direction, lest we arouse the women's sus-

---

*Customs are far more complex than the law. In certain rich country families there are young Bedouin girls who have been 'rented' or 'bought' from their families and given food and lodging in exchange for domestic services. In a tacit contract of this kind it is understood that the girl will be free when she marries. And in order to discourage possible suitors and keep her as long as possible, the 'owners' may shave her head. (In Islamic countries, as in many Mediterranean lands, hair is a powerful erotic symbol.) Often, however, the master of the house keeps these little girls – half-slave, half-free – for his own personal use.

picions. She joined their singing, then laughed with them as if nothing had ever happened, as if it were all a joke. During the dancing she seemed perfectly gay and clapped her hands, in time, like the others.

Then, as Naïma tells it, at the end of this entertainment she went back to the car to give an account of what she had been doing. And we never saw Rima again.*

The White Spring

From the right-hand exit from the open space which extends from the lower part of the village down towards the desert, one can detect, in the distance, beyond three or four stony ravines, a mangy oasis, hardly more than a watering-hole. This is the so-called White Spring, the home of old Omar, the true custodian of the tomb and shrine of Sidi Sultan.

Since ascertaining his name we have heard frequent mention of him, but no one has been able to tell us exactly how he lives. It seems that, at some earlier time, he led a more brilliant existence, that he came often to the village and took part in offerings and festivities. The disappearance of the camel trains after the First World War, the settling down of the nomads, the closing of the Algerian frontier,† all these things have lessened

* A year and a half later, in 1964, we had some news of her. Everyone pretended to have forgotten who she was. Finally an old woman of the Qadduri family told us that she had been stung by a scorpion while washing clothes in the *wadi* and had been taken to Tawzar for medical attention. An old man told us, on the contrary, that she must have died after the bite, before anything could be done about it. This seems more likely. Other people – including Ridha, the grocer – say that she was ill for a long time and no one could save her, not even Sidi Sultan, to whom Iimra often addressed prayers on her behalf. The simplest conclusion is that she died, somewhere around 1964, before the celebration of the feast-day of Sidi Sultan, about whose ritual she was the only one to inform us.

† The end of the Algerian war did little to ease the rigidity of the boundary lines between the two Arab countries. Beyond the mines the frontier between the two 'sister' countries is often uncrossable. The fact that they are competing in the search for oil has caused them to stick to the boundaries staked out by the French colonizers.

the flow of travellers, particularly those making religious pilgrimages, in this part of Southern Tunisia. Now Omar is a *khammes* like any other, except that he lives apart.

Occasionally Omar comes by night to Shebika. Because he walks with difficulty, his feet make a noise as they drag over the pebbles of the narrow alleys and the square. No one knows where he goes or what he is after, although people imagine that he comes to get food from the grocer. He inspires a certain fear, and no one wants to run into him in the night. After we had finally identified him Si Tijani explained to us that Omar had the reputation of being a sorcerer and of harnessing the power of Sidi Sultan to his own ends. But none of the villagers openly subscribed to this explanation.

When we started out to the White Spring we found that it was a good deal farther away than we had thought. We had to go down into three ravines, filled with large masses of rock, and up again on the other side, around a cliff and across an area of stones which have fallen from the mountain and form the bed of a rushing stream that flows over them for a few hours every winter. The palm-grove of the oasis turned out to be bigger than we had expected. The foliage has been dulled and dirtied by the dust borne by the desert wind, which does not strike the oasis of Shebika in the same way, doubtless because of a different exposure. The trees are widely spaced, and the fertile area is narrow and not well shaded. There is also a smell of rot, due to the fact that the heat has sucked up the muddy water too fast.

The custodian of the tomb is there, sitting on a stone in the middle of his field and watching us approach him. He knew perfectly well that we were coming and why. Beside him there crouches a young boy whom we have seen hanging around Shebika. Doubtless this boy serves as his messenger and spy. Omar is not as old as we had been led to expect; he is simply worn. His role is that of an old man and it has been imposed upon him. He must be about sixty years old, and there is an openly hostile look in his eyes. Salah is the first to go up to him, with Khalil following later.

Omar says to Salah that he 'works like everyone else and knows little of what is going on'. He looks mistrustfully at the

Europeans of our group, but is reassured when he learns that they really come from Europe. Actually he fears more his fellow-countrymen from Tunis who are wearing European dress. While we wait, a short distance away, and a rising wind blows even more dust on to the palm-trees, Salah attempts to overcome Omar's ill-humour. They sit down, leaning against a cluster of young date-palms, with their backs to the wind, and indulge in some theological considerations. That is, Salah has to listen to a harshly and aggressively pronounced lesson.

'There are four things,' says Omar, 'that separate us from God and lead us to hell. These are : "I am and we are; I possess and we possess." I have no right to say "I'm hungry" or "I'm not hungry"; "My father was such and such" or "My grandfather was such and such". Man possesses nothing; everything belongs to God, and he succours us in both wealth and poverty.'

'The men of Shebika used to own land. Now they own it no longer. Is their life better or worse than it was before?'

'The people of olden times had more patience than those of today. They didn't sell their land, even if they were reduced to eating desert grass. Neither palm-trees nor goats did they sell, under any conditions whatsoever. The nomads were very patient.'

'If someone goes two evenings without his dinner, won't his relatives help him?'

'Nobody helps anybody any more. There's no trust. God has said that if three or four people come together and discuss things in a spirit of honesty, God is with them, but if it's to lie and deceive one another, they are blinded by Satan. The man of today changes character several times a day. There's no truth, no trust. God assures our sustenance and we worship Him. He has said : "I created man; worship me." We aren't immortal. God distributes life and death as He wills.'

'You say that nowadays there's no trust?'

'Yes. Among a thousand persons only one is trustworthy. Once, when a man wasn't worthy of trust people avoided him. How can things go, when out of twenty people it's hard to find one that's any good? Things can't go well this way.'

'And what do you say of the youth of today?'

'One day the Prophet Muhammad was sitting with his cousin Ali. The Prophet said to Ali: "Come with me to visit my little daughter." And Ali answered: "Never mind about her, cousin." Then Muhammad said: "You're wrong, Ali. God helps the man who helps his own family; when a man doesn't help his own family God doesn't bother about him.'

'What do you mean?'

'That there's no more truth, no more trust.'

'Particularly among the young, isn't it so?'

'It's a sign of the times in which we live; among old and young it's the same.'

'You mean that not only is there no more trust, but also that men no longer give thanks to God?'

'Exactly. There used not to be so much importance attached to money. People had patience. They endured everything and thanked God, both for wealth and poverty, because they knew that He was all-powerful.'

There is a silence. Omar turns around and asks about the rest of our group. Salah assures him that we are neither policemen nor tax-collectors nor government employees of any kind. We only want to find out about and help Shebika. Then he goes on to tell him about his own birthplace and parents.

'Once upon a time,' says Omar, 'there were men who travelled from place to place in order to learn and to enrich the knowledge which God had given them. We received them gladly.'

'We're not just like them, but you can treat us the same way. We too are interested in everything that is done in God's name.'

'But you,' said Omar, 'you don't have the faith of your forefathers. You've turned away from God.'

'I want to know about Sidi Sultan, the holy spot of the village.'

'There's nothing to know about Sidi Sultan. No one understands Sidi Sultan nowadays, and I even doubt that there's anything in the tomb. Once upon a time, yes, Sidi Sultan was the heart of the village. Now it's nothing, nothing, I tell you, just words ...'

Salah lets some time go by. Omar coughs, asks for a cigarette, lights it, but remains silent. Then he repeats that the village has no *halq*, no core or kernel or pole or centre. Salah continues to sound him out:

'We've asked everywhere for the true story of Sidi Sultan but no one has been able to tell it to us.'

'Sidi Sultan came from Saqiyet El Hamra; he was a descendant of Al Hassan and Al Hussein [both of them descendants of the Prophet]. He died here on his way back from Mecca, and a paper was found upon him.'

'What was written on the paper?'

'I can't tell you. My grandfather died at the age of eighty and my father at the age of eighty-six, I myself am sixty-four, but neither they nor I know anything about Sidi Sultan, even if we are the custodians of his tomb. I've heard it told, but I don't know it at first hand, that just before he died Sidi Sultan asked that his body be loaded on the back of his camel and said: "Wherever the camel kneels down, there you're to bury me." The camel knelt down at the site of the tomb, and water spurted out of the ground, so that the site was named *Ain el Naqa* [Camel Spring]. They say that Sidi Sultan did good deeds. Visitors come to see him, and sometimes they bring invalids who bathe in the water and are cured.'

'There are real cures?'

'Yes. And then some people ask that their sons not be taken for military service and things like that. There you have all that's known about Sidi Sultan. Oh yes, now I remember another of his miracles. Every year there's a *zarda* in his honour. Once my father brought him a castrated billy-goat, and all of a sudden the goat ran away and couldn't be caught. That's why they say that Sidi Sultan won't accept a castrated animal and people bring him only male sheep. They say – but I wasn't here to see – that he did all sorts of good things, that he was very devout. Fate brought him here, and here he was buried. We don't know whether he came alone or with his family, because none of us ever knew him personally, not even my uncle Ibrahim, the oldest man of Shebika, Ibrahim Al Qadduri.'

'And who's actually in charge of Sidi Sultan?'

'I am.'

'And before you?'

'My father, and before him my grandfather.'

Salah knows that truth is elusive, above all in men's memory, and that at Shebika they don't like to talk about a certain glorious period of the past. Sidi Sultan may have lived at a time of power or of war some hundred and fifty years ago, when the South had a life of its own, based on the circulation of camel-trains. But after Omar's story he has to admit that the *halq*, the hard core or kernel which he hoped to discover in Sidi Sultan, has no real significance, at least today.

When we think more about it we realize that the figure of the holy man fades away before the word which designates Him. *Sidi* means lord or master; *Sultan* comes from the word *sulta*, which means domination or power; in this case it is 'He who can', He who has the power to answer prayers. This title has more importance than his personality or even his identity; there is no use searching for an historical character – a war leader of times gone by or a rebel against the French – such as Salah hoped to find. Just as the name of another holy man of the Jerid, Sidi Shabaan, means 'the lord who is satiated', an adjective which has an almost mystical value in a country where hunger is endemic and permanent, so the name of Sidi Sultan refers to a power which, if they follow certain rules, the villagers can appropriate for their own use. Of course the religion of Islam is remote from these magic practices, but it cannot completely dismiss them. Often, as is the case at Shebika, they are mingled. The attendants of the Mosque and of Sidi Sultan form a sort of alliance.

The name of Sultan is not unlike that which Marcel Mauss borrows from the language of the Melanesians to designate that category of the collective consciousness – power and value – which constitutes a background and a definite action known as *mana*. If it is true, as Marcel Mauss says, that 'in magic, as in religion and linguistics, unconscious ideas are those that lead somewhere',* then the designation of this collective power, in a pure state, personalized in a symbolic character whose content

*Outline of a theory of magic in *Sociologie et anthropologie* (Paris : Presses Universitaires de France, 1950 and 1966), p. 109.

is as thin as that of the other marabouts, satisfies the common will to classify things and to use a social substance to regulate relationships among men.

In these regions, where what we call history is known only through the tendentious accounts given by the radio, the impact of events which affect national groups and nations is deposited like layers of sediment in the collective consciousness or the implicit imagery of the life of the village. Jacques Berque has frequently noted how, during the phase of colonization, the life of the Maghrib, at every level, contracted and fell back upon its basis. The pages which he devoted to this contraction in his book *Le Maghreb entre deux guerres* * are particularly striking inasmuch as they fit the reality of today, such as it may be dis·covered by any administrator educated to Western technical values and the principles of modern government. In reaction to the new politicians' efforts to involve even the remotest sections of the country in its economic, administrative and psychological transformation, the single village and family often fall back and turn inward on themselves. Hence the bewilderment of many a local administrator who, like his European predecessors, is forced to rely on 'personal action', not to mention coercion. During our five-year study we saw many examples of this predicament at Shebika and in the Jerid.

There are conclusions to be drawn. The custodian of the tomb said angrily that nothing was left of the past, that no one remembers it, not even the elders of the village, not even himself. But what are the famous 'traditions' so often brought up as an excuse or a justification? 'Sidi Sultan no longer amounts to much because we amount to nothing,' Omar rightly told us. What, then, is Sidi Sultan? A vague magic power, occupying a certain place amid a life that monotonously and despairingly repeats itself, leaving no room for any revolt. Going away (for a man, since we have seen in Rima's case that it is impossible for a woman) simply means exchanging the poverty of Shebika for the poverty of the tumbledown outskirts of Qafsa or Tunis. Independence and foreign economic aid can, no more than did

---

* Chapter I, Part one, *'Dispute pour les bases'*.

colonial rule, make for an immediate new way of living, especially for men and women over thirty. Even on the other side of the frontier, where the oil-wells are, the life of the village people has not changed. They have simply moved to the outskirts of the big cities or to other villages. Only a very few of them have found 'jobs'. *

But their situation does not hinge upon tradition. Just as Sidi Sultan was the heart of Shebika only insofar as the village itself existed as a living entity and, when this ceased to be so, survived only in hazy descriptions, so, ten years after Independence, tradition is dying out all over the Maghrib. Even the term itself, with which administrators constantly justify the slowness of progress or the impossibility of its achievement, may be called into question, for when we search for its concrete implications we cannot put our finger on them. If the cult of Sidi Sultan still really existed, if the efficacy implied by its survival had a genuine basis, then we might justify both the actuality of the constant, inscribed as a filigree over a succession of generations, which we call tradition, and the importance of the theocratic or sacred element of which P. Massignon speaks in relation to Islamic society. But Omar said, quite violently, to Salah : 'Nothing's left, nothing. When people come we let them make an offering. Why not? But Sidi Sultan no longer answers their prayers. The old ways are gone; the bonds are loosened. We go through the motions, but what of it?' And he added, with real anger : 'The radio has killed everything.'

The radio, yes; we shall be returning to it later. But, above all, the successive arbitrary and disorganized administrations of the Beys, the French and the present-day government, which claims that everything has changed, when it has not yet laid the groundwork for change. Of that which may have been a refuge during the period of foreign occupation there remains only the outward shell, and nothing to justify its existence.

Why, then, speak of tradition? Human societies, at whatever stage they may be, are dominated not by history or tradition

*Like the awlad Nail, of whom Émile Dermenghem has given such a striking description in the chapter *Les Filles de la douceur* in his book *Le pays d'Abel* (Paris : Gallimard, 1960).

but by the internal structure of backgrounds, by the moving shape which momentarily constitutes their existence. If we admit that *diachronic* elements designate a law of distribution of facts and their cause in the succession at a single tempo equivalent to the philosophers' 'becoming', and that *synchronic* elements define the actual constitution of all the aspects making up a structure, then we must conclude that the living reality of a narrow group such as that of Shebika depends less on the existence of diachronic elements than on its actual synchronic composition. The word 'tradition' loses all significance, because it does not designate the real existence of a constant or of an active deterministic action of the past on the present, but only the contemporary traces, reveries, and beliefs shared by a few people in a group of which they are only the momentary and diversely accentuated components.

The collective reality of Shebika is a poor thing, but, miserable and deteriorated as it may be, it is the framework of community life. The combination of all the present-day factors – family, work, hope, expectation, magic, religion – rules over everything pertaining to both the conscious and the unconscious, including the factors of the past. As far as tradition goes, we can speak of it only in reference to the de-structurization of all the forms which were more or less solidly established when the Maghrib received the impact of a foreign conqueror's culture. Fragile and deteriorated structures are giving way, and men can find no support on which to lean in a tradition made up only of words that have lost their meaning.

4

THE CONFRONTATION

Shebika in the South : the South in Shebika

The South? Yes, a ruin. Ever since the eleventh-century invasion by the Hilali, who cut down the trees and destroyed the wells, the South has had poverty for a second nature. Nine centuries of gradual decline and surrender to the nomads, who, amid a growing 'Saharization', have tried to construct, in small units, a mediocre culture. The period of French colonization wrought few changes. The iron and phosphate mines did not benefit the natives; the railroad brought only a few tourists; the army a few buyers. Shebika is the typical example of a community which, over and above persistent catastrophe, in spite of the traditions which only accentuate its decay, gives proof of a will to live of which no one so far has made use.

In 1956 the newly independent government of Tunisia tried 'to do something for the South'. In imitation of Italy's *Cassa del Mezzogiorno* there was set up a 'Central and South Tunisian Bank', an institution which existed only on paper.* But it was publicized over the radio, and the people of Shebika learned that a movement to help them was under way. And, in a language which makes little distinction between reality and wishful thinking, intention and action were easily confounded.

'It's like the train,' says old Ahmad.

'What train?'

'The train of the Frankawi, which started coming all the way to Tawzar. We went to have a look at it and to see what would happen.'

'Well, what did happen?'

'Nothing. Men change, but God doesn't change. The way of

* The Banque du Sud was in fact set up in October 1968 to aid development in Southern Tunisia. (Ed.)

God is the straight way, and we are bidden to obey the master of the world.'

'But God allows change.'

'Yes, but men don't allow it.'

During the early years of Independence a sort of fever ran through Southern Tunisia. Salah Bin Yussif, Bourguiba's Southern collaborator, had not yet broken with the idea of 'local internal autonomy'. When he spoke over the radio everyone in the South recognized his voice. But in the long run he did nothing.

'He turned out to be just like the others,' says old Ahmad. 'He spoke from the city and in the city he got into a quarrel. He was just like all the rest.'

At this same time the new young leaders were beginning to realize that there was no solution to the problems of the South in mere paperwork administration, and international experts bore out their views. It was possible to improve the condition of the villages of the central steppe, of the Sahil, of Cape Bon and of the rural centres such as Medjerda and Enfida, but the problems of the South were insurmountable. In the first place, there was no over-all study of the region, only abstract charts and statistics and a few pages in geography textbooks.

A good deal later, in 1965, it was decided to face up to the problem by joining Qafsa, Medeneen, Sfax and Qabes into a single unit of economic development. We shall omit the extreme South – Burj Bourguiba – a military region, where oil-wells are now gushing, and concern ourselves with the region of particular interest, on which the first serious economic studies date from 1962. These studies, let us note, do not take into account the social framework and the real human potential of the region. At this point, after much stumbling, the government has set up a scheduled plan for the solution of the most urgent problems. Within ten years Shebika should achieve a certain balance, that is if the government has and invests the necessary money, something of which there can be no guarantee.

The most urgent need, obviously, is for water. The annual rainfall of 5.87 inches in the Shirb, 3.55 in the Jerid and 3.9 in the

Nefzaona, allows for no regularity in the harvests; only about one in every five is comparatively successful. There is water everywhere underground, but wells – deep wells – have to be driven and better use made of the existing springs. On this score Shebika is fairly well off, with its spring and its man-made irrigation ditches. The position of the village is such that it receives most of the summer storms, although there is no reservoir in which to gather the water. With a limited amount of effort the land beyond the oasis, now cultivated by the Bedouins, could be made regularly and remarkably fertile.

The poverty of the soil is a more serious question. All through the South the clayey earth (*dab-dab*, as the nomads call it) forms a crust which is easily eroded by the wind. The oases are, of course, more productive, but there is a lack of fertilizers with which to make up for the age-long overworking of the land. Shebika is aware of this need and demands its satisfaction. Everyone knows that fertilizers are the key to greater productivity.

'The most serious problem,' one of the administrators of the Plan told us, 'is the human one, as represented by malnutrition, obedience to ridiculous and outmoded customs and the young people's tendency to sell off arable land and go off to seek their fortune in the North. The newly irrigated areas – of which there are many – do not attract enough nomads or inhabitants of ruined villages. If we complete the projected dams: that of the Jir Wadi near Qabes and that of Sidi Reesh near Qafsa, which should irrigate five thousand acres, if we successfully carry out our *jussur* project of channelling the natural streams, then we shall have opened up new areas to agriculture. But who will make use of them if the local people can't adjust to new ways of living?'

There are expectations, also, of the improvement of five million acres of pasture land, of which one half is actually good. Here there are presently 800,000 goats and sheep and 300,000 camels, but these figures could be easily tripled, if care were taken not to crowd too many animals into one sector, where they quickly exhaust the flora, and to provide watering-places.

This improvement would give an even tenor of life to the whole region.

In this sector, too, Shebika is ready to accept change, if it is prepared in an orderly fashion. And the nomads could quickly organize systematic exchanges which would allow for a more rational utilization of the pastures at the foot of the mountains and along the lost *wadis*.

A transformation of the oases is something more difficult to imagine in view of present conditions of land-ownership, the sub-division of lots or parcels and the fact that some of them have more than one owner, as we have seen at Shebika. But the creation of a new, geometrically planted oasis as an extension of the orchard of today, is a project which the men gathered round the *qaddus* are willing to envisage.

'We've been promised a new oasis.'

'Planted with new trees, one here, one there, like dancers. The trees wouldn't choke each other off, and there'd be enough shade in which to plant peppers.'

'Where would it be set up?'

'Down there, beyond the road leading up to the village, at the bottom of the ravine. And then in the other direction, near the house of the custodian of Sidi Sultan. Water can be brought there; all that is needed is digging.'

'All of us must work in the new oasis, while holding on to the parcels of land we hold already.'

'There'd be no more need to divide the water. It would flow for the benefit of everybody. At this point the irrigation ditches are all destroyed. When the water from the spring was channelled, the ditches in the oasis were not reinforced. Water flowed faster into the oasis, and the ditches were damaged.'

'And then new palm-trees have to be planted. There are no *digla* (date-palms) with soft fruit, such as is saleable abroad. Our produce is all of an inferior quality.'

The transformation of the oases was begun, without fanfare, in 1965, in such important localities at Qafsa and Qabes. But there is as yet no sign of it at Dakash, Naftaani, Tawzar, or, quite naturally, at Shebika. The farmers, grouped together in co-operatives, have made joint purchases of water and agricultural implements. But there is as yet no cooperative for production, and this may be the weak link in the system. There may have to be large-scale elimination of the presently over-crowded trees. The ideal figure is fifty trees per acre, and now there are around 300, because each succeeding generation, for motives of prestige, has increased their number. And no land-owner can be expected to give up over two-thirds of his trees without compensation. The cost to the government of transforming the oases has been calculated at 1,200,000 dinars for every thousand acres.

'We belong to the Jerid. If they do something for the Jerid, we'll be glad to join in,' says Ali.

'Instead of going to work in the city, we'll get rich here, if it's God's will.'

'Rich you'll never be!' says old Qaddur. 'You can't be rich, and neither can any of the rest of us.'

'Who knows? Only Allah. If the government wants to help us, we can enlarge the oasis.'

'Then there'll be taxes, and all that goes with them.'

'We belong to the Jerid. If they help the Jerid, we're sure to be included.'

The government is interested in the South. The unfortunate thing is that it does not have enough men and women trained to counsel the people during the difficult phase of transition. This is a fact which we have constantly called to the attention of official circles. *Unless young Tunisian university graduates go into the villages and oases of the South for a period of one to two years in order to help the inhabitants to adapt themselves to new social conditions, then the changes now under way will have no meaning.* Administrators alone are unable to cope with the situation. Eventually they will have to resort to coercion, and thus to undo from a social point of view what they are striving to accomplish from an economic one. The truth is that, after four years of on-the-spot study, our group of young Tunisian sociologists lost the typically optimistic self-assurance which it had picked up from the ruling class in the capital city and realized what a gap there is between a political programme and a social reality.

The Effect of the Investigation upon the Investigator

During the third year of our study of Shebika, at midnight of
one of the nights which we always spent at Tawzar before going
on, the next morning, to our destination, Naïma, the most gifted
of our women researchers, had an attack of nerves. A doctor
was called, but by this time she was calm, and we stayed with
her for the sake of giving her reassurance.

'You must realize that here is a girl who had never before left
her sisters. This expedition is something entirely new for her.
Every time that she wants to come with us she has a real fight
with her parents. Her father has a fairly important government
job, and her mother is kind and understanding. They're ready to
do anything to "open her eyes", as they put it, that is, to make
her into a modern young woman. In fact, they plan to send her,
alone, to Paris, so that she'll get to know Europe and finish her
schooling under the best possible conditions. Because they come
from the Sahil they're more up-to-date than the rest of their
countrymen.'

This last statement is a hard fact. The Sahil, the region between Susa and Sfax, is the birthplace of two-thirds of the
leaders of modern Tunisia. Here the same trade is practised by
one generation after another; for a thousand years the men have
been craftsmen, weavers (in Muqneen and Qasr Hilal), fishermen
(at Mahidiya), small farmers (reminiscent of those of Attica).
The Sahilians (to whom we must add the inhabitants of the
Karkinnah Islands, birthplace of Farhaat Hashid, the trade-union
leader assassinated by terrorists before the achievement of
Independence) are born hard workers and administrators. Unlike the middle-class city-dwellers and the Bedouins, with their
sparse notions of time and space, they have all the virtues of
stability and continuity, derived from regular work, and some
notions, however summary, of the value of money. As Jacques
Berque has so intuitively put it, the independence of Tunisia is
'the fruit of the olive tree', the tree proper to the Sahil region.
It was at Qasr Hilal, on a wintry day of the month of Ramadan
in 1934, that Bourguiba, then a young lawyer from Monastir,

founded the Neo Destour. It was the Sahil that provided the most stable, even if not the most heroic, fighters for Independence, rather than Tunis, where the middle class was torn between integration with France and a violent revolution without any long-range political strategy. Again, it was with the support of the Sahil that, during an 'historical' congress, Bourguiba overcame his chief opponent, Salah Bin Yussif, the Southern Muslim who admired Nasser and predicated Independence upon hostility to Europe and a return to traditional values which, in all probability, existed only in his religiously inflamed imagination. And in today's government men of the Sahil – the sons of craftsmen, fishermen and small farmers – quite naturally hold the first place and just as naturally oppose the Bedouins – the steppe- and village-dwellers – who appear on the scene after the battle is won, applaud the victory, but are not organized in such a way as to benefit from it.

Naïma's father is a Sahilian, a veteran of the fight for Independence. He wants his daughter to live the life of a modern woman, but our expeditions to the South worry him.

'At the beginning,' one of Naïma's friends tells me, 'he was impressed and pleased by his daughter's interest in the country and the South in particular, which neither he nor most of his colleagues know at first hand. Later, when she told him that the people of the South mustn't be left in a state of abandonment, that volunteers were needed to live with them and see them through their difficulties, he became uneasy. We were making a big mistake, all of us, in his opinion, by attaching ourselves to this "scorpions' nest" of which his daughter spoke so eloquently. He wasn't against what we were doing, but, as a sophisticated city-dweller, he felt that his daughter's future lay elsewhere than in the lost wastes of the South, which had contributed so little to the achievement of Independence. Hence there were tensions within the family, which came to a head every time that we went down to Shebika. Nothing overt, of course, but an atmosphere which made Naïma nervous, perhaps because of the special relationship which exists in our cities between a father and his eldest daughter. Because she felt the weight of her father's disapproval of her new scientific vocation she was upset and at odds with herself. Her brief crisis, aggravated by the panic of her masculine companions, who were unused to any demonstration of emotion on the part of a young girl, was the direct result of this interior discomfort. Never again were there signs of anything wrong. Shebika had made its mark upon her, but she was quick to regain and retain her calm.'

Now Naïma is relaxed and smiling. She is listening attentively to a friend of Salah, as he sings a Bedouin song, accompanying himself on a tambourine. The contact which she and her contemporaries have made with the mainstream of life has aroused in them emotions which their mothers never knew, although Naïma's mother did advanced studies and works as a schoolteacher. Her encounter with the South and Shebika has taught her that her generation is not and cannot be self-satisfied, that, in her own words, 'the country can't be really independent until people like those of Shebika have reached a certain educational level'. But there has never been, in Tunisia or any other Muslim country, a movement like that of the late nineteenth-century *narodniki*, a return to the people, a voluntary renouncement of class privileges for the purpose of living with the peasants and educating them. Muslims may imagine such conduct but they can give it neither philosophical nor practical expression. Naïma knows that Khalil and Salah feel just as she does. Because her spirit has not yet been dulled by adaptation to the habits of a ruling class already set in its ways, because she thinks of herself not as the beneficiary of a new social system but as a fighter, like her admired father, she knows that she has not only rights but also duties. The idea of duty only occasionally takes shape in her mind, but its strength is sufficient to make her a member of our group and one of our best investigators among the women of Shebika. She does not simply ask questions; she wants the answers to serve the government in its attempt to improve the lot of the villages of the South.

Naïma is only one example (perhaps the most striking) of the influence of Shebika upon our Tunisian researchers, young people from the city but in most cases of country (but not – except for Salah and Khalil – Bedouin) origin. This influence came out quite clearly in the course of our many discussions, above all those held after we had been coming for over three years to the village and had established a relationship with its people, a relationship, however, which in the South has to be constantly reinvigorated if it is not to weaken and perish.

Of the fifteen Tunisians who worked with us over a period of five years, only one – a cardiologist's daughter who had made a tourist's visit to Jerba and Tawzar – had ever crossed the mountains. And yet ten of them had peasant grandparents, a fact which gives some idea of the extent to which the country has developed since Independence. Only Khalil, Salah and Naïma had kept up any connexion with the countryside, and the relatives with whom Naïma corresponded were fishermen of the Karkinnah Islands, who had already crossed the theshold of modern life. As for the parts of the country which our young people knew (except for Salah, and for Khalil, whose uncle owns land at Zaghwaan), they are all vacation spots on Cape Bon or in the Sahil. None of them had dreamed of going to the country for the purpose of social study. Indeed, as is true of all the ruling, upper middle class, they fled and even feared nature in the raw.

Obviously, then, the first discovery of the village was a shock. Some of the young men and women who came with us at first were scared away by what they heard about snakes, scorpions and the other dangers of the desert. At a deeper level, none of the survivors found it difficult to establish or keep up a relationship with the people of Shebika. On the contrary, in spite of the poverty of the *khammes'* vocabulary, there was never any linguistic misunderstanding. Perhaps because this region is profoundly Arabic in speech, whereas to the west, in the mountains of Algeria, the Kabyl language is still alive.

When we speak of 'resistance' it is that inherent in the process of study: the difficulty of knowing the real number of inhabitants, of calculating a family budget, of appreciating the significance of Sidi Sultan. For the most part, the village yields itself to the investigator, and often he is the one to take refuge in concealment.

'After a year, I didn't have the heart to say that we could do nothing for them, because I knew they would have to wait for years before anything happened.'

'I didn't want to lead them on with false hopes, but I couldn't bear to leave them in their misery.'

'We knew that they had years to wait, but they were all expectation. We talked about them in Tunis, but the economists and students at the School of Government laughed at us and said they weren't really important. What answer, then, were we to bring back? We taught them a lot and they say that we've helped them to understand their situation, but sometimes I feel that we've deceived them.'

The contact with Shebika brought about, in our researchers, a real transformation. It is natural that the person or persons who are the objects of research should be affected by the research process; natural, also, that the researcher should adapt himself to the local situation, but quite out of the ordinary that he should be directly affected by it.

In this case the effect was one of what might be called erosion or undermining. Young Tunisian students derive their image of themselves from foreign standards (up-to-dateness, efficiency, pragmatism) and from attitudes characteristic of their newly independent nation (centralization, systematic and purposeful self-development, a belief in education). At Shebika they did not lose their faith in these things but they were forced to see that they did not have the same value throughout the country. Before coming to the South, no longer as tourists but as analysts, not one of them had realized that the ideas professed at Tunis, which hold the ruling class together, might not have universal application. Their ingenuous and generous consciences were put to a rude test. They did not come to doubt that change was possible, but the concrete existence of the people of Shebika taught them two very important things. First, 'the government must realize that the South can't be ruled in the same way as the North, and that our education has been of too abstract a character'; second, 'we can't but feel responsible for these people who are part of ourselves'. Shebika, then, obliges the educated young Tunisian, ready to enter the ruling class, to think twice about some of his country's problems.

These second thoughts may be forgotten as he becomes part of the highly persuasive power structure, but perhaps he will remember that a nation of the Maghrib, such as Tunisia, cannot be built up without consideration of that portion of its society which now has only a marginal existence.

The influence of the investigation upon the investigators was, of course, not immediate but gradual and insidious. It was subject, also, to flux and reflux, as opinions and attitudes were modified. They began to doubt that government officials of intermediate rank, with their urban and bureaucratic prejudices, could do any good in this far-away region. They saw that it would be wrong to neglect the existence and cohesive power of long-standing communities, even if they are presently in a state of decay. They developed enthusiasm for the role of pioneer, even if none of them could, for the moment, embrace it, because, whereas a French colonial teacher or administrator found adventure in his assignment to the South, to a young Tunisian city-dweller it represents a form of exile. They faced the reality of a world impervious to change, petrified by pauperism, for which the simplified ideology of the Neo-Destour movement had ill-prepared them.

'I'd rather talk to the people of Shebika than to the denizens of the old section of Tunis,' says Munira. 'They're more spontaneous and sincere. In the city there's falsity; they have all sorts of wrong ideas. You have to lie and cheat, while here they're being cheated. And I've come to feel more deeply Tunisian; I've learned things about ourselves and our traditions of which I knew nothing before.'

'Really nothing?'

'They think I must be very rich because I live in the city and dress in European style, because I have a fountain-pen and camera. They asked if I'd let them have some clothes and stockings – oh, yes, they wanted to pay – so that they could be like me.'

'Words mean more at Shebika,' says Ridha, one of our researchers. 'In the city you can say what you want, the words don't really matter. But here every word has its full meaning and you have to be careful what you say. Not only us, but the

radio and the government too. At Shebika there are no stereo-
type responses. In all the projects in which I took part in the
city, the people questioned came up with ready-made ideas.
Probably it had to be that way. Whereas at Shebika they have
nothing to lose by speaking straight from the heart.'

'For instance,' says Badra, 'the women of Shebika never complain of their troubles. In the city, you can't talk to a poor
woman without her trying to arouse your pity.'

'Isn't that because the people of Shebika have no means of
comparing their lot with that of others?'

'No. They're stuck in a condition which they know is miserable, but they've made a sort of situation or culture (neither of
these is the right word) out of it. In the city everyone has to
live like everyone else, to be obliterated in the general picture,
and when someone protests it's to testify to his individual
existence. Here they have nothing to hide; poverty isn't as
shameful as in the city, where everyone is trying to keep up
with his neighbour.'

'They don't envy us,' says Naïma. 'The women covet my
clothes, my ring, my hair, but none of them, as far as I can
make out, wants to change places with me.'

'These women,' says Badra, 'never harp on their troubles.
They speak without shame or reticence of dead children and
incurable diseases. There's something worse than poverty and
that's the habit of poverty, but they talk of it quite happily as
if it did not affect them.'

'That's just how they differ from city people,' says Khalil. 'In
the city every poor man or woman you meet is trying to exploit
his poverty. At Shebika, and throughout the South, they don't
use money or the lack of it as a basis of comparison, although
they have a good enough notion of how people better off than
themselves live and what they would need in order to have an
equally good start in life.'

In the city the density of the population makes the wilful
display of poverty inevitable. Slum people have a vague awareness of the fact that they are a thorn in the flesh of a government which aspires to raising standards of living and doing
away with poverty. The calculated exhibition of their woes is a

form of blackmail which, ever since the time of the *plebs* of ancient Rome, has been practised in the seaports of the Mediterranean, where poverty is a sort of stock in trade. Actually the Destour government is probably the only one in all Africa to attempt to make a radical change in the decayed life of the urban and rural masses. The measures it has taken are less spectacular than unenforceable interdictions of begging and shoeshining, but they are very real. The essential problem is not in the choice of courses to follow, for the government's purpose is very clear: to do away with poverty in order that there may be no fertile ground for the development of subversive or revolutionary ideas. The only choice is that of methods. And today no native-born technician would consent to leave the city and live, for a year, the life of the people of Shebika in order to help them, with his daily presence and practical advice, to find, on the spot, the means of changing their destiny and their surroundings.

'Is that really a desirable thing?' asks Munira. 'Perhaps, inasmuch as we have brought them a theoretical and schematic view of a better world. But they were aware, already, of its existence, and of their own abandonment. Is our tardy interest in them actually beneficial? Our visit is only a moment of their long expectation. And why should we help them in particular? We must help the whole population. Preferential treatment would smack of charity and paternalism; it would only increase their feeling that they are left behind in relation to the new social reality.'

'Yes, but it's not a question of preferential treatment for a limited group. It's a question of whether you and other university graduates are willing, within the framework of a plan to improve the whole South, to leave Tunis and go out like pioneers, applying your technical ability to a place like this one.'

'Our position would always be that of an ethnologist, a stranger. They'd look on us as people who take an interest in their customs and habits in order to maintain them.'

'True,' says another. 'And then we'd need real authority. The governor would have to listen to us as if we had political power, not just as if we were experts and consultants in that the admin-

istrators listen to them politely and then do exactly as they, or
the party leaders, choose.'

'Do you think your presence among them over a period of
several years has been helpful?'

'So they all say,' puts in a young man. 'But they don't always
speak freely.'

'If they did,' says one of the girls, 'they'd get into trouble.
Already they've been reproached for having told us too much.
But our being here has at least afforded them a certain release
and liberation. The idea that there are people who take an interest in what is to become of them may be helpful in the long
run.'

'Words are dangerous, in any case,' says Badra. 'An awkwardly phrased question or a "wrong" tone of voice can ruin
everything. The "questionnaire" approach scares them off at
once. The best thing is to get *them* to ask the questions. They
ask and we answer, and then we have a right to question them
in our turn. If we show total ignorance of their tools and utensils then they're induced to tell us how they use them. The
poverty of their language is all to the good. For instance, the
women act out their relationship with objects in order to explain their use to us. If we tell them that something is beautiful
then they show us something still more beautiful.'

'Words don't change people's lives,' puts in Ridha. 'Neither
does the radio. You have to come here and be close to us. On
that point I agree. But it would make trouble in Tunis. And then
we have had our own ways which hold us back, our group
allegiance, which leaves us less free than we may seem.'

'Don't let's fool ourselves. We've changed some of their ideas,
so they all say, but what are we going to put into their place?
Their poverty has a cohesive quality; they're held together by
a sort of system.'

'You mean that there's a "poverty" culture as well as an
"affluent" one, that it has a strongly centripetal quality by
virtue of which men adapt themselves, when the old traditions
are a dead letter, to a state of inanition and continuous want?'

All our young researchers agree that since they have come to
know Shebika they view their country with a different eye,

that their particular brand of Islamic society has acquired new meanings. They now realize that the image they – along with other intellectuals, politicians, administrators and technicians – had formed of the typical Tunisian, has to be modified. And yet to modify the image one has of the typical member of one's own society is not so simple; it entails a rupture with the underpinnings of both present-day conditions and aspirations for the future. The image current in the capital is built up on several political and economic stereotypes, which tend to bear out the slogans of the Neo-Destour party and the theories of growth common to the intellectuals of all the developing countries. Some of these are: opposition to outworn traditions artificially maintained by the colonialists; a more equitable distribution of incomes and goods; an inevitable improvement of the standard of living in response to the apparent efforts of government agencies; a form of nationalism in which Islam is held up as a civilization rather than a religion; the necessity of producing educated leaders and, to this end, the broadening of elementary education by the elimination of illiteracy and the multiplication of schools. This optimistic vision of things leads the ruling class and its successors among the younger generation to be ruthless in regard to the means with which they propose to achieve their ends and blind to the actual possibility of achieving them. ('The peasants' way of life has to change drastically, if necessary by force,' said Salah when he first arrived on the scene.)

It was this optimistic vision that the temporary sojourn in the village of Shebika altered and corroded. The young researchers, hitherto easy in their consciences, came suddenly up against the phenomenon of pauperism. This they could not dismiss as a 'disappearing, retrogade tradition', because they had to face the fact that it derives from the gap between official promises and the total absence of their fulfilment, where over a million inhabitants of the South are concerned. The people of the steppe are of this number, in spite of the fact that many of them do not have permanent homes or trades.

It was at this point (the spring of 1964) that Jacques Berque defined to young government employees and students of the University of Tunis the principle of 'Maghrib authenticity', which he considers the necessary basis of the renewal of the young nations of North Africa. According to him this *as-sala*, or authenticity of the Maghrib's individual and collective being, is based, beyond laws and religion, on a general attitude bound up with a group of beliefs, ideal values and human relationships ordered by a coherent, although invisible, logic. In speaking of the Bedouin or nomad who comes, looking for work, to the city, Berque notes that the suburban slum plays an all-important role in his urban initiation. With it go a sudden 'Islamization', the practice of a hitherto neglected religion, the veiling of women, indicative of entrance into 'respectable' urban society, the discovery of regular employment and working hours and also of the public services (hospitals, dispensaries, etc.). It is in the slum suburb that the man of the steppe makes the acquaintance of modern life.

But in the course of this apprenticeship there occur a dispersal and dissolution of some of the characteristic Bedouin attitudes; of the almost mystical qualities of the relationship between man and man and between man and the outside world; of the essential tenets of faith and of the participation in a type of life which seems incompatible with any other. The government, meanwhile, acts as if the authenticity of the groups of the steppe was merely a sign of their backwardness and one to be eliminated rather than a positive element which might contribute to an original new synthesis. 'Beware,' says Berque, 'of discouraging or perverting the Bedouin, of destroying his authenticity. Otherwise you will be impoverished, half-Westernized and unable to give any content to your national identity.'

Many technicians and technocrats are taken aback by Berque's ideas, because they are more intent upon Westernizing their country than upon achieving the social synthesis without which its development is only a verbal abstraction. To recall the existence of a concrete content, of a collective existence not merely traditional but on a level with the situation of the present day, calls for integrating the Bedouin personality with the contemporary metamorphosis. And this means treating the Bedouins not like the surviving fossils of dead societies but as groups which constituted, in the past, provisory and intermediate syntheses. Few politicians or technicians are ready to make this effort. Their Western education (including the very ideas of national Independence and economic development) turns them away from everything that they consider part of a discarded past. They are in error on this very point, in regarding this transitional culture, born of pauperism and frustrated expectation, as belonging to the past alone. Didn't Franz Fanon, in his opposition to the nationalistic ruling class, see here the only ferment capable of breaking down crystallized structures?*

Whether or not Berque's contention hit the mark, it came, for us, at a most timely moment. It helped our investigators to understand why they had been so deeply touched by the people they were investigating, to see that these people formed a part of the life of their country. In the past, visiting the South only as tourists, they had never imagined anything of the kind; on the contrary, they had striven to thrust what they had seen out of their minds. Their new awareness of involvement in the 'poverty culture' did not result in opposition to change. It took shape, rather, as a doubt that the government could do anything to bring it about, since it insisted upon relegating the old structures to a vague, mythological past instead of admitting that they were very much a part of the present.

About this *as-sala* or authenticity our young people were not in complete agreement; quite naturally, since it conflicted with some of the unquestioned ideas on which they had been brought up.

'You can't talk of authenticity,' says one of the young men; 'only poverty counts at Shebika. When people haven't enough to eat they lose their originality. They're perpetually anxious, and they've made me anxious too.'

A young woman, Jawida, has more definite ideas:

'What's backward isn't the preservation of traditions but the failure to replace them with others. A culture – with its beliefs, techniques, customs and traditions – forms a whole, which must be understood by the society that is trying to develop it. Traditions stand for certain values, often essential ones. They

* *Les Damnés de a terre* (*The Wretched of the Earth*, Penguin Books, 1967) and *L'an I de la Révolution algérienne* (Hatier).

will disappear when new values are brought in. The thing is to propose new values.'

'But on what basis can you "propose" anything? The "development" of which you speak is what was called in nineteenth-century Europe the "cult of progress". But it has little to do with the village people's very real expectations.'

'How can one way of life be more authentic than another?' asks Jawida. 'We are "authentic" with ourselves and with others. Unless we speak of contact with Nature, which is always authentic to a certain degree. The people of Shebika commune with a rough form of nature. They may be authentic in this way. But authenticity depends on the degree of real participation in the surroundings. A Paris street-urchin or a Tibetan monk can be just as authentic as a man of Shebika.'

'Just imagine life in Shebika as it will be in a few years,' put in Khalil. 'Don't forget that this is Tunisia. If there is rapid development it must, for the time being, be in the line of tourism; there's no other choice. Imagine the opening of a café for tourists, as someone in the tourist office in Tunis has suggested. This would be a great shock but a superficial one. A café can't change a people's mentality by bringing in something new in the place of something old. But it can cause a deterioration of values and, later on, a deterioration of the group. People would come from Tawzar for a cup of tea at Shebika, just the way they go now from Tunis to Sidi Bu Saïd.* The children would leave school in order to shine shoes and sell post-cards, desert roses, frogs and "authentic native-boy smiles". Café tables set out around Sidi Sultan and a vending-machine next to the *qaddus*. ... Why not? But let's first give the people of Shebika a chance to achieve self-realization in this nature which is such a part of themselves. Let's make it possible for them to choose the values that will develop and transform them.'

'I think we have here sufficient authenticity,' says Badra. 'The fact that economic decay hasn't undermined the values of the community is a sign of good social health. Future develop-

---

*A well-known village in the outskirts of Tunis where André Gide, Paul Klee, Henry de Montherlant and many artists and journalists used to live.

ment must be built up on these values rather than ignoring them.'

Ridha's opinion is more subtle, no doubt because he is a student of history and has difficulty adapting himself to sociological analysis, which is not of the process of becoming but of 'things as they are'.

'Authenticity is being hard pushed by geographical and economic considerations. The values of which you speak, when they are crystallized, may be obstacles in the way. Authenticity is positive only when it is achieved within the framework of development. Just now the inhabitants of Shebika are affected by some elements of progress (the radio, telephone, etc.), which shake up their social structures without really transforming their way of life. Our guide, Si Tijani, says that the young men, because they listen to the radio, no longer want to work on the land; they're attracted by the bright lights of the city. Shebika's present way of life is falsely authentic, inasmuch as it illustrates the failure of a system. "Authentic" and "falsely authentic" may seem to be contradictory terms, but they describe a complex social reality.'

In any case, something has deeply stirred our young people, something that has shattered the images of themselves and their country, particularly its backward South, whose inhabitants cannot be simply forgotten or eliminated from the over-all social picture. Jacques Berque's words disturbed them, just because they reflected a truth of which they themselves were aware without wanting to admit it: namely that the three years at Shebika had not only made them keener observers and more sensitive investigators, but also that they had acquired a different concept of their own country which, from the city, had seemed very easy to transform. Shebika got under their skin, and every return to it made them slightly nervous. Before this they had tried to escape, via European culture, from the Maghrib; now they felt that integration with the European ruling class was a sort of treason.

'I don't know what this village has done to me,' says one of the girls; 'it's always in the back of my mind. The slums of Tunis are a miserable sight, but we know that they're on the way out. But the South won't change unless we make a special effort. Shebika is the image of our responsibility. It's as if where politics leaves off, sociology begins.'

The Ya Awlad

From the very first day they were called *ya awlad*, or children. For the first two years of our study the people of Shebika considered them as visitors, looking them over out of sheer curiosity. In these parts, 'to look is to steal', and our researchers were held at arm's length. Except for the girls, such as Naïma and also the young Frenchwoman baptized 'Christ', who was popular from one end of our stay to the other and of whom the villagers speak even today as 'the woman with fair hair and blue eyes who had no children at an age when other women are mothers several times over'. There is an immediate understanding among women, and for a long time afternoons spent in the houses and courtyards were much more fruitful than discussions with the men.

'They're children of Tunis,' said Nawa. 'They look and look at things without knowing what they see. There we are, and they don't seem to know what we're doing.'

'Do they really seem not to know?'

'Well, they ought to know, that's certain. How do their own mothers cook? But they're wrapped up in their work, without any idea yet of getting married and having children.'

'Tunis is a big city.'

'What does that mean, a big city?'

'Something very large. Many houses, and all sorts of different things. Music everywhere. And people going around in cars.'

'And the *ya awlad*, the children?'

'They're children, just like any others. They don't know what it's all about.'

Two years later, we asked Nawa the same questions.

'They care for us. They put in a word for us at Tunis. We know that.'

'Who told you?'

'The people from Tawzar. They told us that we shouldn't open up the way we did with you, that we ought to give you a better picture of Tunisia.'

'Who told you, exactly?'

'A representative of the government. They may not give us seeds if we go on talking to you this way.'

'Can they really do that?'

'That's what they said, I told you. But we don't need their seeds this year.'

'Their seeds don't sprout,' said another woman, laughing. 'So what about the *ya awlad*, the children?'

'They've been good to us. They tell us how things are with them and we tell them how they are with us. They're people we can talk to.'

'And the government man?'

Nawa did not answer. She looked at Salah, who was walking across the square, at Naïma, who was photographing the grocery. Then she gathered up her veils and went off in the direction of the Mosque and her house, whose rickety gate is just beside it.

'Is that true? The man said you shouldn't answer our questions?'

'He said we shouldn't give you a bad picture of Tunisia.'

'Is it a patriotic duty to conceal the fact that you're poor?'

Others told us the same thing. The governor is at far-away Qafsa, but some official from Tawzar came down at least twice during the course of our five-year investigation and tried to persuade these people to speak less freely. This is what they told us by way of an explanation for the fact that they couldn't talk to us any more. We let several months go by, and when we came back everything was the way it had been before. But no longer did they call our young researchers *ya awlad*. Now they were 'the young ones who have come to find out what's going on in the South'. The change in their attitude was reflected in their rationalized mode of expression. They no longer regarded themselves as objects of outsiders' curiosity; they began to question and think things out on their own account.

'We know now what you're doing, and that it's actually

helpful to us,' says Ali. 'We need to talk to you. It makes us happy. The young people are good to us. Of course the girls aren't dressed the way they should be. They're always talking and laughing together and we don't always catch what they say. But they go to see our women, and the women like them.'

Little by little the villagers began to view our group in a different light; their attitude changed along with that of their interlocutors; they began to feel that they were not merely objects of curiosity but participants in a meaningful common effort which reached beyond the confines of Shebika. No longer did they simply take the researchers aside to display their poverty, as during the early months; knowing that they had sympathetic hearers they went more deeply into their whole situation.

'They're children, yes, but they wish us well. We want them to know what we can do. Today we haven't a single millime, but through them we may have better things in the future. They say they want to come to Shebika to work with us. They'll never do that; nobody has in the past. But they want us to become more like themselves. At first they asked all sorts of irritating questions. Now *we* ask *them* how we should go about certain things, and they find out at Tunis before giving us an answer.'

'Yes,' says Muhammad. 'We live differently, because we look at the way we're living.'

5

'THE RE-OPENING OF THE GATE
OF EFFORT'

The Future

On our very first day at Shebika we were shown the school-house, a plain, rectangular, one-storey building, built around 1960. Of its two rooms only one is used for classes, since there is only one teacher, and the other serves as a storage place.

The old men – Ali and Qaddur – took us to the yard in front of the school-house. They touched the stones with their fingers and pointed to the inside, where some thirty children were listening distractedly – turning their heads from side to side and pinching their neighbours – to what the teacher was saying. But they were at school; they were learning the history and geography of their country and, of course, how to read and write in both Arabic and French. The teacher, wearing a shirt and trousers, moved to and fro in front of a map of Tunisia. The day was oppressively hot, and the children wriggly in the way of all the children of the Maghrib. Most of them came from Shebika, particularly the boys, since among the eight girls two were daughters of Ridha, the grocer, and the rest came from the Bedouin encampment. The little Bedouins have to cover several miles, on foot, every day, and yet they are the most regular in their attendance.

'We have a school and also a *kuttab*,' says Qaddur.

'Does every family send the children to school?'

'Yes, if they have reached the legal age.'

'Before Independence you didn't have a school, did you?'

'No.'

'Why do people send their children to school, anyhow?'

'So they'll make money. If I send my son to school, he'll become a teacher. He'll have a salary and get married.'

'Do your great-grandchildren go to school?'

'They have to. And in any case it's a good thing.'

'Do the young people who have gone to school stay at Shebika or do they go away?'

'I can't tell you that. In any case, all knowledge belongs to God, and it is divided into two parts: hidden knowledge and visible knowledge. Hidden knowledge was hidden by God and it has five parts: law-making, benevolence, rain, spirits and *jinn*. Visible knowledge has three parts: politics, charity, and the knowledge of Satan. The knowledge of Satan has four subdivisions: the knowledge of Satan proper, the politics of philosophy, geometry and industry. But these last four exist only in Europe.'

'So geometry and philosophy belong to the knowledge of Satan?'

'Industry and geometry are for those who have denied their religion. We have the law. As for the Jews, they have everything. The Jews have two books.'

'Do you think that the young people who have been to school should stay here or should go away?'

'If they can go, let them go.'

The school and the radio are the two most important things of Shebika, because in them there is tangible evidence of change. This can be seen, every day, in the barrier between parents and their children who have learned to read and write and very often, when they are about fifteen years old, take over the few existing radios.

This is no slight acquisition. None of the eighteen young men of Shebika who have seen military service, all of whom own transistors, would dream of giving up the power of turning the knob and choosing a programme. These young men belong, of course, to the first educated generation. The next age-group, that of boys between twelve and fifteen years old, has won control over the radios owned by five or six of the village families, and this thanks to the unrecognized but very real superiority of anyone who can read and write and explain some of the things going on at Sfax or in the capital city of Tunis. The explanations are far from complete; often they echo the words of the school-teacher and run something like this:

'Bourguiba has asked the people of the Sahil to trust him, because he wants Tunisia to be rich and flourishing', or 'We must prepare for great changes'. In any case, they contain more than is to be learned from visiting local officials or from the National Guards.

The school, then, relays the voice of the radio. And yet it is the school that is at the heart of the change, not only because it brings possession of a knowledge hitherto confined to a very small group of wise or educated men, most of them in the field of theology, but also because it integrates Shebika in a greater whole, in the living body not of just the South but of Tunisia. Even if a child doesn't know much about his country he perceives it as an organism to which he belongs, and the shape of this organism, first seen on the school-room map and then retraced, in his free hours, on the sand of the central square, modifies the totality of his concepts. Of the fifteen mature but illiterate heads of families in Shebika only one can project himself into the context of Tunisia, this long upside-down triangle whose apex plunges into the Sahara and whose base – with the excrescences of Bizerta and Cape Bon at either end – faces Sicily. And this is because he has been several times to Tunis. The school-children, on the other hand, and the young men who have seen army service, can relate their life in Shebika to the shape on the map, which is further enlivened by what they are told of it over the radio. Their personal centre of gravity is shifted from the village to Tunis, the bright centre of national life, as they have learned about it at school and literally heard it on radio programmes. An important modification of the individual's view of his *own* world is brought about by the language of radio and the school-room, a language made up of signs, images and ideas which attach him to the equally real world outside, all the more fascinating because he does not know it at first hand. The implicit knowledge thus acquired owes nothing to the village; it is the skeleton of a new and startling awareness of a broader frame of reference.

Within the narrow confines of Shebika (and for that matter in the whole Maghrib) two images clash: one defined by immediate surroundings and a religious orientation, the other, more abstractly known, which puts the individual into his wider geographical context. The immediate surroundings, as we have described them, include El Hamma and Tawzar to the south, Tamerza and Redayif to the north; they touch the mountains, without crossing them, but extend beyond the Algerian border. Across this area, which the villagers cover on foot except for the rare occasions when they get a ride in the jeeps of the National Guards, there lies the vector that joins it, spiritually, to Mecca and the East. In this picture Tunis is vague and far away, confused with the pressure and coercive power exercised by every government since that of the Turks.

The country's real geographic proportions are abstract. Even the young men who have done their military service at Tunis or Bizerta cannot trace their route on a map, place any of the major towns or even locate Shebika. The notions of north and south and of topography in general are as alien to them as if they were complete illiterates. And the mystical distance to Mecca is even vaguer in their minds than in those of their elders.

As for the school-children, their insertion into a space ruled by the abstract topography of the map is definitely accomplished. They place Shebika in the South and Tunis in the North; they know the whereabouts of the big towns and the roads which lead to the capital. The polarization of this wide area is that which has been taught them in school, and it testifies to their integration with a European world which they adopt without the slightest hesitation. Hence the attitude of superiority which they sometimes strike up towards their elders. They feel sure that the world in which they feel at home is the only one with any meaning. The universe of the illiterate has become alien to them.

It is quite conceivable, then, that there should be a barrier between these two visions of the world, which nevertheless coexist without too much difficulty. The elders, illiterate as they may be, hold the command posts of the world in which the young people still live and exercise control over them. The young do not feel oppressed or even bothered by this control, but a sizeable part of their existence is at a different level from that of the community in which they admit to living. They are in a state of expectancy, waiting to be integrated with the rest of the nation. This split in their lives and personalities must not be left out of account for too long, particularly if the development of the South does not follow upon that of the North and Centre. In this case the 'forgotten men' might fall into a state of embittered frustration.

When the school-day is over the children leap from their seats and run, school-bag in hand, through the cemetery and then either up to the square or, in summer, to the *wadi*, where they chase small animals or splash about in the water. Tunisian law is very strict: schooling is to be spread as widely and carried as far as possible. The Neo-Destour educational policy is a signal success. The children, on their side, are extraordinarily receptive and quick-witted. School means much more than the acquisition of knowledge; it feeds the dream of 'coming up in the world', 'advancing from one social class to another', and, meanwhile, of running away or, in any case, going to the city.

'What's your name?' we ask a fifteen-year-old boy.

'Ali Bu Amin.'

'What class are you in?'

'Third.'

'What do you want to be when you've finished school? A farmer, a grocer, or a teacher?'

'A teacher. I want to leave Shebika and go to Sfax where our teacher comes from.'

'And you, what do you want to be?' we ask the grocer's son.

'Anything, as long as I don't have to work in the oasis.'

'Would you like to be a carter?'

'No, I certainly wouldn't.'

'How would you like to be in charge of Sidi Sultan?'

'No; I want to get away from Shebika.'

'Why? You don't like Shebika?'

'No.'

'And you?' we ask the son of Iimra.

'A teacher.'

'And where would you like to teach?'

'Not at Shebika.'

'At Tawzar? Tunis?'

'That's it. In the city.'

'Do all of you want to be teachers?'

'No, I want to run a school.'

'Whereabouts?'

'At Qafsa.'

'And you, young woman, what's your name?'

'Rima.'

'Are you a good student?'

'Yes.'

'What do you want to be later on?'

'A nurse.'

'At Shebika or somewhere else?'

'Somewhere else.'

The children are already, in their imagination, escaping from Shebika. What they will actually be able to do with their book-learning is another matter.

During the French protectorate the school, above all the *lycée* (for the boys of Tunis or of the Sahil who were able to reach it), was a powerful instrument of social advancement, following in the wake of earlier traditional or aristocratic educational establishments, such as 'Khaldounia' in the Medina of Tunis. Bourguiba, Bin Salah, Massaadi, Masmudi – all the leaders of the movement for Independence – were projected by the French secular schools into the ranks of the older élite, which they made over, just as they later made over the original Independence party. This élite was a shadowy affair, because, in spite of the schools, the ruling class, under the Protectorate, was that of French government officials, the military and the settlers. But what a triumph for the son of a rich native of Tunis or of a fisherman of the Sahil to come back from Paris with a diploma which neither a French sergeant nor a settler, in spite of his social superiority, could ever hope to obtain for himself or even his children! This budding native élite furnished the members of the Neo-Destour movement and impregnated it with resentment of the colonial *status quo*. There was a contradiction between the colonial policy of the Jules Ferry government and the educational system which it built up and which was to foster the nationalist movement that would turn against it. At the same time the schools played on the conscience of the settlers' children and weakened their belief in the right to conquest. After the achievement of Independence the new government remembered this lesson and applied it in reverse. Against the traditional aristocracy and upper middle class (the *baladi* of Tunis and Sfax) it started to raise up a new class which owed everything to the public school. This social advancement brought into the ruling circles an ever larger number of university graduates and technicians, of whom our young Salah is a good example. There remains the great body of the semi-literate, the semi-educated. To them the new government has little to offer, because in an essentially agricultural country the process of industrialization, however much effort is put into it, cannot move as rapidly as the development of its educational system.

It is reasonable to suppose that the proportion of the 'chosen' or most favoured individuals at Shebika will be the same as that in the rest of the country, where only five or six per cent of the children can hope to go to the university, a percentage which is shrinking as the number entering the primary grades grows. The others, in view of the general situation of the South, have little chance of finding work commensurate with their abilities. It is more likely that they will swell the ranks of the half-baked or semi-educated, some of whom will forget what they have learned for lack of an occasion to use it, while others shut themselves up in frustration.

As things stand the school at Shebika serves above all as a means by which to attain a security and stability which the precarious character of life in the South (more obvious to its inhabitants since the radio has given them an inkling of the possibilities open to people who have more of a chance than they) makes eminently desirable in this period of promised but unfulfilled change. Thus every family, without exception, hopes that its children will become government employees. The public school fosters the myth of public service. Only one of the fathers of a Shebika family has any further aspiration, namely that his children should hold on to their land, but in order to 'cultivate it on a large scale, like engineers'. This one is, understandably enough, Ridha the grocer, who thinks that another of his sons should go into business and speaks knowingly of the university's Business School. All the others consider that 'education is money', that is, that it leads to a 'safe and sure' life, in which a monthly salary and an old-age pension are ideals whose pursuit justifies hours of sitting in the classroom in a way in which they and their contemporaries could never have imagined.

The men of Shebika and of the tents below have a particular psychology. The life they know is fraught with uncertainty, with drought and famine. The dream of a diploma which guarantees, once and for all, the right to a regular pay-cheque is not unnatural, and makes for the willingness with which they send their children to school. The father's projection of himself into the future of his son implies not only his certainty that the son will survive (which is in itself a step forward) but also the hope of seeing him solidly installed in a government office. The expectations which one generation has of another makes for a logically chronological and historical sequence very different from the ties of earlier days, which grew out of a group structure anchored in an unpredictable cosmos.

After Salah had escaped from the fascination of Sidi Sultan and stopped trying to find there the motive power of Shebika he transferred his interest to the school.

'The parents are waiting even more eagerly than the children. The children are sure that they will live in the way described in their school-books.'

'At least they hope so ...'

'They know it. But the fathers are waiting for the all-over change which will lead to fulfilment of this promise. The past represents an important dimension of the group's existence and also of its self-awareness. But there is also the future. The school represents the future, and the way the children are going to help bring it about.'

Ridha, another of our researchers, says:

'These people can't imagine how things may or will happen. They think that education has the power of a magic wand. The children know that they are penetrating the world of books, the books that come to them, through their teacher, from the Ministry of Education. All the parents know is that the ability to read and write is everything, that there is no other problem.'

The school, then, is an opening. It is self-sufficient, and most of the children are caught up in its mechanism; even if their home life is spent among the unschooled. Salah questioned Al-massi, a reputedly gifted seventeen-year-old boy who has reached the point where he is ready to go to some city or town where he can take what are called 'middle-level' courses, leading to a special skill. Almassi is persuaded that all doors will be open to him. Not that he can become a Cabinet member or a doctor, as some children imagine, but certainly an agricultur-alist or a surveyor, for he has seen surveyors' maps at Tawzar. He doesn't want to go too far from Shebika, since his family will always be here and he wants to keep an eye on the plot of land which his elderly father owns in the oasis. In five or six years, he says, the whole situation will have changed, because practically everyone will know how to read and write and have a trade of his own.

Almassi is not the only one to believe that the coming changes will not lead, as the younger children imagine, to his leaving the village. Like those of his contemporaries who have seen military service he thinks the wisest thing is to stay put and obtain aid from the government. According to him and his friends, the reason why the government has not helped the village before is simply the ignorance of its people. From now on, he believes, there will be a rapid change. His ideas are actually somewhat sophisticated. For the problems of Independ-ence he has no concern; he is indifferent towards what his elders call the 'events'; he relegates them to a distant past with which he has no connexions. Things as they are, he believes, are no different from what they were before, and the technical experts from abroad have come to Tunisia because they have a better life there than they had at home. He goes so far as to believe that there is no deep-lying difference between his country and the United States of America. He has been taught at school that all the independent countries are equal and that Tunisia has the same number of votes as any other at what is for some reason called the 'Tribunal of the United Nations'. To him it is the most natural thing in the world that he should become a technician or an engineer and thus be like everyone else. The 'others' (his relatives and friends at Shebika) are poor simply because they are 'stupid', because they have never wanted to learn to read and write.

Certainly the school is a primary instrument for the construction of the future. It makes for an insurmountable gap between those who are over twenty-five years old and those who are under. To the latter it makes 'natural' and 'normal' that which their unheeded elders consider 'monstrous' : the fact of attaching more importance to school than to prayers, the idea that a woman can do the same job as a man and that a marriage can be made by choice rather than by arrangement. This vision of the 'normal' life is built up on present-day information, for there is a strong tendency to consider the text-book picture of life as a reality. In other words, the radical quality of the school is felt, above all, by those who do not go there but send their children, the men who lived through the colonial period and – actively or inactively – the struggle for Independence, who know that the atmosphere in which their children are being brought up cannot possibly be the same as that which they knew themselves.

The school is not the only determining factor of change at Shebika. Military service is equally important. A dozen or so young men have experienced it and of those to whom we talked – not without difficulty, for most of them took no interest in our research and avoided us without giving any reason – the majority hoped that Shebika would change as rapidly as possible. They know something of their country, chiefly the barracks where they were stationed in the North, and they have some idea of organization and the life of a city. Their acquaintance with army discipline is probably what made them mistrustful of us, for they are not at all prejudiced against foreigners. On the contrary, when they do talk, they say at once that foreigners like ourselves are beneficial to their country. Like all the local men, they are *afraid of words*, or rather held back by the paucity of their concepts and their inability to express themselves in the presence of people who deal in ideas with which they are not acquainted. Shebika has got to change, they know that; like the rest of the country it must 'get in the swing of progress'. Exactly what they mean by 'progress' they do not say, although they speak vaguely of hygiene and sanitation and the conditions of work in the oasis. They are working as *khammes*, but they feel sure that the government will improve their status. The young men of their generation have no intention of going away. Some of them saved up part of their army pay and have bought or are buying a couple of date-palms, which they will cultivate on their own.

These young men who have learned the ways of discipline and hygiene in army barracks, who have had the totally new experience of living with other Tunisians who do not come from the same group, still feel that, if they belong to a larger community, it is as representatives of Shebika. Unlike their juniors they are not projected, by the school, far beyond the village. Their limited but very real acquaintance with the country as a whole has enabled them to measure their ambitions by their ability to achieve them. They definitely admit, however, that change is both normal and inevitable and that it entails no break with tradition, since 'It doesn't forbid honouring our parents or observing Ramadan'. The party and the government, they think, are there to settle problems which are above their heads. But how long will this passivity, born of military training, endure?

Some of them have, after all, seen countries other than their own. In 1962–3, when there was trouble in the Congo, Tunisia sent a contingent of troops which played a not unimportant role among the United Nations forces. Those who came from the South were shipped off to the heart of Africa after six months or a year in the barracks of Tunis or Bir Bu Riqba. It took us months to ferret out the two young men of Shebika who were among them and even longer to persuade one of them to talk. They weren't hiding from us, nor were they afraid we might quiz them on military secrets. They were hesitant for the usual reason, because they couldn't find words with which to tell their experience, and perhaps because the impression it had made upon them was still so vivid. The one we finally managed to question was Abdelqadir, the fellow who runs the sewing-machine in front of the grocery. He is timid and retiring, as if the short absence from home had blocked his verbal power. This is how the 'skinny soldier', as we called him, answered us:

'Yes I'm the one that went to the Congo. I was there for eleven months, and I have plenty to tell. It would take hours and hours to give you the whole story. Here I have nothing. I'm very poor, and I only wish I could find work.'

'Since you came back, have you stayed all the time in Shebika?'

'Yes.'

'In the Congo, did you see peasants?'

'No, there are peasants here, in Tunisia, but I didn't see any in the Congo. It's very different down there. First of all, there's rain, rain such as you never see the like of at Shebika, or at Tunis either. The country isn't at all the same; there are no peasants, only trees and water, a lot more water than you find here, water everywhere. There are large areas where you can walk for hours without seeing anything but trees. It's hard to tell how people find their way.'

'You mean there are big forests?'

'Yes, forests.'

'You don't want to tell us about the forests?'

'I don't know.'

'They didn't exactly scare me. But they're unlike anything we have here. Before we went down there they told us about them. But they were different from what we had expected. There are leaves everywhere. I saw them even in my sleep, leaves full of water.'

'And what about the people?'

'There are people there, among the leaves.'

'What kind of people?'

'What kind? I can't exactly tell you. People that don't have a God like ours. They have villages, all right, but built with leaves. Some of them are very tall, and the women don't cover their faces. They are much noisier than we are. They call each other with drums. As a matter of fact, we did the same thing during the war.'

'Would you like to live with them?'

'I don't know. To live there you have to come from there in the first place. They're people like us, like the way we were when there were fights between the villages. That's why we went down there, so they wouldn't fight among themselves.'

'To prevent a *jaiysh*, is that it?'

'A sort of *jaiysh*, yes. I don't think they believe a man's a man.'

'What do you mean?'

'They have to do with men, but only those from their own village are men like themselves.'

'To you every man's a man?'

'Every believer, yes.'

'Is that all?'

'Plus all those that see God, even the God of the Christians.'

'What about the men of the Congo?'

'I don't know. And then they live in the forest. Can you imagine me living in the forest? Where would I put my camels? And down there I wouldn't be able to sleep at night. There are leaves growing everywhere, growing very fast. That's all I have to say.'

Young Abdelqadir came back from the Congo to Bizerta and finished his military service there. He returned to Shebika a year ago.

'Why did you come back to Shebika?'

'It's my home, that's why.'

'What kind of work do you find there?'

'It depends on what comes along. Something new every day.'

'You don't have regular work?'

'No. I go one day to work on the roads, another in the oasis. If anyone asks me to help him, I go along. If I have nothing to do I lie down beside the wall and sleep.'

'How do you imagine the future of Shebika?'

'Of Shebika?'

'Yes, right here.'

'It's a very poor place.'

'How did you think of Shebika when you were in the Congo?'

'I thought about it as the centre of the world. Tunisia's everything to me. The dust of Tunisia is more precious than all the gold of the Congo.'

'Are you permanently settled, now, at Shebika?'

'No, I'm on a prolonged furlough. I'm still attached to an army post not far away.'

'What kind of work do you do?'

'Work by the day. For instance, I cut wood in the mountains or pick dates in the oasis. And if there's nothing doing, I just take it easy.'

'You said this is a poor place. Would you like to see Shebika become richer?'

'Yes, of course. I'd like to see the same things here that I saw at Tunis.'

'And what do you think should be done to make things better?'

'The means of improvement are in the hands of the men of Tunis, not mine.'

'How do you imagine Shebika in the future?'

'With many more houses and with cars and buses and moving-picture theatres. I'd like to see people better dressed and fed, and above all I'd like to see better quality building.'

'In your opinion, what's necessary to bring all this about?'

'It has to come from Tunis. They've got to take thought for this desert, to start building and creating jobs ...'

'You don't think Shebika can do something for itself?'

'No, I don't.'

'Why not?'

'Shebika's too poor.'

'It needs help, does it?'

'Yes, help from the government.'

'And how do you imagine Shebika ten years from now?'

'By that time it ought to have improved. Things ought to be better.'

'What, exactly, will be better?'

'Housing, clothes, food and jobs. Men shouldn't have to work just by the day, hired for one month and then laid off for the next. They ought to have steady employment, all of them on the same basis.'

'What do you mean by "the same basis"?'

'I mean there should be work for everyone, not that some fellows should have jobs and others be unemployed. Everyone would like to work steadily.'

The other men of Shebika may not have travelled so far, but in front of the grocery or under the portico, old and young, when they are not lamenting their present poverty, indulge in dreams of the future. Everything leads them to it: the radio, the newspapers which their children read aloud and the government officials who come their way. The word 'tomorrow' has taken on a mythical value, on a world-wide scale; no longer does it have the typically Mediterranean meaning of indefinite postponement.

This is because of the ideology of the Neo-Destour party, which has replaced the slogan of 'Independence' with that of 'development'. Development is spoken of in terms of a battle against outworn traditions and also a change of living conditions. But the leaders, who know that the change-over from agriculture to industry is for the moment purely theoretical, have had the wisdom to say that 'there must be a change of heart before there is a change of institutions'. They wish, they say, to avoid the mistake of building up a new social structure before the people are willing to give up their old ideas and adapt themselves to new ones. A change of heart implies a change in men's view of the future; it means winning their allegiance to an acceptable ideal and then, when it is accepted, breaking with tradition.

We have said before how dubious we find this word 'tradition', and how hard it is to pin down the concrete things which supposedly embody it. At present, when various groups meet and combine in fragile, temporary structures, the only signs of a continuing past are certain verbal prescriptions (respected in proportion to the prestige of the prescriber) and oral affirmations of the survival of a supposedly ancient order. The word 'tradition' itself is in danger of serving to justify certain political or administrative policies. For many rural groups find it insurmountably difficult not only to adapt themselves to a new mode of life which has been imposed upon them but also to envisage the new human relationships brought about by the change.

The new 'way of life' (such as that of Sidi Bu Saïd, which is, on the whole, successful) has usually been thought up by urban administrators. The idea of settling the nomads and turning them into peasants calls for administrative, economic and technical measures conceived with scanty regard for the human element involved. The construction of 'in-gathering' villages for the nomads is all too often an exercise in virtuosity for the benefit of some native or European architect. Thus, north of the Matmata or on the road between Qafsa and Qassireen, there are blocks of incredibly ugly buildings, cement cubes in geometrical formation, low-price 'housing projects' which take into account neither the needs of the nomads nor the architectural style suited to the Mediterranean region. For instance, in the typical building of this whole 'cultural area', the patio or courtyard, where the women might continue to wash and cook and create a little world of their own, has been systematically left out. And the furniture offered to the new tenants is usually not at all what they need. In certain recently built 'units' the newly arrived nomads use the chairs as tables and continue to sit on mats laid out on the floor.

This, of course, is only a symptomatic detail. But there are many more of the same kind in the economic life of the country. At Sidi Bu Saïd the recently settled nomads insist on growing tomatoes and other fruits and vegetables, such as bring them immediate gains, instead of slower-ripening produce. In the North the attempt to set up rural cooperatives failed because of lack of confidence on the part of the members. (In certain cases they were taken over by government employees or local land-owners.) Officials blame a backward tradition. But there is no organized resistance to progress, no effort to maintain principles of long standing or acquired by the preceding generation (as is the case in countries with a widely scattered peasant class and, at least partially, between Susa and Sfax, in the Sahil region of Tunisia). In the uncertain present in which these scattered groups live the past plays no part. At the moment of entry into the economic and social no-man's-land where the government is pushing them, these groups undergo in their own way the effects of the inevitably ambiguous policy of a nation which wants to create conditions favourable to economic development but which cannot, in the space of a few years (or ever), industrialize the countryside and make it over. A mentality can be worked upon and prepared for change, but the change itself cannot take place unless uprooted individuals are provided with actually acceptable new structures in which they can find self-expression. Groups can be drawn into new enterprises, even enterprises contrary to what they habitually consider their own interest, but not unless there is, at the same time, an enrichment of human relationships. *The intensity of social life has always more weight than economic advantage.*

Economists, administrators and experts of various kinds speak of 'brakes on development', but this is a phrase intended to make acceptable the *inevitable* slowness of its rhythm. The so-called traditional groups enter into an exclusively *verbal* universe, one growing out of the gap between a government desirous of overturning the structures of a society and the actual means for doing so, which allow only for narrow and shallow rectifications. As might be expected, the administrators make up for the slowness of change by an accentuation of the ideology behind it, and this is what creates such a shock at Shebika and other villages. As a result they take refuge in certain forms of psychological and social behaviour not necessarily long-standing, which are then crystallized and hardened. The government proceeds to discover a 'resistance' which it strives to overcome; the peasant detects in the government a familiar coercive force which he immediately recognizes as that of the city trying to impose its will upon the steppe.

In all the young countries of Africa – at varying levels of intensity – this same drama is being enacted. Out of the confusion of independence, development and industrialization there arises a misunderstanding by virtue of which the former period of colonialism is blamed not only for the exploitation of the market-place but also for the delay in the 'inevitable modernization'. To try to modernize the countryside is reasonable enough, but to assimilate this reorganization to an 'agrarian reform' is a misuse of language of which the village groups concerned are not unaware, since they are given no chance of new and richer participation. The so-called resistance is simply the projection into rural life of the difficulties incurred by new governments which have an ambitious programme without the means of carrying it out.

At Shebika, for the moment, the dangers of hardening 'resistance to change' are very slight. Perhaps on account of its relationship, through marriage and property-ownership and the exchange of services, with El Hamma, Redayif, Tamerza and the nomads, the village is eager to participate in whatever is going on, and no distinction is made between its existence as a social centre, that is, its collective well-being, and the notion of prosperity. Military service, the school-house and the radio have pushed the whole village towards a future of which it knows only a few external signs.

The impact of change is powerful, but it is not yet conceptualized, because, even if the people can *imagine* life in a factory or a big city, they know from experience that the suburban slums hold few attractions for a peasant from the South. This feeling must be peculiar to Shebika, because it quite surprised Salah, most of whose family had left the desolate region of Qassireen for the outskirts of Tunis. Shebika and a few other villages are proud enough to believe that they themselves can be the starting-points of collective development.

The collective idea is present in the picture of the future envisaged by all the men and most of the women of the village, but not by the children. Of the thirty heads of families whom we questioned everyone said quite positively: 'The government must develop Shebika on the spot. ... We can become as rich as anyone else from our work, if only we're given the tools. ... Why should we emigrate to other sections if we can enrich the soil of the oasis, build dams which will assure us water the year round and reconstruct the village? ... At Tawzar they don't want to modernize according to the wishes of the oasis people, but we want to live better than we do now and so we're ready to start in immediately if some help is given us. ... I don't want my children to go away. If I get to be rich enough we can take trips to Tunis and Sfax. We may even own a car, and there'll be a good road all the way to Tawzar.'

'Before military service,' says the 'skinny soldier', 'I wanted, like all my school-friends, to go to Tunis. Then I saw Tunis and the way people live there with my own eyes and I said to myself that I didn't want to be like them. They're people that don't know how to live. Si Tijani himself says so: "At Tunis they don't live; they just run around in circles and then die." I want to stay here and have the government give me my due, the amount of land that I want to cultivate. I listen to the radio, you know.'

Strangely enough, the women, particularly those between twenty and forty, are the most impatient. They don't want their children to grow up in Shebika, 'because people live differently now in Tunisia', and 'the men ought to get on with the job'. Although they themselves don't want to leave they admit that their children, at least the boys, should go away 'if there's still nothing doing here'. In the five years we have known them they have changed considerably. The very women who, at the beginning, so violently opposed the departure of Rima now grant that 'a girl can go anywhere that there is a home and a job waiting for her'. It is important to them that in the cities the government has not clamped down on the celebration of Ramadan. Obviously, within the last few years the school-children have had a great influence on family life and have broadened their mothers' horizons.

'My son knows what's going on at Tunis,' says one, and another: 'We know that some day we'll live the way they do in other places.'

In a village like Shebika the teaching of the Quran has greatly declined. But the villagers know enough to see in it a dynamism for which Westerners were long unwilling to give it credit. As has often been said, Islam is an all-pervasive religion as well as a civilization, and it is sensitive to the atmosphere around it, static during the periods of debasement, which Ibn Khaldun had begun to analyse, but dynamic when new political factors affect the collectivity. The saying 'Let Allah wipe out or strengthen what he will' can perfectly well imply a return to energy and dynamism, to *fatah al ijtihad*, 'the re-opening of the gates of effort'. Perception of the future as the advent of a new collective reality, unpredictable in nature but better, at least, than the conditions of the present day is stimulated not merely by a revolt against poverty; it comes out of the latent dynamism of the 'social electron' of Shebika. Already the villagers no longer have their centre of gravity in the present state of things; they are looking for it in a projection of the future, and it is upon this hopefulness that the government should base a genuine social transformation. The school-house is the matrix of this future that is waiting to be born.

Shebika face-to-face with Shebika

'Now we talk,' said young Ali. 'We talk, among ourselves, *about everything*. Your questions shook us up.'

Ali was leading us along the *wadi* towards the spring, where the women wash their red and violet veils. We jumped over the water, with Si Tijani at our head, moving elegantly but with a touch of awkwardness due to his age and garb. Sure-footed but leaning on his stick, he burst into throaty laughter.

'In the beginning,' Ali went on, 'we didn't know exactly what to think. You Europeans, of course, were visitors whom we were glad to see. But the young people from Tunis. . . . They asked us just as many questions as if they too had come from far away and didn't know about the simplest things of our everyday life. We thought they must be making fun of us. Then we saw that, even though they were Muslims like ourselves, they had no respect for God.'

We were passing in front of the first waterfall, the one that comes down from the opening in the semi-circle of mountains at the spring. Si Tijani poked at the mud with his stick in order to stir up the frogs. Ali, continuing to walk, told us that our first questions had caused considerable indignation, but that the villagers had made allowances for our group because of its foreign members. Foreigners, God willing, had always been welcome at Shebika. A boy like Salah, on the other hand, was an anathema to them; he might have been one of their own sons and yet he pretended to know nothing. What difference was there, after all, except for the fact that he knew how to read and write? That was no excuse for not knowing that the hour of prayer is established by tossing a cap into the air, that for want of anything better you play checkers with stones or pieces of camel dung. Yet after we had gone away the men of the village, lying under the portico, repeated our questions. Mockingly at first: 'Salah asked me why we kill a camel in such or such a way'; or: 'Khalil wanted to know how many dinars pass through our hands in the course of a year.' Then they put the question again, imitating the speech of the questioner. The question was there, words calling for words in reply, only they didn't have the words at their command. But by repeating the question over and over it ceased to be a question and became words, like so many others. All this until the day (Ali couldn't say exactly which) when Salah said that he, the student from Tunis, had everything to learn from the men of Shebika, that he had neglected things more important than reading and writing, things that they knew and he didn't.

We had arrived by now at the open space at the foot of the mountains and the spring. We were climbing up a path paved with crumbling gravel into which Si Tijani stuck his stick, striving to keep a footing on the less slippery, larger stones, those not blown away by the wind. Ali had discovered the lair of a mountain goat and was anxious also to point out a cave where people had hidden during the epoch of guerrilla warfare. He walked with the rapid springy step of a true Southerner, accustomed to covering incredible distances on foot. Above our heads birds were flying towards the mountain-tops, heavy birds that alighted frequently on the ground and covered some of the distance by running.

As he walked Ali told us that the men had held long meetings to find out how much money they actually made and to talk about the impoverishment caused by their marriage customs. They had talked about life in general and what we might have said to a young girl that made her want to leave Shebika. She might as well have gone, said Ridha the grocer, since she had died from the bite of a scorpion.

When we reached the top of the hill and sat down in a circle to smoke, we looked at the semi-circular formation of dried, reddish rocks and the triangular expansion of the *wadi* at the juncture of the bases of the two steep mountains. A light cloud of smoke was rising from the invisible Shebika below. Out of his trouser pocket Ali took a newspaper which we recognized as *Afrique Action.** In it, a few days earlier, we had published an article, with photographs of Shebika, whose purpose was to draw the government's attention to the plight of the South. Someone had brought this copy of the paper from Tawzar and, after a general inspection, it had come into Ali's hands. Few of the villagers were able to read the text, but all were sensitive to the illustrations. They had never dreamed that our stay, in spite of its length, could create any more of a stir than the frequent passage of minor government officials and technicians, which had never produced any effect whatsoever.

When the paper first came, Ridha attempted to translate parts of the article from French into Arabic. But even so, Ali assured us, most of the content escaped his audience's understanding. Now Ali opened it at the page which carried the photographs of the village. The article spoke, naturally, of the poverty of Shebika, but also of the attitude of expectation of the whole South, and this latter point the translator had failed to render. Now, holding out the paper, Ali asked us for a further explanation. He was still excited by the illustrations and, waving the paper in the air as if he were signalling to Shebika, he said: 'That's us! That's us!' Then, staring again at the illustrations with the attentiveness of someone who is unused to seeing a portrayal of his immediate surroundings, he pointed out old Qaddur (now dead) in one of the first photographs which we had taken, and then a group of children. Laughing softly to himself he said that now the villagers were more aware of their

* Now *Jeune Afrique*, a French-language weekly published in Paris.

identity than they were before. This, they knew, was Shebika, and it was time for Tunis to take its existence into account.

At this point we got up and started to move on. Ali's real purpose was not to show us the lair of a mountain goat but to lead us to the other side of the barren mountains, where there was no path other than that traced by the passage of a huntsman like himself. Si Tijani continued to puff peacefully at his pipe, walking as if the movement of his legs was independent of that of his body and pausing at intervals to observe the tracks made by snakes on the ground.

Finally Ali pointed to something sticking up over the mountain-tops – three or four metal skeletons gleaming in the sun. He explained that 'Americans' have settled into this deserted spot and are drilling for oil. They have already laid out a road leading to Redayif on the other side, and thrown up wooden shacks in which they live. No one can see or hear them but they are there. Two or three men from the village have wandered around the camp, but they have seen nothing but a dozen or so men in oilskin suits working at shiny machines. Nothing more. No workers are being hired and no food is purchased on the spot because everything is brought in by truck on the hastily built road. Nothing is sold, either. A man from Tamerza saw the drilling operation at night, when the whole site was brilliantly lit up. Ali was impressed. He had never seen anything like this : so big an operation set in motion so fast, so small a number of men to work such big machines. What struck him most was the silence, and the isolation of the site among the mountains.

This phenomenon has been the object of considerable discussion at Shebika, where they say that if oil is struck, then life will be the way it is on the other side of the border, in Algeria, where people are living in new houses, with electricity, and drawing monthly salaries which come to as much money as passes through the hands of all the men of Shebika in a whole year.

How does he, Ali, envisage this change? He has his own ideas, based on personal observation. He saw Sfax before the construction of the refinery, when people lived in straw or slat huts in the swampland. When the refinery was built many of these had to be torn down, but their owners moved into something better. They found work either at the refinery itself or in the stores and workshops which grew up around it. Everything changed, and he feels sure that this will happen in Shebika. The people will stay put, because for them there is no place like Shebika, but they will have new houses and electric current such as there is at Tawzar. There will be a new Mosque and the tomb of Sidi Sultan will be repainted and restored.

We looked up at the shiny aluminium structures sticking up over the black rocks. Birds were chirping all around us. As we walked back, Ali told us again that hopes for a change were high at Shebika. He pulled the newspaper out of his pocket, and we sat down among the rocks in order to translate the article for him. He knows now that it contains a description of the village, a mention of old Qaddur and Si Tijani, that there is emphasis on the most urgent needs: seed, fertilizers, a dispensary, a road. Nodding his head, he approves. He has learned, as Si Tijani told us later, that you have to state your needs and insist upon them if you want to obtain satisfaction. He is glad that we have stated the case for Shebika. As we continued on our way he went on:

'This piece in the paper has made for a lot of talk.'

'How could there be talk if people didn't know what it said?'

'Well, they knew that it was about Shebika, about us, all of us. We need to know that we are talked about.'

'And what did people say about the article? What effect did it have on them?'

'You mean, did they read it? No. But they understood that Shebika was being talked about in Tunis and everywhere else that the paper goes. All over the world, probably.'

'No, not all over the world.'

'Well, we don't know how many places there are in the world. But it's a good thing to make it known that there are people in Shebika.'

'And the oil: if the Americans strike oil, what do you think will happen?'

'Oil? That would make us all rich. I'd open up my land and say to the government: "Come and buy it! There's oil underneath." I'd buy land somewhere else and build myself a house.'

'I wouldn't be so sure,' put in one of our researchers. 'The subsoil doesn't belong to you; it belongs to the government.'

'All right. But the government would have to pay for it, at least for the top level.'

'Not as much as you may think. If there's really oil on your land, you'd get hardly enough money to buy yourself another piece somewhere else.'

'That's not the point,' said one of our occasional collaborators (Salah's friend who is nicknamed 'Lenin'). 'If oil is struck we shan't get rich, but our standard of living will be such that we can go to spend our week-ends in New York.'

No one answered right away. Then another student raised an objection:

'Doesn't it depend upon the distribution of wealth?'

'What difference would distribution make? We'd all be millionaires. Like in Texas. Not because the oil would be ours, but because it makes everyone rich.'

'Not like Texas. Like Kuwait.'

'Yes, Kuwait. That's what I meant. In Kuwait they live in tents for two months a year, in order not to lose the habit, and the rest of the time they live in the palaces they've built for themselves.'

Si Tijani translated this exchange, which was in French, to Ali, who laughed silently to himself as he walked along and finally answered:

'They know how, in the cities. As for us, we'd have a new village, and electricity, and that would be a good thing.'

'Which is more important,' asked one of the researchers, 'that Shebika should be written up in the newspaper or that we should strike oil?'

'That people should talk about Shebika,' said Ali.

'You can't imagine the importance of this article,' said another researcher. 'They haven't read it, but they talk about it as if it were an event. Under the portico, near the *qaddus*, while you were up in the mountains, we talked it all over. "It's not just a question of words," they said; "it's a matter of realizing that this is no longer a place that nobody knows. Through these pictures other people have seen Shebika, just as surely as if they'd been here. People have come before and taken pictures, but nobody knows what happened to them; they simply kept them at home. But this time they're in the paper. The governor of Qafsa and his friends at Tawzar will discover that people know about us. They won't be able to speak of us in the same way as before." '

'And so people said that this is a good thing?'

'Yes, a good thing. They say that the village will never be the same again. This article has changed them radically. They're beginning to say that they must behave in the way that's expected of them. While you were gone I took part in a discussion with the nomads. For the first time the men of Shebika took a strong hand. It was a question of putting out some goats to pasture with the camels, and we told the nomads that we could find men among ourselves to look after the goats if the fee for pasturing was too high. I had the impression that they had acquired a more definite idea of how they should live together, of how they should carry out the various roles of the village. The thing that impressed you most five years ago, the fact that the people of Shebika didn't believe in anything, that they were living haphazardly, this seems to be no longer true. In the last six months there has been considerable progress, and the newspaper article has been one of its factors. They want to live up to it. That's more important to them than striking oil.'

About the drilling, Ali was quite right. Out of thirty *khammes* whom we questioned twenty-eight said that 'striking oil is less important than the fact of there being talk about Shebika', because 'talking about Shebika means talking about human beings, and that is pleasing to God'. 'Yes, oil is a good thing, and the radio has told them that it is Arab and it's up to them to dispose of it as they please.' The young man who said these words was one who had seen military service and never moved without his transistor radio, wrapped in a red wool case.

'That the oil is here or elsewhere, in the eastern or western Arab countries, what does it matter? It's all Arab. That it should be found at Shebika or somewhere else is of no importance; the Arabs are all brothers; it's Muslim oil. If the Europeans came here it was because they knew that the Arabs had this wealth. They're still coming, armed with dollars instead of guns, all on the oil's account. If the Arabs were to hold back the oil, cars wouldn't move, airplanes would be grounded and machinery would come to a halt. Except in the Arab countries everything would stop running. That's what has the rest of the world scared and makes the Arabs the most important of all peoples. If the oil didn't flow you'd be stuck . . .'

Not all of them are quite so apocalyptic, simply because they don't really understand the nature of the oil-wells. 'A sort of mine,' some call it; 'a hole, like the kind you drill for a well, with great basins in which to gather the oil, hammers that drive enormous nails into the ground, without stopping.' Then, because the oil-wells interest them less than the newspaper, which they pass from hand to hand, examining it as if they were reading, especially the photographs, a chorus of voices arises from under the portico.

'Look, there we are!'

'There's Qaddur, sitting on a stone. God's house and Qaddur.'

'He's all alone. They should have put in the others.'

'Once upon a time a German took pictures of God's house, with the children.'

'We can ask for more money from Tawzar, since we're in the news.'

'God willing, it won't do any harm.'

'There's the *qaddus*! The *qaddus*!'

(The speaker exclaims as if he were discovering for the first time an object only five or six feet away, or rather as if seeing it in a photograph had revealed it to him.)

'We're poor, really poor. When the government people see it they won't let things stay the way they are.'

'God's house is small, smaller than the rest.'

'You can't tell what the effect will be. You can't say.'

'There's Ismaïl's tent, with Ismaïl.'

'Ismaïl's dead.'

'There he is, though, with the tent.'

'God willing, he isn't like Qaddur.'

('At this point I felt I had to say something,' says the researcher who taped this conversation. 'Our pictures were old, dating from our first trip. Since then two of the men we photographed – old Qaddur and old Ismaïl – had died. This might have led them to think that a photograph brings bad luck. So I changed the subject. I asked them what was the first thing they'd like to see changed if the government really decided to do something for Shebika.')

'What could be different, you mean? The first thing would be to clean the streets and put new roofs on the houses.'

'In the newspaper they picture the houses just the way they are, falling to pieces, no better than caves in the mountains. That'll show the government people in Tunis how we live and who we are.'

'The Minister of Agriculture ought to come here and give us seeds.'

'And tools.'

'Yes, God willing, tools.'

In any case, as one of our researchers put it, the very existence of the article, the fact that they had got into the news, transformed them. Or, to be more exact, it forced them to be more 'Shebikan', to play their roles with a purposefulness which they had not heretofore imagined. Yesterday and the day before we saw two meetings under the portico of the heads of the most important families. One was to choose two men to be sent to work on a public works project at El Hamma, the other to settle the problem of the goats which were supposed to be put out to pasture with the Bedouins' camels, a service for which the Bedouins had asked too high a price. Once upon a time such meetings were practically unheard of. Most of the men sprawled indifferently on the ground, without seeming to listen, while the decisions were made by two or three of their number, always the same. Now, for the first time, there was a broader meeting, with a discussion. The choice of the two men to benefit from the public works jobs was based on the needs of their families and, as for the affair of the goats, the Bedouins, for the first time, got the worst of it, since the men of Shebika threatened to find a shepherd among themselves if necessary. It wasn't very solid or definitive or conscious, but the knowledge that Shebika exists somewhere outside itself changed its inhabitants in their own eyes.

If, then, the newspaper article stirred up the miserable and inert life of Shebika, this is because for the first time in years the villagers felt that they were drawn into an event in the outside world which concerned them. Many groups and villages of the Maghrib decayed when an order from the city (promulgated by the Bey, or the French colonial administration or even the new national government) forbade them to indulge in the traditional *jaiysh* or guerrilla warfare. During the period of disguised conflict these groups and villages existed by virtue of their enemies. Underpinning the state of war among non-historical peoples there is doubtless the hostility that one group nurtures towards another simply because the latter mirrors its existence, and it feels in some way mutilated by this alien conception. The resulting hostility (equivalent, perhaps, to one group's urge to show itself to another in a guise different from that which the other expects and thus to regain some of the substance which it believes its rival stole from it) falls to pieces, of course, when a government imposes so-called pacification. Subsequently the rival groups decay all the more rapidly, because there is no longer any need for them to prove their existence to each other. They fall back on themselves, no longer bothering to play their former collective roles or even the multiple roles within their group. In other words, they let themselves go and disintegrate. We may be led to conclude that a *human group has its own structure only from the moment in which it enters into competition with other groups which owe their structures to the same rivalry, or when it receives certain information which causes its decayed social organism to crystallize into an organized and logical system.*

During the first phase of our investigation (two and a half years) the men of Shebika lived in a state of abandonment such that it was almost impossible to proceed to a reconstruction of their way of life. This low estate affected not only their everyday practices and religious rites but also their conscience. This implicit force, which makes for observance of the rules and also for an impulse of collective renewal, (that is, insofar as it is not, as Durkheim thought, a mere negative pressure or form of coercion), was dead. The new national government which replaced a colonial administration (in this remote border-post, one of a military nature) left this and all other such groups as undeveloped as they were before.

One of the most important things which, paradoxically enough, prevented them from being completely wiped out by the impact of a government administration was the recourse to a drug, Indian hemp or hashish. *Takruri*, as it is called here, has long played a determining role, as have the use and abuse of its substitute, tea. The indolence which pervaded the whole South on a hot, heavy afternoon (even in winter, although less visibly, because it was hidden away in private courtyards or under the portico) was the chief characteristic of the groups whose substructure had been wiped out by a foreign government.

The effects of *takruri*, smoked in carelessly rolled cigarettes, is well known. But we must take into account also the fact that tea, formerly rejected as sinful by the 'unwashed peoples' of the Maghrib, is now drunk there as a drug. The custom of tea-drinking originally spread because it calmed the peasants' endemic hunger. This was at the time when tea (which, under the influence of English trade, had, in the nineteenth century, replaced coffee in Morocco) was spreading from the empire of the Sherifs to the Saharians, Tripolitanians and Tunisians. At this same moment, during the 1912 war between Italy and Turkey, many Tunisians were emigrating towards Egypt, or towards the ancient 'Ifriqiya'.* The fact that tea was taken up at Shebika before its use was widespread in the whole region is not at all unlikely, that is, if we consider the close relationship between nomads and villagers.

From this time on tea – a powerful, bitter brew quite dissimilar to that which we know – was an intoxicant no less strong than *takruri*. These two drugs have a deep social signifi-

*E. G. Gobert, *'Usages et rites alimentaires des Tunisiens'*, in *Archives de l'Institut Pasteur de Tunis*, XXIX, 1940, p. 20.

cance, for they allow their users to release their pent-up energy in the form of dreams. Drugs form, indeed, a sort of bond among debilitated social groups among which long-since superannuated structures still survive in some sort of ghostly fashion.

During the struggle for Independence all sorts of new things forced themselves upon the attention of Shebika. The word 'independence' itself had a mythical meaning, postulating the autonomy of long-standing groups and its accompanying frustrations, which call for compensation. Then there was the call for a total change and renewal of a society that had to be torn out of its 'colonial immobility'. Momentarily these brave slogans lent Shebika a new purpose, evidenced by its participation in or at least approval of the nationalist uprising. As is often forgotten, this uprising continued, in remote parts of the country, after it had stopped in the cities. In 1958, after the French had recognized Tunisian autonomy, members of the new Bourguiba government, together with French army officers, had to be sent on a countryside mission of pacification.

Subsequently, however, the new government was not in a position to effect the changes which it had called for so urgently. A country can't be re-structured within a few years, especially one like Tunisia, richer in politicians and administrators than in monetary wealth or natural resources. The fact that the South lingers in the state of stagnation of the last hundred years is no reflection on the new government's very real effort to transform it. But the inevitably slow pace at which progress filters down into the Centre and South has led their inhabitants to think that they are neglected. Some family or village units break up and set out (like the family of our Salah) for the cities; others stay put and give way to the gradual decay and somnolence characteristic of a group deprived of its structure.

When we first came to Shebika, in 1961, decay and somnolence were at their height. The people were living in the paranoic state which grows out of a discrepancy between real life and the group reality. The government had forbidden the use of *takruri*, which formerly had channelled dissatisfaction into daydreaming; the only drug left was tea, which has a way of stimulating rather than calming frustration.

It was through the newspaper article that Shebika recovered its own image. The fact – or at least the idea – that the far-away central government had seen a picture of Shebika gave the village new life and impelled it, to some degree, to restore its old mechanism. In other words, the physical solidity of the group exists and can be seen and experienced only in a moment of crisis. But, at this point, the reinforced structure, which implied the functioning of the various roles that make up the system and both the collective and individual consciences of its members, overflowed its limits. It tended to destroy a fragile and temporary equilibrium and to build up a new one based on the *expectation* produced by development, or rather by the prospect of development and change as seen through the eyes of a microscopic group.

The most striking evidence of this change and of the temporary structure brought into being by a startling piece of news (the appearance of the village in a newspaper) was in the comment of young Ali when he said that ever since that day 'we talk, among ourselves, about everything'. Shebika talking about itself, bearing witness in words to its structured existence ... here we have a positive demonstration of social dynamism, functioning, alas, in a vacuum.

The Quarry

Then there was the episode of the quarry ...

This time, when we arrived at Shebika at the morning hour when old Ali and the Mosque attendant were usually lying in the narrow shaded area at the foot of the walls, we found the square empty and the water of the *qaddus* flowing peacefully, alone. The grocery was closed down, but more definitively so than we had ever seen it, with a lock on the door, and the sewing-machine had been pushed into a corner. Ridha, the grocer, had said to us: 'Only an earthquake could prevent me from being there or my uncle from replacing me in case I have to go on a buying trip to Tawzar.' But now the door was shut and locked and all the village houses seemed to be empty.

What surprised us most and roused us – we didn't know exactly why – to indignation was the discovery of the muezzin's checker board, with its pieces of camel dung, thrown down haphazardly at the foot of the Mosque's wall, on the square. We went back to the jeep and listened to the silence of the deserted village, over which there hung the cold smell of an imperfectly extinguished fire. In all the years of our visits to Shebika we had never found it abandoned in this way.

The most incongruous thing of all was the silence. There was no sound, even when a child ran down from the direction of the grocery, crossed the square without looking at us and hesitated for a moment before running around the Mosque towards the place where the cliff on which the village is built slopes steeply down into a conglomeration of stones. Khalil ran after him and disappeared from view. Something new was afoot, of which we knew nothing, and which estranged us from the village. When Khalil came back, after catching up with and questioning the child, and told us that all the men of the village were holding a discussion down in the quarry, then we knew that a new Shebika was emerging from its cocoon.

As we went down the winding path we saw the hundred or so men that make up the male population of the village and of the near-by tents standing among the stones, leaning on pick-axes, not as if they were going to work but rather as if they wanted and were waiting for something. They raised their heads and stared at us as we made our way awkwardly down the path. They made no gesture, but stared at us expectantly as if they had been waiting for us to keep a long-standing appointment. At this same moment we saw, above us, lined up at the foot of the houses which overhang the cliff, all the women of the village, in their red and violet dresses, standing quite motionless with the children tugging at their skirts. Crowded together in a solid mass, they stared mutely down at the men below. They were simply there.

When, armed with our notebooks and our tape-recorder, we reached the centre of the group of men, we felt empty and disarmed, because for the first time we were confronted by a phalanx of hard, stubborn faces, by the whole of Shebika. Finally Muhammad came forward to shake our hands and tell us that 'they had things to say'. We sat down among them, on the stones, as if inviting them to follow our example. A few, followed by a few others, did start to take a seat, and there was a general movement in our direction. Finally they re-grouped, some sitting on the rocks, others leaning on their pick-axes or stretching out on the ground. Usually they were all smiles, but today their faces were stony and unyielding.

They broke out talking, in hoarse voices, all together. The new, hard look on their wrinkled faces indicated that something had happened, a purely exterior event, perhaps, but one that had drawn to the surface unsuspected resources deep within them, greater than those which they applied to their work in the oasis or to the apparent nonchalance of the summer days. When we finally persuaded them to let one of their number speak for all, something in them relaxed and they were content to nod their heads in approval. This meeting in the quarry lasted for two whole hours.

We learned that 'they had been pushed to the limit of endurance'. It all began when a representative of the governor appeared upon the scene. He had looked at the houses and the school, taken measurements with a long wire handled by two young men, counted the paces that it took him to cover first one distance and then another, and finally gone away without any explanation. Two or three days later some trucks arrived, bringing with them hooks and pick-axes, some of which the men were now holding in their hands. They showed them to us in a brusque, almost violent way which we had never seen before. They had been told, they informed us, to break up the stones and haul them away from the quarry. A foreman – a certain Nureddin from Tawzar – was to come to oversee their work the next day and to stay at Shebika until it was finished. They were to work five hours a day and to receive the customary wages. The villagers were delighted. For a long time they had been hoping to get in on a construction project, and this one, they thought, must involve the rebuilding of their houses,

which for two or three generations had been falling into dis-
repair. At last the government was taking an interest in them,
and they were inspired to work harder than ever before. They
looked forward to wages of three hundred millimes a day, and a
pound of American semolina. The care of the oasis was abandoned, because they were sure that everything was going to be
different. And so, for two weeks, they hewed rock out of the
quarry and broke it up into approximately equal pieces. Actually they quite enjoyed this sort of work. It was more strenuous
than that of the oasis but it was regular and well paid.

And now, or rather the day before, an engineer from Tamerza
had come to tell them that the newly cut stone was not for
the repair of their houses but for the construction of a building
to lodge the governor's representative or the National Guards
when they came on a tour of inspection. At first they went
right on working, persistent in their belief that engineers would
be coming to show them how to rebuild their houses, with
trucks of cement. But the man from Tamerza, perched on a
wall above them, kept shouting down that they weren't working for themselves but for the governor. When their ears had
been filled with the words of the man from Tamerza and when
they remembered how the first government man had taken
measurements in the public square, they decided to stop working. That evening a car arrived, bringing an engineer from the
Public Works Office and a National Guard. Once more they were
told that the project was for the government building. This,
they said plainly, they didn't want. They were glad to work
together, but on their own houses, not on a house for a stranger. Of what use could it be? To lodge a man from Tunis or the
Sahil, a man with dark glasses and a tie, repeating to them what
they had already heard over the radio? Might he not force them
to pay taxes? Why should they lodge a man who had no reason
to be there unless it was to spy on them and prevent them
from doing the things they were accustomed to do?

When they had told us this they all began to talk at once,
demanding that we take notes on what they were saying, because 'it ought to be discussed and put into print in order that
Bourguiba should know what is going on and stop it'. Because

they, the men of Shebika, didn't intend to work for no purpose. Calming down somewhat, they spoke, in a sing-song manner, one after the other, leaning on a bucket or a pick-axe or sitting on a rock, within their eyes the stubborn look that country people put on when they have made up their minds about something and will not be budged from it.

'What we need, God willing,' said Ali, 'is to fix the roofs and walls of the houses. As it is, during the winter, rain falls directly into the rooms and we have to sleep on boards in one corner. After that we should build a flight of steps from the grocery down to the square, because there, too, water runs like a *wadi* in the winter. The houses need roofs as strong as that of the school, and sloping, on account of the storms ...'

'Electricity, that's the main thing,' said Hassan. 'With a year of hard work we could put in poles all the fifteen miles or less from El Hamma. There are motors, too, which make electricity, and we could perfectly well build one like the motor I saw running twenty-four hours a day at Tawzar.'

'Never mind about electricity. What we ought to do is drill a well beside the spring, in order to provide more water for the oasis. Then we should plant trees farther into the plain. The Bedouins have sown wheat at the foot of the mountains and tapped water from the oasis before it goes into the rocks, underground. There's no reason why we shouldn't enlarge the oasis.'

'It takes tools. If they give us the tools, we'll do the work. But I mean work for ourselves, not for others.'

'We need new seeds. And machines to dig up the earth and thresh the wheat, to drill a well and make electricity. We ourselves don't know how to use these tools, but we can learn, and our children will make others.'

'Why does the governor come to bring us presents only once every two years? Presents are all right, but there are things that ought to be ours by right, just as they are other people's.'

None of the speakers asked for food, or tea, or tobacco. They spoke only of seeds and machines and tools. All of them thought they could fulfil their desires if they had the proper tools. Tools seemed to them the clue to any real change in the village life. As the 'skinny soldier' told us, 'This is a desert, but all sorts of things can be grown on the desert if you have the will to work and the tools to work with.' Not one of the villagers seemed to dream of making a personal fortune. They were wrapped up, all of them, in the idea that they had a right to the same tools as those owned by other people, the people they had heard about over the radio or from their children.

'When the engineer came we told him that we'd work for the government after we'd rebuilt our own houses. This was our most urgent necessity, and we knew it better than any occasional visitor. He examined the houses, counted up those that are in the worst condition and said he'd report on them. But the National Guard told us that the governor's representative was dead set on throwing up an administrative building, and nothing else.'

'We don't know how to read or write, but we know that our houses are in ruins, and that nowhere else in the country do people live in houses in this condition. If we didn't have building material, we wouldn't have anything to say, but we have stones from the quarry, and all we need is wood and cement. But we're not going to work on a house in which nobody will really live. We worked for the school-house, but we aren't going to work for a government building.'

They went on and on, saying the same thing over and over, until the sun began to sink low in the sky. The main thing was that they were there, without stirring, and that we were there with them. Finally one man spoke up and said:

'You've talked to us about a lot of things, and you must understand why we're doing what we do. You asked all sorts of questions, and then you wrote about us. Why must we stay poor? After all, we're not beggars. Once upon a time the men of Shebika were land-owners.'

They looked at one another. There they were, with their wives above them, the cold winter wind billowing out their veils. And they, the men, stood leaning on just the sort of tools they had always wanted to possess, lent to them, ironically enough, in order that they might build a house not their own.

'The government's all right,' said one of them. 'But if they come here they'll find out that we can do as well as anyone else, perhaps better, and there's no reason why we shouldn't be treated the same way.'

'Bourguiba's never been here,' put in Bashir. 'He's never been anywhere in the South except when the French put him in prison. Down here we want to remain good Muslims and at the same time to enjoy some of the good things of modern life. It's hard to know what the government's after. The radio speaks all the time about the well-being of the people, but it seems as if the people would have to scramble for this well-being themselves.'

At this point a man confided to one of us that our help was absolutely essential, above all our calling their plight to the attention of people in high places. In the final analysis, we had set them on the way which they were following today.

The men were standing around us, with strained faces, their ghandurahs wrapped around them as protection against the wind. For the first time they were putting into a form intelligible to us, and also to themselves, ideas which, once they found verbal expression, became concrete demands. They presented these ideas in a dramatic way because, in the course of presentation, they acquired a life of their own; the speakers began to envisage what action they might take once they were fully aware of the many necessities to which they were entitled. An old man, who had not spoken before, suddenly shouted, almost angrily:

'To think that there are sorts of things in the world we might like to have but don't even know about!'

Later on we heard different reactions. But on this particular day the men of Shebika made us feel that they wanted us to take note of their needs and present them in the appropriate places after we had gone away.

We went back to the city and tried to meet the 'responsible officials', those agreeable, precise, often efficient men, more concerned with government procedures than with the human beings regulated by them. (Actually it is, in many ways, a good thing that this government should be so solidly installed in a country which had never previously known anything like it,

which was hardly aware of its own national existence before
the leader gave it a *name*.)

'Those people down in Shebika,' one such official assured us,
'are a bunch of fakers, of ham actors who took advantage of
your presence to say whatever went through their heads. For
one thing, there was never any question of building a house for
the benefit of the governor's representative. The idea was for a
warehouse in which to store grain. The Party would have made
some use of it, of course, but it would have served, also, as a
distribution point for medicines.'

We objected that this didn't respond to the inhabitants' desire to rebuild their own dilapidated houses. But the official
only shrugged his shoulders. They had received the same wages
as anyone else for their work in the quarry and they ought to
be grateful to the government for this opportunity. As for the
governor, they should have no complaints on his score, since he
made an annual distribution of seeds and drugs. In fact, a medical truck went all over the countryside, offering care to sick
children. We told him, of course, that this truck had paid only
one visit to Shebika (after being stuck several times in the
desert sand), and then in order to show a film on trachoma.
The people of Shebika, he insisted, had always been hard to
please. They preferred lying around in their rat-hole to working
in the mines at Redayif. (This is a point commonly made by the
Bedouins, and we learned later that our interlocutor came from
a nomad family on the other side of the Jerid, towards Douz.)
In any case, he told us, we were wasting our time. The men of
Shebika would prolong the quarrying operation in order to continue to draw regular pay. For this reason, too, they'd throw up
the projected building and in due time it would become indispensable to them for the storage of grain, dates and seeds. We
said that seeds, instead of being held in storage, should be distributed to these same villagers who claimed that for years
none had been given to them. Here, too, he insisted, the villagers had pulled the wool over our eyes. They had been given
seeds, but they had proceeded to trade them for sheep and
goats (for their meat) or used them to pay off debts. They
traded everything that was given them with either the Bedouin

or the shopkeepers of Tamerza; they were a bunch of liars and bluffers, and the only reason why they didn't want the warehouse was because they were afraid of anyone getting to know their business.

(If the building was really intended to be a warehouse, then there was something else against it. Wheat grew on the plains and was cultivated by the nomads, the very nomads who had bought into the oasis. A warehouse would serve them rather than the village, which was already humiliated by the fact that they were encroaching upon it and making it into a colony.)

But the official brushed all our arguments aside. These were petty, parochial problems, he said impatiently. We had been ill-advised to take them up instead of interesting our students in the great national questions, such as the future installation of Destour socialism in the countryside.

'The people of Shebika are left-overs from the past,' he said. 'If they don't adapt they'll be swept away. At best they'll make up their minds to go to work in the mines or in the towns. Eventually a hotel for tourists will be built on the bank of the *wadi* and they'll be all too happy to have jobs as cooks or bell-boys.'

'We know that the construction and maintenance of hotels is the main bulwark against unemployment, but the work it provides is menial and unproductive. The people of Shebika would be better employed as farmers or weavers, right on the spot. A hotel creates jobs, to be sure, but none that develops any special skill; it simply shapes a servant class, one that is torn from its peasant roots but that, for lack of a definite skill, will never be able to fit into an industrial civilization.'

'These are irrelevant considerations,' said our interlocutor: 'the real problem facing this Shebika of yours is how to integrate with socialism. Of course this is a national issue, not a local one.'

On this problem – integration with neo-Destour socialism – we might have had something to say, based on what we had heard in the village during our last year of research, when the Party had changed directives and even headquarters, and the press and radio were filled with explanations of the new state socialism. We had tried to find out, naturally enough, whether this socialism would fit in with the hopes and expectations of the people of Shebika. And, in this light, we saw that the episode of the quarry indicated a receptivity to 'socialist management' greater than all the rehearsed speeches with which the 'local yokels' of Central and Southern Tunisia greeted the visiting big-shots from the North.

First, one must understand what 'socialism' means to a man of Shebika, not as a word or concept (although the five years during which we took root in and studied this village did help its inhabitants, as they themselves said, to put their hitherto unexpressed thoughts into words), but as a factor of everyday life. At the beginning of our investigation we were astounded to find that most of the approximately forty-year-old men whom we questioned (both land-owners and *khammes*) knew what was meant by the direct management of collective production and the responsibility which it entailed. 'That means I'd work the land together with my neighbour; we'd sell our dates together and then, please Allah, I'd get my share', or 'I'd keep an eye on what my neighbour was doing and he'd keep an eye on me, so that we'd all reap the same benefits.' There were also less precise definitions, such as: 'There would have to be one man to keep accounts – Ridha, the grocer, no doubt – but he'd have to give up his store and concentrate on book-keeping', or 'If anyone wanted to keep all the profits to himself, we'd simply give him his share; then we'd get together to say: "Here's your wheat and your goats, but this is my water."' Nureddin, a land-owner, and Muhammad, a *khammes*, were the most articulate of our interlocutors.

'When I was looking for work for my son,' said Nureddin, 'I found only my parcel of land in the oasis. I wanted him to go to work somewhere else, and I went with him to Tawzar and Dakash, but everywhere they told us to go back home, because he'd never find work anywhere else. Of course, there was the job of harvesting the dates, but the Bedouins are moving in on that during the two-month season. There was nothing doing in the way of public works – either road-building or electrical installations. My son didn't go to school, because we didn't have one when he was little, and he hasn't done military service either. So I brought him back to the land which God gave us, and he works on it with me. If we had a cooperative of some kind, he'd do something more, I'm sure. He wouldn't be a mere dirt-farmer if we had machinery. He's gifted for machines.'

'Machines?' echoed Muhammad. 'God has seen to it that we're no worse off than the rest of our brothers. There's no need for a cooperative here in Shebika, because we already own most of the things we need in common. Of course, we might be better off if we all got together, than if we honestly divided everything among us. But that's something to be discussed not only with the government but among ourselves.'

This sort of conversation revealed to us a whole level of new experience to which we had had no clue. The men of Shebika knew more about collective and cooperative farming than we had imagined, even after four years of research among them. In groups of this kind levels of belief or awareness seem to emerge when their total experience is caught up in a movement of or a stimulation to change. The richness of a group is not measured by the complexity of its stable structures but by the variety and flexibility of the classifications with which it seeks self-understanding through the world to which it belongs, by the number of its real or imaginary acts of participation, by the widely different levels which are manifest in its collective life, whether hidden behind other beliefs or out in the open. The Shebikans' 'preview' of cooperative management came out, under our questioning, as the product of common experience, built up amid the need and expectation of taking part in something new. It was, in itself, an attempt at rational construction, however awkwardly expressed. The inner significance of the words of a conversation has greater wealth and concrete meaning than a system of pure logic proper to our European categories.

On the other hand, it is clear, upon analysis, that the clear vision of autonomous collective management took shape and became a concept during two historical events, one of which is little known while the other was verbally publicized throughout the Maghrib.

The first was the protest movement of 1955, before the achievement of internal autonomy and independence, which crystallized the discontent of the *khammes* of Tawzar and Naftah and even led to a strike, the first ever to take place in the Jerid. In the protest demonstration two hundred men gathered to demand a reorganization of the labour system. But there were no consequences either in this period of nationalist agitation (when the demonstration was actually put down) or even after Independence was won, since the local Destour leaders were at this time and in these places mostly large-scale land-owners. But the effect produced by an action of this kind, its far-away echoes and repercussions, seems to carry weight and create new symbols or attitudes in proportion to the number of organized groups which receive the shock. The repercussion of a dynamic message is weaker among a scattered population than among agglomerations or communities, where it is expressed in concrete attitudes or even in previously thought-out practical ideas.

This event of 1955 is, as we have said, little known, but it concerned the Jerid as a unit and roused opinion on a familiar and concrete problem, common to the whole region. The second event, the spread of Algerian ideas of autonomous local management and socialist cooperatives (both undertaken by the government of Ben Bella) is a very different matter. But it reached Shebika, first through the Algiers Radio, which explained these policies at great length almost every day, and second from across the border, in the reports of travellers. Whether the Algerian experiment in rural socialism was or was not a success is irrelevant. What matters is the contagious idea that a new social and economic group could be built up in the Maghrib countryside and permit the existing villages to alter their structure without dropping out of existence. Knowing the internal cohesion of Shebika we could see that the idea of an on-the-spot change-over, of a redistribution of the village's fundamental social elements within the already established forms, could not fail to be attractive.

But if, in 1964, socialism was an actual and determining factor of Shebika's collective expectation, further analysis did not reveal in what technical terms the villagers envisaged its achievement. Here, again, we ran into the expedient of recourse to the government, into the passivity characteristic of a region where, ever since the collapse of the wandering rebel tribes, all initiative has stemmed from the big cities. 'Let the government give us tools and send us engineers!' or : 'It's up to Bourguiba to say what he wants; if he says the word, we'll do it', or again 'It's hard to say anything unless the governor comes and tells us : "Here's what we're going to do, here are the seeds, the stones, the cement, the machines and the money...." '
In other words, Shebika is counting on government aid in order to carry out the self-development which its long-dormant dynamism suddenly demands. One cannot ask the villagers to perceive the contradiction between a state socialism, held back by an unenterprising centralized government, and an independent action which calls for a radical and fundamental reform whose nature they only dimly apprehend.

As always, it is at the level of daily life that such contradictions come to light. The governor's representative or his subordinates at Redayif and Tamerza (of which Shebika is an administrative dependency) decide to centralize the distribution of seeds and the storage of the harvested grain at this strategically central point. The warehouse or granary is also to serve as a party headquarters. But the villagers, who ask nothing better than to participate in some collective enterprise, if only it remedies their own desperate condition, lay down their tools and start talking. It is clear for all to see that there is a contradiction between the abstract plans of the central government and the needs of a locality where no government official has ever lingered long enough to explain the government's aims and help the inhabitants to embrace a new type of economy. The upshot can only be coercion. And this is the result of the inanition of petty bureaucrats, the lack of imagination of officials who seek to apply the verbal norms of an abstract, urban socialist doctrine, calling for a complete reversal of the country's political habits such as the apparently monolithic structure of the 'Destour Socialist Party' cannot yet put into effect.*

When we came back in 1966, a year after the end of our investigation, we saw how the pro-socialist attitude of the people of Shebika had changed, not so much in reference to their experience as a whole as to one of its aspects.

In 1966 there was a whole new situation which, a year later, was to be that of the whole country. The people of Shebika had foreseen its consequences inasmuch as the change in their mentality had accustomed them to conceptualization and to a certain rational and practical view of the immediate future. The new situation was brought about by the transformation of all the groceries in the country into cooperatives. This step was justifiable in the framework of the national economy, inasmuch as it was to lead to similar measures in other sectors of the production and distribution of food, or at least to the creation of new organisms in which the ruling class and the big land-owners were not to play a preponderant role. But we found the people of Shebika in a state of absolute (the word is not too strong) despair. Let us listen to the words of one of our friends, a very poor *khammes*:

'If they do away with the groceries, where are we to buy oil and tea? At Tawzar they told us we'd have to buy packaged tea and oil by the bottle. But where are we to find the money to pay five hundred millimes in cash for a quart of oil? We've never put out more than a hundred millimes at a time. Where, I ask you, are we to find the money? We never have that much to spend. It means we'll go further into debt. But who'll be the creditor, if Ridha goes out of business and a cooperative steps in? You can't go into debt to a state cooperative.'

The dozen or so men whom we questioned all had the same misgivings. They didn't have enough cash to make any but the smallest purchases. And the government didn't seem to realize that the economy of their part of the country was based on complicated exchanges. There is also another and more serious drawback.

*When I spoke of these problems to a higher-up in the government, he smiled and said: 'This isn't China and never will be.'

'If Ridha is drawn into the cooperative, what about the money we all owe him? He'll have to be paid. He can and will wait, but eventually we'll have to pay up and we can't do that all at once. They're crazy there in Tunis.'

'No,' said a younger man, 'the government has a point. Ridha will no longer lend money. The government wants us to manage our affairs in such a way that we can buy things for cash instead of on credit. If Ridha stops lending money he'll only be doing what the government has set forth over the radio.'

We never did learn what were the villagers' true feelings towards Ridha. Although he is the focal point of all the exchanges within the village and between it and the Bedouin encampment, nobody ever talks about him. As for Ridha himself, he didn't seem to be worried. When one of us asked him for his opinion, he went on wrapping tea without raising his eyes. If this was what the government wanted to do, he said, there must be a reason, and he would fall into line.

We were puzzled by this self-assurance. But soon it was explained to us. 'Ridha's "in" with the government. He goes all the time to Redayif and Tamerza, and has joined the Party. He's better educated than the rest of us and probably he'll be put in charge of the cooperative and even of the entire village.'

*

We learned the sequel to 'the meeting in the quarry' when we came back to the Jerid – but not to Shebika – two months later. At the gasoline station of Tawzar we met one of our Shebika friends, Bashir, who hung on to the door of our jeep until we got out and went to drink a cup of tea with him. We started to question him, and he, of course, at first held back, pretending not to know what we were driving at. Finally he broke down and talked, uninterruptedly, until night, with the many details of his story lending it impressive power. From what he told us that day (which we later verified on the spot) we found out that 'the meeting in the quarry' had much greater significance than we realized at the time.

After we left the quarry the discussion continued. There was no letup in the opposition to the governor's plan for a combined granary and party office, which took no account of the fact that the village's private houses were falling to pieces. The women, too, stayed where we saw them, along the walls on top of the cliff, with the cold winter wind billowing out their wide red and violet dresses as if it would carry them away.

At a certain point the men looked at the sky and saw that the sun was close to the horizon. The muezzin, who had been working with them, hurried up to the Mosque to give the call to prayer. From below they could not hear it, but they managed as best they could, among the rocks, to prostrate themselves in the direction of Mecca. After they had got up someone (no one remembers who) said that it was all very simple. They would use the stones for their own houses and not that willed by the governor. Then they went back up the hill.

The next morning they returned to the gorge and began breaking up the rocks with picks and hammers, reducing them to very small pieces, preferably of the same size. This is something they know how to do, and it doesn't bore them. Time went fast, and finally Muhammad's wife, Nawa, came down with cups and several pots for tea. She stayed no longer than was necessary to hand these over to her husband for distribution. Later on, the women and children came out and took up their stance along the edge of the cliff, as they had done the day before, with bare feet and the children clinging to their skirts.

The wind was colder than on the previous day; clouds were scudding across the sky from east to west, as is usual at this season. The men drank their tea, rested and then went back to their stone-cutting. The foreman, who had put in a brief appearance, disappeared and they did not see him again until around three o'clock in the afternoon, when an engineer of the Department of Public Works brought him back in a jeep and then took him away after he had heard what the villagers had to say. They were not disturbed by the lack of supervision, but went right on working until the evening prayer and the hour for supper. From time to time they paused, leaned on their pick-axes, looked over at the tea-kettle, boiling in a place sheltered from the wind, or teased old Ali about the awkward way in which he tackled the rocks. In short, they behaved just like any group of men working together.

According to Bashir's story, it was almost dark when a dozen National Guards, whom no one had seen arrive, were seen standing near the Mosque. At the lower end of the ravine, towards the desert, two trucks were parked, with more Guards standing beside them. The villagers had stopped working in order to say their prayer; now, turning their heads, they saw one or two Guards, looking, in their khaki uniforms, like giant grasshoppers, climb up the side of the mountain.

The Guards moved into formation around the quarry. (Here, too, Bashir's story was confirmed by other on-the-spot reports.) As darkness fell the women uttered far-sounding guttural cries. The men knew that the women were voicing an appeal of some kind, but they made no reply. They left their tools on the ground and huddled together to protect themselves from the oncoming cold. The Guards, too, stayed where they were. The headlights of one of the two trucks played on the huddled group of villagers in their grey ghandurahs.

Nothing happened, on either one side or the other. No one spoke; those who had cigarettes lit them, cupping their hands to shield the match from the wind. Cigarettes gleamed, too, among the National Guards, who stood among the rocks at a slightly higher level. At this season the desert night is almost phosphorescent. Probably an observer could have made out the group of villagers, huddled together in the quarry, the National Guards scattered nonchalantly around them and the women above.

Nobody stirred. They were all *there*, waiting. The men stayed all night with their tools. Probably they did not even speak among themselves, because there was nothing more to say after the declaration that they wouldn't build a warehouse for the governor until they had repaired their own dwellings. Since this had been said, there was nothing to do but wait. Words, after all, make their own way.

When the sun rose the women had long since disappeared; the men were sleeping, huddled together, and the guards lay rolled up in their blankets. Suddenly a parcel, wrapped in news-paper, was thrown down from above. It opened up, as it hit the bottom of the ravine, revealing clusters of dried dates and loaves of bread. This was the only parcel to arrive in this fashion, because shortly afterwards the Guards scattered through the village.

During the day the men continued to cut stone, but lackadais-ically, just to show that they were still working. At noon they divided the bread and dates, and boiled water for tea. Sud-denly they realized that Ridha had not come down with them the previous day. Doubtless he would send them some food ...

Meanwhile the Guards, posted slightly above them, passed their tin plates, stacked with rations, from one to the other, in silence, staring down at the scene below. Then they lay down and smoked, interrupted from time to time by some order, which they transmitted by cupping their hands over their mouths. The women, too, it seems, took up their stand, not in the same place as the day before, which was now occupied by the military, but on the rooftops – the famous caved-in roof-tops – whence they too looked down in silence. Altogether there was a sort of ladder: the women at the top, with their veils blown by the wind, the soldiers in the middle and, at the bottom, the men of the village, resting among their tools and occasionally bursting into laughter.

There is no way of knowing how long a time passed in this way, how long the two groups of men remained in such proxi-mity, exchanging occasionally such commonplace remarks as: 'The wild goats know a passage over the Hand of Fatimah [one of the overhanging mountains]', or, looking in the other direc-tion, towards the plain: 'Ismaïl's camels are going up towards the *shatt*.' In any case, time went on so, until an old man who had come to work with the others simply because he didn't want to be left alone on the square, turned suddenly over on to his right side, with his mouth swinging wide open. The men around him understood what was happening, but they didn't budge. It was the old man's fate to die at this particular moment and their duty to stay where they were. Little by little, the old man's body completely crumpled, until the corpse lay, stiff and cold, on the stones. Then the others stopped working and crouched in silence, with their ghandurahs over their heads.

There must be some sort of extra-sensory perception which indicates to the living the presence of death. For the National Guards seem to have realized that the old man stretched out on the rocks was dead although his companions continued to crouch, motionless, about him. In spite of no apparent change there was a certain stiffening of attitudes. But, actually, nothing happened, and the old man might as well have died in his own courtyard.

Here Bashir's account is, necessarily, very confused, and even more so for what came after. According to him, the men (of whom he was one) stayed for five days and nights in the quarry, without anything happening. On the basis of other information we calculate that the time was no more than three days. Bashir claims that he slept a large part of the time, because 'sleep takes the place of everything, including food and work'. But he spoke, no doubt, of the somnolent state so common among the people of the South, whose eyes remain wide open even when they are functioning at a reduced capacity.

'Eventually two other men died as well, of cold, or hunger, or of some ailment they already had. Who could know why? On both sides there was an attitude of waiting. The only movement was among the women, who leaned over from the rooftops to look down, and occasionally that of a Guard who circled the quarry in order to speak to a friend on the fire side. At night the truck headlights lit up the mass of bodies huddled together against the cold. But on the third night the Guards did not turn on the headlights, doubtless in order to save the batteries. The cold was intense, especially in the early morning, when the wind blew from the desert. But the men of Shebika were less exposed to it than were the Guards, who lay down in their greatcoats or rolled up in a blanket, but without sleeping. But in the morning the men of the village were very excited when the women appeared on the scene.'

'Because the women came down the hill to join them?'

According to Bashir's story, the women did play a part. At a certain moment they decided, quite suddenly, to go down the ravine and bring water and dried dates to their menfolk. It seems that they arrived from the far end of the village, farther up the mountain, in a solid phalanx, walking hip to hip and very straight, with jars of water on their shoulders and their heads tossed proudly back. The soldiers let them by, not as if they were giving them official sanction but as if they did not see them, as if they were moving through another world. The women went down into the gorge without helping themselves with their hands, the jars still on their shoulders (of course women are notoriously more agile than men). When they reached the quarry they mingled with the men, who were standing there motionless. Nothing had happened before and nothing happened now. The men were dead set against building any house other than their own, but they were stuck in the quarry and didn't know what conclusion there might be to their venture.

'The women mingled with the men, and they all walked up the path through the ravine. They passed right in front of the soldiers, who didn't know exactly what to do. They went to their homes, and later on the men went down into the oasis to carry out their customary day's work.'

'But there were the dead men. What did the soldiers do?'

'Nothing.'

'What did they say, then? They must have said something.'

'There was the old man, of course, the one who died the first evening,' Muhammad said, later on, at Shebika. 'He was working with us. During a moment of rest he lay down and, by God's grace, he stayed lying. We didn't want to carry him away before night. After . . .'

'Were the National Guards there?'

'Yes, they were there. They usually are at the start of any work project, so that the Bedouins won't come and steal the tools. When the project is completed the tools are taken back to the army trucks. The tools belong to the Ministry of Public Works.'

'Nothing happened, then?'

'We worked and slept, as on any other project. The Guards were there, as they always are . . .'

Questioning proved to be difficult. 'Nothing happened', as Bashir put it, but there were the three days in the quarry and the three deaths.

'Yes, there were deaths, all right. Allah called three souls back to him,' said a young woman called Fawzia. 'To die of illness, or for some other reason, is all the same; it's God's will.'

'But all three men died down in the quarry, didn't they?'

'The bodies were taken to the cemetery in the shroud from the Mosque. That's God's will.'

*

'The fact is,' said a man from Tamerza who is an employee of the Ministry of Public Works, 'they're a bunch of lazy good-for-nothings.' (But Tamerza hates Shebika as El Hamma hates Tamerza and Redayif hates Metlawi. . . .) 'What if some of them did die? It's because they're too stupid to know how to cook. The old man died on the job, that's true, but he was the only one. Then they raised all sorts of trouble, because the National Guards told them he couldn't be buried before evening. They're lazy, that's all, I tell you. And now they have the nerve to say that they want to live like the rest of us and manage their own affairs.'

*

'I don't know,' said the Mosque attendant. 'I don't know what actually went on. They went down into the quarry. The National Guards came along. Our fellows broke stones. They did the work that God and the government sent them.'

'Yes, they broke stones,' said Iimra's husband, 'but not for the governor's house. They didn't go for that. The stones have lain for six months in a quarry [we had seen them], and nobody's doing anything about them. As a matter of fact we haven't been paid the wages of three hundred millimes a day, which the government owes us.'

'And the semolina?'

'We got the semolina.'

'And the Guards, what did they say?'

'Nothing.'

'None of them spoke up?'

'No, there was nothing to say.'

'And in the village, didn't anyone talk about it?'

'No, nobody.'

'How about the three fellows who died?'

'Old men are liable to die if they spend a winter night in the open.'

'Then they wouldn't have died if they'd been at home.'

'Who knows?'

'And you still haven't built the "governor's house"?'

'Oh, no.'

After this, time went by, the opaque time of the South, which wipes out events and spares only ritual gestures, the abstract repetition of the usual or generally admitted customs. As if the outer forms of an unlettered society were only a residue of experience (when man has no other outlet) and but one (the least important) aspect of collective and individual existence. What, after all, are organized structures, other than that to which man hangs on in order to maintain the cohesion of the group and to bear witness to his belonging to it? But experience overflows the limits of cohesion, as do also the fact of being together, the living tonality of the community or society, without which these structures would be mere vague signs towards a permanent link with forgetfulness.

When we came back to Shebika we tried to talk about what had happened. Bashir stared at us in astonishment and said nothing. (But everyone knows that Bashir smokes hashish and is a teller of tall tales.) As for the others, they laughed and pointed to the stones, still piled up in the quarry and waiting for some administrative decision as to their disposal.

The Expectation

In *Division of Labour in Society* and *Suicide*, Durkheim says that in every phase of history there is 'a deep-down feeling of the relative values of different social services', as they meet the collective and individual expectation. For him this expectation is one with the 'common conscience', which regulates a man's particular needs and desires. At the moment when a society is in the process of transformation, when there is 'increased prosperity' or, on the contrary, 'economic disaster', needs are exacerbated and desires are excited to the point where the former way of life can no longer satisfy them. And yet at no time does man have a greater need of 'welcoming structures' than when 'traditional rules have lost their sway'. It is understandable that there should develop a morbid condition, which upsets the habits hitherto imposed by collective constraint but leaves no outlet for the expression of suddenly awakened spontaneity. 'The state of instability and anomie is worsened by the fact that passions are least disciplined just when they need discipline the most.'

This state of anomie is actually painful. Groups and individuals are faced with a new set-up which cannot be dealt with on the basis of their past experience, and they have not the means of integrating themselves with it or even of modifying their own organism by way of adaptation. Contrary to the opinion of too many sociologists and other experts working in a strange country, the change does not take place in the society as a whole but throughout the web of diversified collective life, in the group microcosms that compose it. It is here, and not at the planning boards (which are good only for highly industrialized countries where the industrial revolution has homogenized society) that there occur the syntheses productive of change; here, too, can be destroyed and lost the hope of development, if the basic 'electrons' halt, harden or simply fade away.

During the colonial period, as Jacques Berque has noted, 'the traditional groups served the man of the Maghrib as a protective cave or shelter'.* At the moment of Independence, which marked the peasant's reconciliation with history, the 're-naturalization' or restoration of a society which had been rendered abstract by the pre-colonial condition of decay and an unbalanced power and wealth structure, this shelter was un-

* Jacques Berque, *Dépossession du monde* (Paris : Seuil).

covered; the door of the cave swung open and the period of expectation began.

The expectation is not passive. Men don't know what they may become, but they feel that something is going to happen. They are no longer content with the old ways, but no new way has yet been defined. The village of Shebika, as we studied it, was in this state of drifting 'without the law', a state rendered more acute by its isolated position on the edge of the desert. The sponsors of development cannot merely rustle the papers of a large-scale economic plan which takes no account of these fundamental facts and indeed fears them. Among most of the country's leaders we found examples of what we called 'the scorpions' nest theory'. They are more intent on presenting outsiders (who may give them financial aid) with an all-over plan than with finding out in what measure the various native groups are digesting all the changes trumpeted by the radio and are preparing themselves for a real change. Of course, in Tunisia, as in the rest of the Maghrib, the ruling class so completely identifies with the West that it reneges its own origins and authenticity, its *as-sala* and the living foundation on which rest the possibilities of changing a too-long immobilized situation. Official circles found Shebika and our interest in it shocking. They could not see why an anomic situation should be considered typical. But just as medical science knows health only through the symptoms which light up disease, so sociology (and above all the sociology of development) finds in anomie (not anomaly or abnormality) a sign indicative of a whole social crisis. As we managed to say to some of the uprooted intellectuals of the big city, Tunisia will become a truly modern country when Shebika has *spontaneously* found the social forms of its adaptation to change.

*

We like to think, also, that our investigation called the village out of a state of passive mediocrity and bitterness into a consciousness of its own existence. Our observation and analysis had a double effect upon their 'objects', which they made into subjects and induced to self-analysis. First, Shebika discovered its own identity, and second, the expectation of change grew sharper and more impatient than ever.

Of this first effect we have spoken at some length. Shebika played out its decayed social existence more and more plainly as we took roots among its people. Certainly there was an element of play-acting, of sly buffoonery, and the spontaneous dramatization of their lot. But for the people of Shebika, playing the social game revived their collective life and restored it to its fulness and plenty, even if this was 'plenty of nothing'. What human group, in an indecisive situation, on the boundary-line between two types of social existence, does not feel impelled to enact its dilemma? Doesn't the dramatization of social life reveal the importance of the change that lies just ahead? Of course, at the level of micro-sociology such dramatizations do not have the power or scope of those to be seen in the political circles of the big cities, where there is a momentary concentration of the collective dynamism which animates the transformation of the structures. At Shebika there was only a revival of old ways and activation of the modes of participation which did, however, lead to the 'affair of the quarry', in which the village found its identity by acting out its collective existence. What reality can fail to manifest itself in dramatic exteriorization?

The second effect of the investigation was even more interesting from the point of view of genuine transformation. The attitude of expectation (which has been characteristic of the Maghrib for centuries) is here the possible forerunner of the invention of new forms of social organization. For this reason we shall pause longer over it.

In a famous text Marcel Mauss defines this expectation as 'a frequent sociological phenomenon with both physiological and psychological overtones'.* People belonging to the same group expect the laws to function, 'the idea of order is only the symbol of their expectation'. They follow the existing economic system and wait for it to work, for the other people to whom they

* *'Rapports réels et pratiques de la psychologie et de la sociologie'*, in *Sociologie et Anthropologie* (Paris: Presses Universitaires de France), pp. 307–8.

give their money to accept it as an essential element in the circuit of exchange. Or else they wait for their prayers to be
granted, for the game to begin according to the rules. 'We may
compare this condition to familiar states of tension : so-called
diplomatic tension, the tension of a soldier standing at attention or on sentry duty.' There is expectation, also, in art, when
it culminates in a 'purge of expectation', the 'catharsis' of Aristotle. (At this point we can better see how individual or collective anxiety reflects the fear of disappointment, whether because the whole system is thrown into disorder or because the
new prospects are deeply disquieting.)

Social expectation, yes, and something more : the state of
patent tension of the peasantry of the young countries of the
Maghrib (and not there alone), since independence has brought
about a change which, even if it is mostly verbal, is real as
well. Long ago, during the 'dark ages' of North Africa, the men
of the Maghrib (Numidians, Zenatas, Kabyls and even Bedouins)
were systematically unaware of the object of their expectation; their collective existence was based on a confused will
to survive. A man constantly subject to invasion cannot expect
anything. Or rather, he is waiting expectantly for the desired
moment when, by some magical process, he can go from country to city. The *History of the Berbers* by Ibn Khaldun is dominated by this propulsion, this excessive eagerness which he
considers one of the causes of Arab decay. A propulsion which,
in A.D. 945, drove Abu-Yazeed, 'the man with the donkey', born
in the vicinity of Tawzar, towards the stabler region of the
Sahil and to the gates of Mahidiya, the capital of the Fatimids.
Here he knocked with his stick at the city gate, while in the
fountain of his palace garden the Sultan played with an eel.
Thirty years before, if we are to believe the chronicle of Bayan,
the founder of the city, the promised one, the Mahdi, Obeid-
allah, had predicted his arrival and this the Sultan knew. Now
he took his time, verified the exactness of the prophecy, then
sent out his soldiers to catch and skin alive in his presence the
man who was endangering the young Fatimid dynasty. And,
after this, he took upon himself the title, which was to become
so glorious in the future, of 'Al Mansur', the Victorious One. The

thrust of the man of the steppe, the man of the Jerid, was broken.

And yet there is, always, in the man of the South, an acute desire, aspiration, or perhaps need, which is in all likelihood the source of his impulse to leave the sands for the city. 'The man with the donkey' is the prototype of the man of the desert, who throws himself avidly on the city and plunders it, or 'if he fails to "make good", settles down in a state of acute poverty'.

This state of mind is not so much one of expectation as it is of frustration. The *jaiysh*, the war for purposes of pillaging which fills the chronicles of the 'dark ages', is even more symptomatic. The victim is a caravan, a lone traveller, the inhabitants of an inaccessible village or nomad encampment. The *jaiysh* is a confession of impotence, of the inability of the steppe peoples to make up a harmonious whole. Its practitioners have no hopes of obtaining anything from the faraway big cities. Like the innumerable 'brigands' of most of the societies we know, they seek to obtain from haphazard plundering that which organized society fails to give them. In the wide dispersion of the steppe peoples there is not even the embryo of unity, only a number of communities thrown back on themselves and upon the hazards of chance. Who, indeed, in 'perfidious Ifriqiya', as the Cairo Arabs call it, has established real power outside the immediate environs of the cities? We have spoken about the Sahil region of Tunisia; in reality it is a suburb of Qairawan, Mahidiya, Sfax and Susa. The nomads seldom set foot there, except in isolated groups, scorned by both city-dwellers and established peasants, who refer to them as 'lice', when they come looking for ill-paid seasonal labour. But who ventures into the plain, the steppe, and, above all, the deserts of the Far South? What political regime – after the Romans, the first Arabs and, for a very short while, the Moroccans – ever tried to unify the region? After the swift and destructive division of spoils on the part of the Hilali a curse settled upon this landlocked area. The Turks did not dare go outside the cities where they had installed themselves except to carry out brief missions of checking-up, repression or forced tax payments. This was pillage fighting pillage. Then, in caravans from farther south, came riches from the heart of the continent, above all slaves, who soon filled the villages. The caravans came from far away and they had to cross, as well as they could, these dangerous regions. No one is going to try to rule over vague human agglomerations which fade away on the surface of an ever more desolate land, whose population steadily decays as the desert encroaches upon it. The Beys sometimes managed to impose order, but nothing outside the framework of episodic alliances and antagonisms. *Jaiysh*, or pillage, is the normal business of people that cannot integrate with society.

Then colonialism came along and did, most assuredly, modify the situation. The pretext for intervention was the pillaging action of a band of Crumirs in the service of the Regency, operating in Algeria. Colonialism, then, upset the balance of forces; and brought with it tools, roads, railroads and, eventually, cars. The desert lands of the South fell back on themselves, on mystical devotion to the marabouts and the daydreaming produced by Indian hemp. It was then that the period of expectation began, but in an unexpected form, drawing its strength from a decaying religion, which was revived as a form of opposition to Europe. The struggle for Independence was, in a way, a phase of the 'long wait', set and kept in motion by Bourguiba.

But Independence was not an end in itself; it opened up a new period of waiting, an active kind of waiting, which demanded circumstances conducive to change. When the peasants were taken away from home and scattered among the work-camps of government construction projects, they were lost and submissive. In their villages, when they remained there, they recovered their *as-sala* or authenticity, stemming not so much from a long past as from awareness of their own collective power.

With Independence and through such new technical devices as the radio (especially the transistor type which was indispensable to the wars of independence in both Tunisia and Algeria, particularly the latter) there came the factor of 'news', of the 'word' which unified and indeed even created the nation. For the first time the man of the South, the man of Shebika was thrust into history. 'We people of this village' became 'we Tunisians', an affirmation and definition of the more abstract 'we Arabs'. He could no longer live or think as he had before; because he knew now that there was a future, one different from the past. And, above all, the realization that there were means of changing the ways and conditions of life made old traditions, whether religious or ideological, obsolete.

Once again, however, the word came from the city, stimulating the desert-dweller's desire to emigrate at least as far as its fringes and also the awareness of those who stayed in the villages.

'We're Tunisians,' said the young son of Ali, 'just like the rest. The government *has* to do something for us. We're waiting to see what it will do.'

The form of this expectation gives proof, if proof is needed, of the dynamic quality of the micro-organism of Shebika. This dynamic quality is latent in villages throughout the country, always focused on a government which has crystallized and capitalized the hopes of change and cannot disappoint them without losing its prestige.

This dynamism is not really social in character. For such blind confidence in the power of the state makes the men of Shebika not unlike the thousands of the unemployed who aspire to no more than a petty but secure government job. In Shebika this, like everything else, takes a very literal form. Nureddin's wife took one of us into a dark room behind the courtyard of her house and pointed out a collection of empty bottles, plates and cracked jars picked up on the roadside.

'They'll be full of oil and every kind of foodstuff that can be preserved,' she said. 'We'll form a cooperative whenever the government gives the word.'

The societies of the various parts of the Maghrib are not inert. In the course of the centuries (which does not necessarily coincide with the course of history) they have shown that they were capable of changing, even if by very slow degrees. Under the stimulus of foreign invasion, a religious conversion or the search for better living conditions they have tried out various social structures, from wandering tribes, to Berber kingdoms, including communities grouped around a marabout and rudimentary shepherd organizations. But this is the first time that the Tunisian Maghrib has tried to *change itself*, on the basis of a logical plan, without any outside stimulus but rather as a nation. Before Independence, in his militant years, Bourguiba strove to plant the nationalist myth outside the cities, where it was born, on the steppe and among 'the quaint characters, known as *fellahin*, barely perceptible among the other Barbary figures'. To these illiterate and inarticulate folk whose respect for tradition was a long-drawn-out suicide, Bourguiba gave a name and a language. By a mere name he endowed them with existence; the phrase 'We Tunisians' broke down all local loyalties, no matter how hardened. In his speeches he proposed a language or mode of expression in which the illiterates could take a place, alongside their fellow-citizens, in a common action and history.

Thus, *by his words, Bourguiba invented a non-existent nation.** His speeches wove the pattern of a fictitious being which gradually came to life in the struggle against foreign domination. In so doing he called into existence groups hitherto abandoned or forgotten. By urging them, verbally, to participate in something new, he made it impossible for them to turn back. At the same time the transistor radio, which brought outside news to places where there was no electricity, made for a supplementary revolution such as to push the peasants ahead, beyond the point of no return.

But, as everyone at Shebika knows, Independence opened up possibilities without furnishing the means of making them come true. Not that the government doesn't think about these things, but it is powerless to act upon them. And it can't admit to this impotence without also admitting that there was a flaw in its earlier claim that Independence would lead to economic development. And so Shebika is condemned to wait on two levels, one official, the other unofficial and indeed secret, based on the government's unconfessed inability to keep its promises.

*He said as much to Jacques Berque and myself when we interviewed him in 1964. Cf: our *'Tunisie'* in *Atlas des voyages* (Lausanne: Editions Rencontre).

The phrase 'We Tunisians', invented by the Independence movement, is left in suspense, and Shebika with it.

Shebika's latent dynamism is not to be doubted. On the contrary, its people have a greater capacity for creating new social
structures and making practical adjustments to them than do
the dwellers in the industrial suburbs of the cities. The expectation and frustration felt by the people of Shebika, and their
dramatic display actually led to broad possibilities of creation.
The advantage of micro-sociology is that it situates the *practice
of transformation* at the only level where men can directly and
really take a hand in bringing about changes such as to permit
a growing expansion of individual and collective freedom. The
spontaneous capability of small groups has not been given its
true worth since Proudhon, and it is here that, today, we
should seek a new way of accomplishment, beyond the illu-
sions and errors of the various forms of state or central government control. Shebika is a 'social electron', which, if it is given
the tools, can create a new situation quite on its own. *The political independence of the new Third World countries must be
followed by social independence*, which today does not exist.
The élite group which won political freedom has become a
petrified ruling class whose very existence broadens the gap
between city and steppe.

The American sociologist, Oscar Lewis, believes that there is
an intermediate stage and that, in the Latin-American countries,
of which he has made such penetrating and graphic studies,
the mediocrity of a situation which cannot presently be
changed leads to the creation of a 'poverty culture'. In this
intermediate state there is a balance between the old social
structures and the dreams of a new life whose images come
from radio, television or contact with the big city. Between
traditional culture and the new life there is a *no man's land*,
described by Georges Balandier as a 'surviving remnant of the
colonial period'.* Under certain conditions it may shut men up
in a sort of mediocrity which curtails change and destroys

*Sociologie actuelle de l'Afrique noire (Paris : Presses Universitaires de France, 1955 and 1963), and *Ambiguous Africa* (New York:
Pantheon, 1965; London : Chatto & Windus).

local dynamism and spontaneity more radically than any amount of coercion or dictatorship. In all the new countries which, once they have achieved independence, measure, with dismay, the gap which – regardless of their ideology – separates them from economic development, there is a similar situation.

Shebika's attitude of expectation should contradict this pessimistic view. But Shebika does not hold the future in its own hands. It is up to Tunisian society as a whole to *want* to save the authenticity of Shebika by calling upon it to make use of its own capacity for transformation. On the other hand Tunisia may betray both Shebika and itself. The village is, without doubt, in an anomic situation, but just such situations are favourable to change, for in them there is a germ of imagination which is lacking in large-scale, centralized government administrations.* Everything depends on whether the more advanced Tunisians are capable of taking root in the village and giving it their aid.

Shebika will be the symbol and proof of the great change in the life of Tunisia, but it is plain that the period of waiting will be long. At least the people of Shebika have an inner strength with which to combat the 'death wish' inherent in tradition. But, in order to face something new, there must be the sort of courage which is born of the willingness to try out emotions and sensations hitherto unknown. This slow transformation has not yet taken place. Fortunately, Tunisia is still open; in many ways it is still a vast work-shop. The people of Shebika, under the portico, around the Mosque and in their cramped, tumbledown houses, must face the supreme trial of waiting. As old Ahmad said to us one day, quoting the Quran: 'God will save men when they have been burned as coal.' And in 1964 he repeated what he said when we came for the first time, in 1961:

'We live on patience.'

*I set forth this theory in *Sociologie du théâtre* (Paris: Presses Universitaires de France), *Sociologie de l'Art* (Paris: Presses Universitaires de France) and *Introduction à la Sociologie* (Paris: Gallimard).

APPENDIX

Problems of Method: the Utopian Reconstruction

This book is an attempt to reconstruct the collective and individual life of a village in southern Tunisia. The project was begun in 1960 under the sponsorship of the Centre of Social Science Studies of the University of Tunis and carried on under that of the Faculty of Letters.

The primary aim was to engage in field-work students who had been used to literary sources and ideological arguments. Indeed, these young people had become so westernized that they were more at home with the metropolitan values of Paris than in their own country. Our aim was to kindle in them a sense of responsibility towards a society whose transformation depended on them rather than on a central government which, too often, especially in the South, acts in an authoritarian manner in order to cover up its inadequacy. From 1960 to 1965, and again in 1966, when we went back for the last time to Shebika, two and even three successive generations of students lived with us in the village.

The influence of their discoveries upon these young people is just as striking as that of our investigation upon Shebika. There came into being a new, reciprocal awareness, favoured by a common language (the same Arab dialect is spoken in both the North and South of Tunisia), a Muslim background, in which religion obviously plays a strong part, and a common political terminology, the terminology of 'development', promoted by the government and transmitted by the radio. The growth of this awareness is an integral part of the project, inasmuch as it became an auxiliary object of our analysis and one which might well lead to future action.

From the beginning it was plain that a statistical approach would be not only inadequate but also actually misleading.

The idea of a sample survey (and to a certain extent the small-ness of the village might have constituted a sample in itself) could only have led to distortion or even outright error. To have looked at Shebika as a homogeneous statistical population would have been to fall into the trap presented by the village's present state of decay. The apparent homogeneity was the superficial mark of the abandonment of the whole of South Tunisia, left to itself and forgotten by a central government which had little inclination for initiating change in so poor a region.

The assumptions of social homogeneity and stability neces-sary to a valid statistical analysis are so restrictive, much more so indeed than several methodologists have admitted, that they force the limitation of this kind of approach to certain stable parts of industrial societies, and make it quite inappropriate for developing communities like Shebika that are characterized by rupture and change.

The fact that the village underwent so many transforma-tions between 1960 and 1966 also rules out the adoption of another traditional approach, that of structural anthropology or sociology. Structural models cannot cope easily with change.

The structural approach currently fashionable in French intellectual circles rests on the assumption that behind visible social reality there exists a fundamental logical order of exist-ence, an unchanging pattern of which the individuals compris-ing the society in question are unaware. But we found Shebika in a state of decay in which rules received only verbal acknow-ledgement, as if they were those of a sort of game in which no one any longer believed. The political and social changes which have taken place in the Maghrib over the last ten or twenty years (especially since the invention of the transistor radio), have discredited the whole complex of 'unconscious collective awareness'. The theory that the apparently irrational and con-fused behaviour of the people of Shebika followed the rules of an underlying logic did not fit in with the unreality of a game that nobody was any longer playing. It was in order to turn us away, to evade disquieting questions, that the men and women of Shebika took refuge in the high-sounding, ready-made phrases of the Quran.

We proceeded in an entirely different manner. First we gathered the greatest possible amount of information on all aspects of the daily life of the village, by observing them continually over a five-year period and keeping detailed notes. All these many observations added together made up the reconstruction which we have sketched above. This was then corrected in the course of discussions in which our investigators analysed and criticized their own conclusions in order to eliminate any traces of personal interpretation.

This continuous investigation brought about a notable change in the village. Hitherto disdained objects, devalued acts and half-forgotten beliefs regained a sort of vitality from the very fact that a researcher recorded them in his notebook and from the subject's realization that they were genuine and more or less accurate clues to his self-estimation. This re-invigoration of the mental and technical equipment of daily life did not, as it often does, lead to a crystallization of traditional ideas. On the contrary, the change was so keenly perceived that the everyday framework was pushed away and, as it were, outdistanced by the awareness of experience. Through the repeated scrutiny to which we subjected him, the man of Shebika developed a new perspective of himself.

But what my team and I tried hardest to do, year after year, was to hold undirected conversations with the village people, in which they were free to 'palaver', in accord with their own often hesitant ways of thinking until they found, on their own, the way to reach us with words. Likewise, as shown in the case of my collaborator, Salah, a son of Bedouins, the researcher from the city was obliged to discover, not without difficulty, the language in which to approach the people of Shebika.*

Our questionnaires and interrogations were, of course, to

*The young women of our group, talking to the women of the village, were quick to discover a common language which it took the men on both sides two years to *invent*. The separate world of women has a direct relationship with *nature* which the men, dispossessed of their land, find harder to establish.

some extent planned in advance, but we soon discovered that
it was better merely to stake out their general direction, since
the course they actually followed came more and more to be
set by the people we talked to. They increasingly took the
initiative until, after 1961, we realized that they were redis-
covering a language – their own language – through the inter-
views.

At the level of micro-sociology (and it is to the tradition of
micro-sociology, the study of individuals in their immediate
social contexts, that our work belongs) the 'case study' of which
Thomas and Znaniecki gave a classic example in *The Polish
Peasant in Europe and America*,* further systematized in 1945
by Kluckhohn in *The Personal Document in Anthropological
Science* † and Angell in *A Critical Review of the Development
of the Personal Document Method in Sociology* ‡ is remarkably
fruitful. The study of autobiographies as complete as possible,
the analysis of the spoken word, the reconstruction of plain
statements and dreaming-out-loud – all these give some idea of
the nature of the personal document and the value of the information which it yields. Such recent books as *Sun Chief, the
Autobiography of a Hopi Indian*, by Leo W. Simmons, *Report
from a Chinese Village*, by Jan Myrdal, and, above all, *The
Children of Sánchez* and *Pedro Martínez*, by Oscar Lewis, show
what levels of richness of detail and also what level of universal
relevance studies like this can achieve when they are conducted
by talented men.

Our interrogations provoked the most notable collective
action recorded in the recent history of Shebika, and this because the motivation of the action came from within. The
repetition of the interrogations from year to year (measuring
such changes and discrepancies as called for explanation) made
for the action in which *Shebika played the role of Shebika*. Or,
to put it another way, the attitudes aroused by repeated ques-

* Chicago: University of Chicago Press, 1927.

† *Social Science Research Council Bulletin*, no. 53, 1945, pp. 77–173.

‡ *Social Science Research Council Bulletin*, no. 53, 1945, pp. 175–232.

tioning led the village to the extreme political limit of self-affirmation.

It was dramatization that allowed the people to play social roles – traditional or non-traditional – whose meaning had previously been lost. Of course, as we said above, there was an element of comedy or even parody in this dramatization of everyday life. How, indeed, could it have been otherwise? Humour and derision must – must they not? – go with the transition from one form of society to another, especially when the former has been for a long time in a state of decay and is marking time in the expectation of an unaccomplished change.

As for the new attitudes which led to what we call 'the affair of the quarry', they are one with the discovery of a new mode of expression. If we admit that there is a link between the texture of real life and the pattern of a group's (and often an individual's) way of speaking, then a new language must bring about the emergence of a new way of life, with all that it implies of hope and expectation. The man of Shebika *gave himself a name* in the larger context of the life of Tunisia when he discovered a language in which to give his new experience expression.

It is perfectly understandable that this double transformation, through self-dramatization and discussion, should define and indeed in part constitute the mechanism of change in a microscopic social organism. 'I want no talk of micro-sociology' was the peremptory dismissal of the subject by a leading member of the government at one of our seminars. And this at the very moment when the first cooperatives were being launched and their success depended on whether the micro-organisms were really working, in such a way that the people could demonstrate both their goodwill and their organizing ability. Certainly at the level of 'large-scale organization' and theoretical planning, the destruction of the outworn structures of an old society called for a broad point of view, far removed from experimentation on a smaller and more concrete scale. But it is not at all certain that Tunisia was ever a unified society and that it was necessary to envisage a total transformation in order to put local dynamism to work. It is possible (although not certain), on the other hand, that the stimulation of microscopic groups to manage their own affairs may be more important than the abstract elaboration of spectacular plans which cannot find a practical application.

Let us add this: Shebika is a microscopic social organism, and as such perhaps a typical cell in the whole, but it is also a rare and special case. The anomic aspect of the village makes for a group of basic facts and symptoms which help us to understand how to work out, at the moment of change, the passage from a miserable and stagnant situation towards adaptation to a new way of life. If, that is, a new way can ever come into being in this region of the South . . .

The five years that we spent in Shebika were, both for the villagers and for the researchers from the city, a truly phenomenological experience of change. That is, the fundamental mental categories by which each side had conceived of change, if they had conceived of it at all, underwent a modification directly as a result of the study. A project on change became, in the techniques that it used and above all in the new language that it generated, an example of change itself. For the phenomenologist, who argues that the conceptual reality that actors present is perhaps the most fundamental form of social life, this is a dramatic experience. A village which had lost what Durkheim would have called its 'conscience collective', its collective identity, gradually became the subject of a change and of a history, a history that lay mostly in the future.

But these facts – multiple checked and re-checked observations, repeated interrogations, free-wheeling conversations, analyses of petty events – cannot be presented in their raw form. A sociological method, in vogue a few years ago in the United States and now in France, consists of an abundance of graphs and tables drawn up on a dubiously scientific basis. It is as if an architect were to leave the scaffolding around a finished building. No one can deny the importance of these quantitative or structural elements; no sociological enterprise can afford to neglect them. But what C. Wright Mills called 'the sociological imagination' lies in synthesizing this data, making sense of all the inter-connexions and fitting them into a total picture that can make them mutually intelligible, a coherent picture, in short, that *reveals* them.

That is why we propose here what one might call a 'Utopian reconstruction' of Shebika ... of a story. We do not, of course, mean that we paint a fantastic picture somehow synthesizing Shebika's past, present and future; that would be silly. It is, rather, an attempt at an act of total social imagination.

Marcel Mauss, speaking of the problems of anthropology, sets forth the idea of a 'total social phenomenon', which, in his view, must pass beyond the conflict among partial or subjective points of view and integrate the various elements into the all-over continuous creation made up by a living social organism. A very profound idea, but one which may remain simply a matter of words if we are content to say 'by way of conclusion' that the facts which we have studied acquire meaning when we have blended them into a whole and that this whole permeates all the facts which it embraces. By such a procedure we should arrive at no more than a truism.

Actually, the only way to understand how successive and dispersed elements make for a whole is to reconstruct it. This task, of conceptualizing the frequently inchoate reality that presents itself to us so that it becomes intellectually manageable, is not easy. What we have tried to do is to capture Shebika in the way in which Max Weber, for example, captured certain aspects of the administrative organization of complex societies in his concept of 'bureaucracy', or in which Karl Marx grasped the actions of particular groups in the idea of 'class'. One must remember that social reality never presents itself *directly* to us as 'bureaucracies' or 'classes'.

We call this reconstruction 'Utopian' because we are forced to use Mills's 'sociological imagination', to set forth a coherent whole (both synchronic and diachronic, structured across time and through time), and because this whole is a hypothetical proposition of uncertain veracity. Even if the Shebika which we have reconstructed in order to depict its *total* reality can be seen to correspond to all the details that our research recorded, and is thus a successful description of the village between 1960 and 1966, it does not necessarily follow that the community will develop in accordance with this model. But, at the very least, our description will depict an organization close to the real one, and will not blind us completely to the possible developments of an essentially unpredictable future. In this way the reconstruction is a *wager* on the village's collective existence. We suggest that our presentation of Shebika in a stage of transition from decay to dynamism (a dynamism which may find no outlet and thus lead into the blind alley of even greater decay) is such as to provide the responsible Tunisian officials with clues to an effective and non-coercive form of action.

In this way, also, our analysis may have an even broader scope. Towns and villages (of Shebika's size or larger) throughout the developing countries are all in the process of passage from a state of decay (which has nothing 'traditional' about it) to one of economic growth and modernization. When we add up what we have seen in Brazil, Peru, Mexico, Senegal, Morocco, Algeria, India and Cambodia, we find confirmation of our conviction that there can be no *real* change where there is no widespread and localized technical progress, where the only development is that of an élite (or ruling class) which is more or less egotistical, more or less militant. The individual town or village is the only true breeding-ground of a change so gradual as to be almost imperceptible, but potentially more radical than one which is claimed to have taken place in spite of the lack of its concrete achievement. But this sociological premiss calls for an almost impossible revision of the political and economic attitudes of the present-day leaders of the developing countries. We have seen how difficult it is, even for more flexible younger men, to give up the advantages of a European-style big city and go to live and work in a rural community.

One last word. Our analytical method covered a wide range, from direct note-taking to the attempt at total reconstruction. We spoke above of the element of invention, of the 'imagining true' which characterizes certain sociological projects. Sociology, when it goes in for such Utopian reconstructions, is on a par with literature. As has been said many times, the nineteenth-century and often the contemporary novel, whether it is 'naturalistic' or 'realistic' (and these are only the slogans of aesthetic ideologies) aims at a totality which includes sociological elements. As Hermann Broch says : 'A literary work must embrace the world as a whole.'*

In this context Balzac, whose world was not crystallized but in a process of becoming, and Joyce (who, according to Broch, fits a world of dreams, desires and other implicit and unconscious elements into a totality constructed by language) followed a process very close to that of a certain creative brand of sociology.

After all, the aim of the classical novel is to organize reality, whether that of individual dramas and their partial values and resolutions or that of murky dream states and psychic visions. Flaubert's imaginative invention of a Madame Bovary is the fruit of a Utopian experience, the reconstruction of a living whole in and around a character who becomes the momentary symbol of this assembling process. Joyce and Proust went on to prove that the same result could be achieved with the matter of the mind, the Self and its complex variations.

In recent years there has been a new turn, one which amounts to a deep rupture. The writer has discovered that invention based on life can have its point of departure in the real existence of men situated in quite specific circumstances – atypical or anomic – and acquire the value of a symbol or myth. This was one of Truman Capote's aims in writing *In Cold Blood*, where he followed up the lives of two murderers whom he deliberately made the pivots of his invention rather than coming upon them in the course of a formal search such as was the basis of the novel of earlier days. This is one of the features which make anthropology and sociology so attractive at the present time. A different life (or one removed by the strangeness of its very everyday quality) becomes the basis and pretext of a reconstruction in which literary expression finds play.

We may most strikingly illustrate this intellectual convergence by saying that *if Balzac and Dickens were alive today they would be sociologists*. That the convergence is not entirely

Erkennen und Handlung (Zürich : Rhein-Verlag, 1955).

recent, of course, is illustrated by Michelet's dramatic reconstruction of history.

At the same time we must admit that the books which really answer the demand for something new can be counted on the fingers of one hand. Many writers, after one or two outstanding works along this line, are tempted by the urge to carry out a particular theory, by pure and impressionistic literary speculation, by calling on the mathematical sciences for a language which confirms and yet replaces sociological imagination. They stray from the path of modernity and follow that of an outmoded positivism or of a mild literary expressionism.

In speaking of the new meaning of what he calls 'myth' and we call a coherent story, a total and Utopian reconstruction, Hermann Broch notes that we are living through a period of dismemberment and fragmentation of the large units of the past and also of the values which made for its general tone and spirit. Our age has a different task before it, especially in view of the fact that currently unleashed techniques may escape our control. 'A world which is in the process of blowing itself up no longer allows us to paint its picture. But since the origin of its ruin is in the deepest roots of human nature, we must portray this nature in all its nakedness, and in its grandeur and misery. This, too, is a "mythical" task.'* If we are not mistaken, the Utopian reconstruction of the poverty of Shebika in which imagination is put at the service of the social reality which it reconstitutes in its story, is one step towards the accomplishment of this new task of creation and understanding.

* Hermann Broch, *Die mythische Erbschaft der Dichtung in Dichten und Erkennen* (Zürich : Rhein-Verlag, 1955), p. 239.